Coaching leadership

Building educational leadership capacity through partnership

Second Edition

Coaching leadership

Building educational leadership capacity through partnership

Second Edition

Jan Robertson

NZCER PRESS

2016

NZCER PRESS
The New Zealand Council for Educational Research
PO Box 3237
Wellington
New Zealand

ISBN 978-1-927231-97-5

Design by Smartwork Creative, www.smartworkcreative.co.nz
Distributed by NZCER Distribution Services
PO Box 3237
sales@nzcer.org.nz
www.nzcer.org.nz

Photography by Jan Robertson

To my daughter, my sister and my mother—
my coaches, my heroes, my friends

"In this edition of *Coaching Leadership*, Jan Robertson has gone deeper and added details and examples that make the book even better. It is accessible, informative and provides a model not only for thinking about coaching but a process for actually becoming a good coach and mentor in a reciprocal relationship. A must read for school leaders—formal and informal."
Dr. Lorna Earl, Toronto.

"This book gets right to the heart of leadership development. This second edition is welcome and even more timely for leaders everywhere."
Louise Stoll, Professor of Professional Learning, UCL Institute of Education, London

"Jan Robertson is one of the most significant contributors in the field of coaching. Her knowledge about peer coaching has been a big inspiration for us in development of a group coaching program. She has already formulated many of our thoughts and experiences in a very clear way."
Marit Aas, National Principal Program, University of Oslo, Norway

"It took me too long to appreciate this coaching model—focusing on individual people and changing mindsets, not just the mindsets of the people I am attempting to lead, but my own mindset as well."
Graham Young, New Zealand Aspiring Principals Programme coach

"How I wish I had known about and used a coaching approach in my years of principalship. What a difference it might have made!"
Nick Major, New Zealand Aspiring Principals' Programme coach

Contents

Chapter 7 Coaching the skills that build trust and understanding

Chapter 8 Coaching the skills that move leaders forward

Chapter 9 Troubleshooting and monitoring the coaching relationship

Chapter 10 Facilitating coaching

Chapter 11 Leaders coaching leaders

Chapter 12 Developing agency and efficacy

Chapter 13 Beyond the boundaries

Foreword

The significance of robust leadership in complex institutional environments such as education cannot be over-estimated. Education is a dynamic context that in recent years has become highly politicised and competitive. Across the globe, the financial, demographic and environmental changes that are affecting all sectors have become acute. In the education field particularly, government responses to these challenges have often been demanding and difficult to interpret, putting extra pressure on leaders at both decision-making and implementation stages.

It is vital in educational settings therefore to ensure that leaders have the best possible help for creating and sustaining strong leadership. Such ongoing leader development plays a crucial role in the health and sustainability of our institutions. As Andy Hargreaves pointed out in the foreword to the first edition of this book, the job of the educational leader is challenging and what can make all the difference is whether leaders have the right kind of support to help them face the challenges of the role. Coaching is seen as playing a key part in that support.

Coaching for educational leadership, as highlighted throughout this second edition, is a powerful constructivist methodology that focuses on leadership practice as an opportunity for learning. As a form of action learning, it provides frameworks for effective change and goal attainment as well as supporting personal and professional development. Jan Robertson explains how coaching is a transformative process that can result in leaders creating new leadership knowledge and crossing borders to "new ways of being and knowing" (p. 244). She explains how coaching supports key leadership principles such as leading change and solving problems as well as enhancing all areas of practice. The book thus encourages the qualities leaders need to succeed: leading with moral purpose, self-belief, continued learning, and guiding and supporting others.

As discussed elsewhere, coaches provide valuable support for the development of leaders, by promoting the necessary courage and bravery to bring about change (McLaughlin & Cox, 2016). Through the skills and expertise of a leadership coach, leaders can find the control and direction needed in times of challenge. Coaches create structure and processes for promoting greater critical understanding in leaders, helping them to brave the problems encountered in multifaceted work environments such as schools, colleges and universities. McLaughlin and Cox point out how, in these kinds of complex settings, leaders need to "make sense of situations that may initially make no sense (p. 141). This complexity leads coaches to ask questions, such as: "Is this a simple problem or is it a symptom of some deeper, more complex issue?", "What can be controlled or influenced in this situation?", "What needs to emerge and be encouraged?"

When educational leaders report their own experiences of coaching, they stress that it empowers them to address the complex issues that confront them in the multifaceted settings within which they work. It encourages deep reflection, enables them to keep in touch with their real values, and promotes the courage to understand and to challenge not only their own thinking but also the existing external parameters that can dog the implementation of decisions. Coaching therefore empowers leaders to recognise and employ their agency more effectively, helping them to be braver in making the right choices and taking the right action. This growth in confidence and self-efficacy promotes new ideas and practices that lead ultimately to assurance and advances in everyday institutional operation.

This new edition of *Coaching Leadership* also draws attention to the boundary-breaking principles underpinning coaching, and these are needed to move leaders from inaction to action, so overcoming their own inertia and the ever-present tendency to be reactive to problems.

The author emphasises how coaching should interrupt the status quo and question all aspects of what educational leaders think and what they do. The designed disruption of leaders' usual modes of thinking and working is what the author calls "looking beyond". It is crucial in complex educational contexts because it enables leaders to observe the environment within which they operate more critically, resulting in more thoughtful communications, better decision making and, crucially, a more robust service to society.

I want to end this foreword by emphasising the timeliness of the discussion of coaching in this book, and commend the advocacy of coaching and the way its potential is recognised here. The relevance of improved leadership abilities is important across the whole work spectrum, but is particularly significant in educational institutions because these have the opportunity to provide role models for our future.

Dr Elaine Cox
Principal Lecturer
Oxford Brookes University
January 2016

Reference

McLaughlin, M., & Cox, E. (2016). *Leadership coaching: Developing braver leaders*. New York: Routledge.

Foreword to first edition

Whenever I have to arrange an appointment with an educational leader I am meeting for the first time, the leader will typically caution me that he or she is very busy and can only spare a few minutes; that there isn't much time. The recurring and paradoxical experience is that once I am through the doors of the leader's office, I then find myself trapped, a captive audience, unable to escape. Over the course of an hour, an hour and a half or more, leader after leader insists on regaling me with stories of their achievements and setbacks, their hopes and plans for the future, their reminiscences and regrets about the past, their long lists of frustrations with the system, and their poignant portrayals of breakthroughs with the students and adults who matter to them most.

Sometimes, after an age of agonizing and complaining about the frustrations of the job—the overwork, the bureaucracy, the lack of appreciation, the imperious superiors with their unreasonable demands, and the "blockers" in their staff who repeatedly sabotage their best efforts, I will then ask the leader I am with whether, if given the chance, they would choose to lead all over again. The response is almost always immediate and emphatic "Oh yes. It's wonderful work. I wouldn't dream of doing anything else!"

Educational leadership is one of the most rewarding and also frustrating jobs there is. The rewards keep leaders going. The frustrations drive them out. What typically tips the balance is whether educational leaders face the challenges together or alone.

Leaders are surrounded by other adults, and in the best communities, they can face the challenges of change together, as colleagues, almost as equals. But even here, so many of the most difficult problems, worries and doubts in leadership are hard to share with or disclose to those leaders whom you're charged to lead. You can't vent your frustration about "resisters" or "blockers" without descending into tittle-tattle and gossip. You can't air your uncertainties about your next career step, or about who might succeed you, without spreading anxiety throughout your community. And, sometimes, in the darkest moments that afflict all leaders, when you doubt your very capacity to lead, it's hard to imagine, outside your own family, with whom you can share any of these feelings at all.

If leadership has always been lonely work, it's becoming lonelier still. The administrators who were once teachers' colleagues have now been forcibly separated by many governments into separate unions and associations, and converted into supervisors and managers as a result. Economic cutbacks and moves towards site-based management have removed the layer of support and mentoring that many educational leaders were once able to turn to. My own research on educational change over 30 years in eight Canadian and US high schools reveals that whereas school leaders were once seen as being larger than life characters who were visibly attached to their schools, that they made their mark upon, and stayed in for a long time, they now are seen as being interchangeable managers who turn over regularly and serve the government or themselves rather than the schools in which they work (Hargreaves & Fink, 2006).

In my own school improvement work, one of the greatest benefits repeatedly cited by leaders is the opportunity that has been created for them to meet once a month with their colleagues and discuss openly, without fear and in an environment of complete trust, their recent achievements, their difficulties in dealing with imposed reform agendas, and their responses to research findings that cast light upon their work. These peer support groups of committed and concerned colleagues are invaluable assets to leadership development and retention. They keep leaders going.

In addition to their form of group support, my colleague Irwin Blumer advises that all school or school system leaders should be provided with a mentor and a coach. The mentor knows your school and its people. The coach is not swayed by their knowledge and experience of the individuals concerned, but understands the job and how people experience it.

This book, by Jan Robertson, is the first of its kind to deal with the theory and practice of leadership coaching. From her years of researching leadership as well as leading herself, Robertson is able to draw on an impressive range of theory and research in psychology, sociology, business management, and organisational development to get to grips with the essence of coaching, the benefits it can provide, and the difficulties of conducting it. Using her extensive contact with leaders and leadership around the world, Robertson puts the theory to work in real life examples of leaders coaching leaders—elucidating how professional development, career development, leaders' motivation, lifelong learning and organisational improvement all benefit as a result.

Robertson is a realist. Neither a Pollyanna professor nor a critical prophet of doom, she deals with leadership and leadership coaching as it is, bringing it to life in ways that will give hope to and also make sense to all leaders who read her work. Practical strategies and guided reflection take the coaches and the coached far beyond the old rudiments of clinical supervision into the complexities and possibilities of leadership coaching today—embedded in rather than separate from organisational improvement and professional development.

Whatever our work, all of us can benefit from the perspective of a critical friend, a coach and an advocate, who stands by our side, gives us pause to reflect, and helps us eventually move forward. Even 9-year-old soccer players get a coach. It's time that all our educational leaders on the front line are provided with one as well. Jan Robertson's splendid book not only advocates articulately for the necessity of leadership coaching, but sets out practically what really good coaching can and should look like.

Andy Hargreaves
Boston College
April 2005

Reference

Hargreaves, A., & Fink, D. (2006). *Sustainable leadership*. San Francisco, CA: Jossey-Bass and Wiley & Sons.

Preface

This book is about coaching leadership, and it has been written for anyone who is interested and involved in improving leadership, teaching and learning—their own and others. Although my focus is the field of education, the principles and practices outlined can be, and have been, used effectively in other contexts, such as learning organisations in the corporate world and public services. Coaching leadership can be understood in terms of a visual language and a metaphoric language, while the patterns and systems of nature can be likened to the practice of educational leadership. These highlight the innate principles of relationship and a certain universality—with ourselves, with one another, and with this land. Chinese people use the encompassing word *li* for these principles. I have enjoyed exploring this notion of *li* through photography and have made these a feature of the second edition of my book. My work in this regard is inspired by author David Wade's interpretation of this concept. The quotes that accompany my photography are from his book *Li: Dynamic Form in Nature* (Walker Books, 2003).

 Coaching Leadership will assist individual leaders[1] wanting to reflect on their own leadership, the consultant working with educational leaders in

---

1 The use of the word "leaders" rather than designated positions such as teacher, principal, head of department, lecturer or chief executive officer in this book is deliberate. The book is about coaching leadership development and so focuses on the leadership responsibilities that all those in education should take up, whatever their position in the institution may be.

the field, senior leaders in an institution who are responsible for leading others and for developing teaching and learning, and classroom teachers wanting to reflect more effectively on the way they facilitate learning. It can help board of trustee members and other leaders conduct appraisal more effectively in schools, and it can challenge those involved in the professional development of educational leaders to critique the way they work. Most importantly, it will assist those who are interested in establishing coaching relationships for leadership development and to improve or change teachers' practice.

Although there are many "how to" coaching books on the market, this book highlights, and builds on, 25 years of research and development in the field of leadership coaching. I first took up academic research when I was in a principalship. The work I did was on effective schools. It whetted my appetite and led me to ask why I'd not previously been acquainted with all this theory and research. During my career I've held many leadership roles in education—senior teacher, principal, assistant dean, head of department, director—and within each there was little specific leadership development, formal professional feedback or critique of my practice available.

While these experiences and roles taught me much about leadership and allowed me to work with leaders of incredible talent, I became concerned, and particularly so at the time of my principalship, at the lack of specific job-related professional opportunities for leadership learning and deep reflection on practice. The dearth of professional dialogue about leadership and learning, particularly within the rural principals' group, alarmed me even more. Sports days, busing issues and other organisational and managerial issues always took precedence over any discussion and debate on leading learning in the school and community. When I moved into the higher education environment in 1989, my study of and research into leadership development began in earnest.

Developing ideas

At this time, both nationally and internationally, there was little national policy relating to, or interest about, educational leadership and its development. With New Zealand's educational institutions moving into self-management as a result of changes in educational policy at the end of the 1980s and beginning of the 1990s, the impetus for management development increased. The government provided one year of professional development support to school principals and their boards, but after the first year of the reforms, individual institutions were generally left to look for leadership support and development from other sources. Much of the rhetoric at the time was managerial, and isolated principals from their teaching profession. However, paradoxically, what they needed in order to *be successfully* self-managing was a greater focus on educational leadership and the ability to build social and intellectual capacity in their institutions.

This paradox created dilemmas for those in education management positions (Robertson, 1991b). Many failed to adapt to the new roles, responsibilities and tensions, and left the profession. Some struggled but found ways of working within the new political context. Others were ready to try new ways of working that took up the intellectual independence offered through self-management, while finding ways to resist, contest or hijack the managerialist ideology that abounded (Strachan, 1999). It was evident that a new type of professional development was necessary for leaders in the new self-managing institutions.

The work of Hallinger and Murphy (1985, 1991) on principalship at this time, along with later work on problem-based learning (Hallinger & Bridges, 1997), influenced my belief in the importance of developing an authentic model of leadership development, especially for use in university-based programmes. This belief led to the establishment of the first educational leadership centre in New Zealand in 1990 at the University of Waikato, when elsewhere the focus was on establishing and maintaining centres for principals and developing educational administration and management qualifications rather than leadership qualifications.

Debate also arose around this time as to whether leadership is a discipline in its own right, and it was with this debate in mind that I accepted a Fulbright scholarship in 1992. The scholarship took me to Vanderbilt University in Tennessee, the Far West Laboratory in San Francisco, the Harvard Principals' Center in Boston, the Washington, D.C. Educational Leadership Center, and many other places where leadership development was both exciting and challenging. The Danforth Foundation was very influential in the USA at this time, impacting on at least 22 university programmes by 1992. Its work focused specifically on "changing the way we prepare educational leaders" (to use the title of a book by Milstein & Associates, 1993), with the aim of making programmes for the study of school leadership more relevant and contextually specific. My motivation for, and commitment to, centring my career on educational leadership development in New Zealand was cemented and ensured.

At this time, too, scholars around the world were interested in New Zealand's full-scale move to site-based administration of education institutions. I was invited to speak at an international conference in Thailand, at Chiang Mai University's Center for Leadership Research and Development, and, later, at other international conferences exploring decentralisation, in Canada, Singapore, Australia, Malaysia and the USA. These engagements allowed me to exchange ideas on leadership development with international colleagues working in this exciting field. Today, there are many strong international networks of scholars working, increasingly collaboratively, to develop the field of educational leadership.

This book encapsulates the ideas drawn from dialogue over many years among numerous educational leaders about professional development through coaching. The empirical data presented in these pages are drawn from one study of leaders coaching one another over a three-year period and my ongoing research and development programmes in this area. These data, the collection of which has been informed by the aforementioned ideas, form the basis of the model of leadership coaching documented in this book. My use of the theory and practice of action research throughout the model's development makes the model a continually developing entity. Many graduate students, all successful leaders themselves in education, health and business, have studied, researched and practised this model, and developed it further in a variety of contexts in the public and private sectors (see, for example, Sutton, 2005; Murrihy, 2009) and also these leaders current case studies in Chapter 11.

The coaching model has been used by teams in early childhood centres, with curriculum development and classroom management in mathematics in secondary schools (Winters, 1996), in higher education departments in New Zealand and Thailand, with teacher education advisers in Indonesia (Fadillah, 1997) and with teacher appraisal in higher education in the Solomon Islands (Houma, 1998). It has also been used in various national development contracts, in information communication technology (ICT) development with secondary leaders in Hong Kong (SAR) (T. Lee, 2002), with groups of school leaders in England, with senior leadership teams in Australia, and with over 300 school leaders in Singapore. In short, the model has been continually and consistently developed and researched across education contexts and cultures over the last two and a half decades.

In the current context, at the time of publication of this second edition of *Coaching Leadership*, the isolation that many leaders in education feel and experience has not diminished. Hattie's (2011) claim that New Zealand has 2,700 islands of individual schools, all operating independently and autonomously, still has cogency. The effects of policies of parental choice, competition, ambiguous educational rhetoric and associated league tables of students' achievement data have worked against collegial collaboration and shared problem solving. Through my coaching leadership work, I continue to find that leaders feel the idea of creating new knowledge together within and across school boundaries is antithetical in this context, even when schools are geographically very close. Rather than supporting and challenging one another to reflect more deeply about educational issues and their own leadership of learning, to share resources among their schools, to experience the benefits of being observed and receiving feedback on their leadership, many school leaders still seem intent on developing all the new knowledge needed to lead future-focused, culturally responsive schools within their own gates.

It's no wonder that Wylie (2012) calls on leaders to collaborate and share knowledge across schools. If educators as leaders are to effectively meet the needs of the 21st-century learners in our schools—learners who are self-directed, flexible, and adaptive, who are creative and critical thinkers, who see learning as a lifelong process, and who, as team collaborators, create knowledge together and value diversity (see, for example, Bull & Gilbert, 2012)—they need to demonstrate the same attributes in their own adult learning communities and through their own professional learning relationships.

My development of the principles and practice of coaching leadership and my many years of simultaneous research into its efficacy (e.g., Robertson, 2009) make clear that coaching partnerships call for a whole new way of *being* in the education context. When educators come to understand these partnership relationships *in practice*, they are better able to critically reflect on and then mediate the learning relationships they have with students, parents and others in the education community. The process is one that works to the benefit of all parties because, as Claxton, Chambers, Powell, and Lucas (2011) put it, educators come to see themselves as learning coaches rather than transmitters of knowledge. Fullan and Langworthy (2014, p. 52) lend support to these findings from my research when they state that "This cascading model of learning through partnership extends through students, teachers and leaders—all learning with and from each other."

The process is also one that challenges the heart of educator identity. Thus, the commensurate process of developing educators who see themselves as leaders, who *know* themselves to be leaders of learning, is of critical importance. The leader *as* learner is a person who has come to know how to create knowledge through collaborative learning partnerships, who is well informed through dialogue and reflection about education issues nationwide, and who takes responsibility for addressing those issues (i.e., is a true system leader in education). Such educators not only have been coached but also have the skills to act as coaches. Because coaching relationships give educators these personalised experiences of meeting their own learning needs, with formative feedback on that learning and its manifestation in praxis, they explicitly understand the transformative, positive change that these relationships and the ability to lead learning bring to themselves and others. These outcomes are evident in New Zealand's National Aspiring Principals' Programme conducted during the years between 2011 and 2016, developed on the paradigm of *Coaching Leadership*, and involving partnership in learning and leadership relationships in schools and e-learning communities. A case study of the programme appears in Chapter 11.

Sustained engagement with others studying the professional development of

"I can honestly say that I have never, through any appraisal system or professional development, been challenged in the ways that I was last year through the National Aspiring Principals' Programme. This was a direct result of my coach's ability to ask purposeful reflective questions."

educational leaders, the many addresses, workshops, and dialogic encounters, both national and international, all in some way informed the model as presented in the first edition of this book. In addition to those I acknowledged in the first edition of *Coaching Leadership*, I would like to thank people associated with this second edition: Caroline Benedet and Andrew Fraser of Sydney Catholic Schools, who have seen the benefits of coaching leadership for senior leadership development and system change over the past four years; the experienced leader–coaches in the New Zealand Aspiring Principals' Programme who have believed in the importance of coaching for generative practice for transformative teacher and system change and who continually reflect with me on the learning process; and my own current coaches, Pare Kana, Loretta Brown and Rosie Walford, who support and challenge me to reflect and transform. I thank with gratitude Bev Webber, the previous publishing manager of NZCER, who believed in the idea I first had for this book, at a time when coaching and learning partnerships was little recognised in international education as a powerful methodology for learning and change, and David Ellis, NZCER's publishing manager 10 years on, who saw the need for a second edition. I sincerely thank Paula Wagemaker for so skilfully editing the final manuscripts. I must continue to thank, too, the many educational leaders I work with in New Zealand and overseas who assist in critiquing and developing the coaching model as they lead the ideas in their schools. Finally, I want to thank my family for the love they give me in life. This would not have been written without their ongoing support.

I have found my journey of understanding change in teaching and leadership stimulating and challenging, and I hope that as you read this book you will become as committed as I am to a model of developing leadership and quality teaching and learning through professional coaching relationships. I believe that coaching partnerships is the main route to shared, capacity-building leadership within any institution, and that it facilitates the development of a particular type of educational culture, a particular type of leadership that is based on reciprocal learning, one that is not only pervasive but also invitational (Stoll & Fink, 1996)—to innovation, to deep learning, to leadership sustainability (Fullan, 2005; Hargreaves, 2004; Hargreaves & Fink, 2004) and to continual renewal. Fullan's recent work (Fullan & Langworthy, 2014), in calling for new pedagogies, now highlights the importance of these learning partnerships in the creation and use of new knowledge.

The structure of the book

Coaching Leadership is structured to assist you to understand leadership coaching, for teachers, for other leaders, for students. It has two main parts. Part One, "Theory", outlines the conceptual framework of the coaching model: its principles, the pedagogy, methodology, and the research. "Practice" (Part Two) presents detailed examples of how to develop the skills and facilitate the process of coaching. It also identifies the challenges you need to consider during and beyond coaching. Ongoing critical reflection about leadership and its development is vital.

Part One: Theory

The first chapter of this section introduces coaching. In addition to providing a definition of the term and the principles behind the model, it establishes the rationale for coaching and outlines the research and development that informs the model. Chapter 2 defines and emphasises the importance of *educational* leadership—the leadership that focuses on the quality of teaching and learning within an education community. It describes why coaching practices build learning and leadership capacity and how leaders then become leaders of leaders. It looks at the reality of leaders' work, which, rather than being inimical to coaching occurring, can be the very reason why coaching is so necessary.

Chapter 3 outlines research and theory on effective lifelong learning and professional development. It looks particularly at how coaching crosses the borders between theory and practice, and between professional leadership contexts, to provide authentic, vicarious learning situations. The fourth chapter presents the research findings from empirical studies on the model of leadership coaching presented in this book.

Chapter 5 explores the theory behind action research and demonstrates how leadership coaching can lead to action research and establish a community of learners within and across institutions. It presents an action research case study of how a principal worked to develop a shared vision in her education community.

Part Two: Practice

The first chapter of this section (Chapter 6) outlines how to select a coaching partner, how to get coaching started and how to develop coaching relationships. It sets out a typical coaching session and a year's coaching programme. It also presents some key ideas from a case study of two leaders getting started in their partnership. The study also demonstrates how the coaching relationship develops over time. Chapter 7 describes the skills of listening, reflective interviewing and context interviewing, all necessary for developing coaching as a professional development practice and for establishing trust and understanding.

The continuing development of skills in the coaching process is set out in Chapter 8. Self-assessment, goal setting, observing and describing practice, giving evaluative feedback and knowledge of the change process are outlined, with the emphasis on deep learning relationships. In Chapter 9, we look at what happens when things do not go as smoothly as was hoped. The focus here is on troubleshooting within coaching and exploring what leads to the success or failure of the developing relationships. This chapter also looks at the importance of continuously evaluating and carrying out meta-reflections of coaching practices; some reflective exercises are given for coaching partners to use for this purpose.

Chapter 10 gives guidance on facilitating the process of coaching and the roles of the coach when establishing coaching relationships with and between leaders. Chapter 11 presents four case studies that show how leaders who have been coached can take what they have learned and coach others to use coaching skills. In so doing, they become facilitators of coaching, people who are able to coach leadership principles and practices with the aim of bringing about transformative change not only for colleagues but entire education systems.

Chapter 12 explores the development of agency and self-efficacy through leadership coaching. The case study presented in this chapter reveals in more detail how aspiring principals in New Zealand schools became supported and challenged in their courage to lead transformative changes in schools.

Chapter 13 questions where to from here and stresses the importance of developing capable leaders as well as leadership capacity in ourselves and in our institutions. It looks at the research on boundary-breaking leadership development and learning and considers how the principles of coaching, learning communities and boundary-breaking leadership link together. Thinking about how coaching can be used as an agent of change and transformation for equity within wider society is the final challenge put to readers.

A little more explanation

Direct quotations from leaders who participated in the research studies and later development work are highlighted throughout the book. These not only capture and portray the richness of these leaders' experiences, frustrations and leadership learning along the way, but also remind you that the ideas in this book are based on empirical research and the real experiences of leaders and teachers worldwide.

The case studies in four of the chapters describe how different leaders worked together, their leadership actions and their subsequent critical reflection on those actions. They demonstrate how these people developed the conviction that they were educational leaders who could act in an alternative, transformative manner, and who, through this new learning, could make a positive difference in education.

The activities included in some of the "Practice" chapters challenge you to reflect critically on leadership. Coaching facilitators (i.e., people who facilitate the learning of others through coaching partnerships) can also use the activities to develop the coaching skills of those with whom they are working.

The chapters are basically chronological in that they detail the evolving nature of the action research studies and the thinking behind the development of the model. I must emphasise here that the book does not signal the culmination of this thinking, but rather, within the framework of "grounded theory", is always only the beginning, never the final word. This second edition of *Coaching Leadership* confirms that claim because it further develops the ideas expressed in the best-selling first edition of the book. This development is as much a product of the comments and reflections of the many leaders who have engaged, whether theoretically and in praxis, with the ideas and model in the book as it is of my own further study into and reflection on them. As Glaser and Strauss, (1967, p. 256) once pointed out, "The sociological perspective is never finished, not even when the last line of the monograph is written. Not even after it has been published, since therefore the researchers find themselves elaborating and amending their theory, knowing more now than when the research was formally concluded."

I consider that my learning in this area will never be complete, and so ideas will continue to develop. As the chapters show, the learning I've gained from how other leaders have applied this model in the field over this past decade (for some examples, see Chapter 11) has helped me refine it, critique it and develop it in new ways. As the chapters also show, the leaders I've worked with developed their coaching partnerships uniquely but had the shared experience of working in critically reflective ways with their colleagues. Their comments (and those of other leaders who have engaged with the model) at the end of their coaching experiences highlight the fulfilment that the more formal professional interaction achieved through the coaching model brought them. The following comments continue to be typical:

> This has been one of the most—no, *the* most!—professionally supportive experiences of my 39 years in the job!

> I hope we keep up this coaching partnership. It's my best development undertaken! Even my staff comment on this.

> We feel we have gained substantially.

I hope your experiences will be equally positive and powerful as you develop and practise the skills of coaching with a professional partner (and perhaps with some external assistance with this process). I believe that after you've embedded the coaching experiences into your own practice, you'll begin to work with others to develop the practices and principles of reciprocal learning through partnership relationships in your leadership.

Jan Robertson
January 2016

PART ONE: **THEORY**

The *li* fissures found in many tree-barks "arise as the result of tension of the outer bark of the tree that is caused by the growth of its inner core".

Chapter 1

Introduction

Chapter overview

This chapter begins by defining leadership coaching as presented in this book. It outlines the reasons why this form of coaching is essential in the current education context and from there moves to an overview of various international leadership development ideas and theories. The chapter then traces the empirical research underpinning the development of the coaching model documented in this book and the key principles and ideas upon which it is based. The chapter concludes by describing the three research studies that produced the model.

What is coaching and why coaching?
Coaching defined

Coaching, as presented in this book, is a special, sometimes reciprocal, relationship between (at least) two people who work together to set professional goals *and* achieve them. The term depicts a learning relationship where participants are open to new learning, engage together as professionals equally committed to facilitating one another's leadership learning, development and wellbeing (both cognitive and affective), and thereby gain a greater understanding of professionalism and the work of professionals.

Dialogue is the essence of coaching and the concurrent improvement of practice. Leaders elect to be coached because they want to improve their practice on an ongoing basis. The coaching model in this book assumes that coaching partners believe they will gain equal, but different, benefits from working with each other as they work to develop and implement their professional and personal goals—goals that are directed towards transformative changes in themselves and their respective institutions.

Underlying premises

Several premises inform the definition of coaching. The first is that educational leaders are often teachers by preparation, and so effective leadership development should include many of the principles that underpin effective teacher development.

The second premise is that professional learning should be a lifelong process. Although leaders may be at different stages of their careers, all need ongoing opportunities to renew, refresh and redirect their educational leadership practice. New expectations and roles necessitate this: the only constant in education, after all, is change. There will always be a need for leaders to change direction—to branch out into new areas of development. New leaders, moreover, need to be able to embrace change for the possibilities and opportunities it can bring. All educators have the responsibility to keep on learning throughout their career.

The third premise is that people who are influential in education should focus, as their main priority, on educational leadership—the leadership that improves teaching and learning. Thrupp and Willmott (2003) describe this focus as "critical leadership", where there is not only reflection on learning but also a "public commitment to doing things differently" (p. 180) and "reflection on wider issues of social structure and politics" (p. 181). This stance requires continual critique of the role and practice of leadership in learning as well as articulation of the dilemmas and tensions faced within that context.

A fourth premise is that effort to link theory and research to the study of issues relating to the first three premises and their leadership practices is the key to successful leadership development, which is why coaching provided by practitioners and academic specialists working in partnership can be very effective. The coaching peers/pairs provide each other with professional feedback and vicarious learning through the observation necessary for leadership development. The academic professional provides the coaching partners with challenges, critical perspectives, skills and theories that support and challenge their developing coaching practices. There must be challenge if the professional relationship that coaching partners develop is to serve an educative purpose. The partners also need to be supported and encouraged if changes in behaviour are to occur. Outside perspectives are thus paramount in bringing effective change to leaders' practice. I explore this facilitative role in greater depth in Chapter 10.

New leaders for new times

In 2005, an increased interest among academic theorists internationally in leadership development and coaching led to coaching being hailed as worthy of respect. Today, coaching has become more mainstream in policy and practice in many education systems, and it's an area now recognised as worthy of the attention it has always deserved (Fullan, 2014). This interest has had particular resonance in New Zealand, where the changes brought about by policy developments in the late 1980s and early 1990s led to a focus on self-management of educational institutions and created particular challenges for leadership. The time was right to begin to explore the use of a coaching model that could help develop and support this new leadership.

New Zealand was the first (and perhaps sole) country in the world to move to full-scale decentralisation of educational provision across all sectors. The advent of self-management in New Zealand required a new type of leader and new ways of developing the skills he or she would need. More specifically, the country needed educational leaders who could

- build capacity and commitment;
- build strong relationships and partnerships, within and between schools;
- focus on learning;
- understand the change process; and
- see the importance of finding new approaches to "doing" and "being".

As Caldwell (2002, p. 843) observed, the need since that time has been for "new approaches to professionalism [that] will challenge the modest levels of knowledge and skill that sufficed in the past, with a vision for values-centred, outcomes-oriented, data-driven and team-focused approaches that matches or even exceeds that of the best of medical practice." For Gronn (2002), "designer leadership development" (his term) based on competencies and standards will not create the types of leaders needed today, for much the same reason articulated by Lupton (2004, p. 31), who contends that "the wide variation between [institutions] ... may give rise for differentiated strategies" rather than to a one-size-fits-all approach effected through the development of leadership competencies devoid of context. Because the context in which leadership operates markedly influences how that leadership is exercised, development and support initiatives need to focus on the local indigenous context—nationally, regionally and institutionally. This focus is not always the case in leadership development initiatives around the world.

The need for relevance and challenge

Essentially, if we are to acknowledge the reality and context of leaders' work, then we must establish the type of professional development that will support these professionals' daily practice. It's important that leaders can see the direct relevance of their professional learning to their practice. Development activities far removed from the reality of leaders' work serve no useful purpose. Educational leaders need to be working with the people, issues and concerns they face daily if they are to fully appreciate the need for and the relevance of change and innovation.

"I can honestly say that I have never, through any appraisal system or professional development, been challenged in the ways that I was last year. This was a direct result of my coach's ability to ask purposeful reflective questions."

Often missing from the theory on effective professional development is *how* leaders can put professional development in place that contains all the principles identified as important. How do we get those in education to see that change and development in their leadership behaviour is necessary and important? The answer is, as the above definition of coaching implies, challenge. Leaders must be challenged to understand and reflect on how changing their practice will make a difference. Peer coaching provides that challenge, and even more so when coaching partners share their perspectives with other such partnerships in learning communities. The variety of perspectives, the development of activities and skills and the presence of support all serve as professional development opportunities that enhance coaching relationships.

The leadership development context today
Reconceptualisations

In 1981, when the Harvard Graduate School of Education opened its Harvard Principals' Center, the USA became one of the first countries in the world to recognise the need for formal leadership development. A decade later, New Zealand opened its first leadership centre at the University of Waikato. Among the governments worldwide that moved forward with a national policy for leadership development, England's took a particularly strong lead with the establishment in 2000 of the country's National College for School Leadership, now called the National College for Teaching and Leadership. A key focus of the National College in those early years was learning-centred leadership and personalised development (Southworth, 2002). A study of 15 countries at that time showed many mandatory or quasi-mandatory programmes developing throughout Europe, Asia, Australasia and North America (Huber, 2003). Today, leadership centres can be found in many more countries around the world; Lithuania, Hong Kong and Norway are just a few of them.

These centres represent a giant step forward from the early 1990s when interest in school leadership preparation and development was of "relatively little interest" outside the USA (Hallinger, 2003). The programmes have also shown major paradigm shifts in leadership development, particularly over the last two decades. While these initiatives have moved a long way from the early days of clinical supervision models (Goldhammer, 1969; Joyce & Showers, 1982), certain elements and key principles of professional learning have survived the test of time (Joyce & Showers, 2002).

Although some policy-makers still tend to favour "informed prescription" of leadership development curricula (Barber, 2002), the education profession now places greater emphasis on initiatives such as learning communities (see, for example, Stoll & Bolam, 2005), coaching and mentoring (e.g., Aas & Vavik, 2015; Tschannen-Moran & Tschannen-Moran, 2010), inquiry learning and networks (e.g., Timperley, Kaser, & Halbert 2014), leadership learning initiatives focused on building human capital in individuals and in institutions (Hargreaves & Fullan, 2012), the self-awareness associated with social and emotional intelligence (Goleman & Senge, 2014) and "data-literate" and evidence-based leadership (Earl & Katz, 2002). In so doing, members of that profession have enhanced their (and other educational stakeholders') belief in "informed professional judgement" (Barber, 2002).

A number of associations and journals continue to focus solely on school effectiveness and improvement. One such professional association is the International Congress for School Effectiveness and Improvement, with its flagship journal *School Effectiveness and School Improvement* (SESI). Some of these associations have added "leadership" to their name to signify a change of emphasis (e.g., BELMAS, which stands for the British Educational Leadership, Management and Administration Society, and NZEALS, that is, the New Zealand Educational Administration and Leadership Society). Similarly, many academic journals now focus solely on the theory and practice of leadership. To date, two editions of the *International Handbook of Educational Leadership and Administration* (see, for example, Leithwood & Hallinger, 2002) have honoured and validated leadership thinking from around the world.

The past two decades have also seen a reconceptualisation of leadership. Sergiovanni (1992) and Fullan (2003a) have advanced our understanding of moral and authentic leadership, while Strachan (1999) and Starratt (2004) have looked respectively at critical leadership for social justice and spirituality in leadership. Gronn (2003) and Thrupp's (2004) call for a move away from "designer models of leadership development" to a more critical focus has been accompanied by calls for cross-cultural and boundary-breaking leadership (Robertson & Webber, 2002; Shields, 2002; Walker & Dimmock, 2002). Leadership *for* learning has also been a key focus (Townsend & MacBeath, 2011) as has the leader *as* learner (Robertson, 2013).

Hallinger (2011) and Robinson, Hohepa, and Lloyd (2009) have since published syntheses of international research on the influence of school leadership. Dempster, Lovett, and Flückiger (2011), Muijs et al. (2014)

and Timperley, Wilson, Barrar, and Fung (2007) have also published syntheses of international research on teacher effectiveness and professional learning. Syntheses such as these, and others, have informed our collective co-construction of knowledge about leadership learning and teacher change and given us a much better understanding internationally of this area.

Key principles and ideas
Reciprocity, structure and support

Different coaching models abound, so it's important when developing coaching relationships to reiterate and maintain the principles underlying the model. The seminal work of Cochran-Smith and Lytle (1993) is reflected in many of the principles developed through the coaching research in this book, which include or focus on:

- the legitimation and validation of educators' practice;
- the development of theory by practitioners;
- the informing and changing of practice;
- the importance of operating at the interface of theory and practice;
- the need to provide support and challenge for changes in practice;
- the need to set up a structure that will help educators become more self-directed in their professional learning;
- the development of a model that any leader can use anywhere and in whatever context;
- a belief in "educators as knowers"—as theory-makers;
- a belief in leaders as lifelong learners; and
- a desire to alter the traditional relationships between professionals, between teachers and students, and among educational institutions involved in learning partnerships.

Several key ideas also inform the model in this book:

1. The process is dynamic, meeting the changing needs of and resulting in new learning for each person. In this way, it's also a reciprocal learning partnership.
2. The coach is the facilitator of the learning process, not the "teacher" of how something should or could be done, unless invited.
3. Instead of being positioned as the expert, the coach is a "learner" in the process. Coaches take their expertise into the relationship

and acknowledge their partner's expertise as they together construct shared knowledge.

4. The coached person takes responsibility for his or her own professional learning and sets the agenda and goals for the coaching sessions.

5. The partners have a good understanding of each other's role and the social, cultural and political context within which they both work.

6. The coaching relationship takes time to develop effectively and sustain, with educational change, innovation and improvement occurring over time.

7. The coaching partners require the interpersonal, communication and coaching skills to work together in different ways.

The role of the coach

Both the person doing the coaching and the person being coached must be taught the skills of coaching and should discuss the principles behind these. When two people in a coaching relationship both know how to coach, coaching is easier, yet schools often want to develop only those individuals they select to be coaches. It's therefore important that the coaches of each partnership not only empower the coached to make their own decisions about their leadership practice but also are overt about the coaching skills in action. Coaches don't tell leaders who are being coached how they should lead but rather assist them to reflect critically on their practice so they can make informed decisions about their leadership. The responsibility for learning is then left in the hands of each leader. Leaders who have been well coached in how best to work with their coaching partners advance their respective professional development and offer supervision and oversight of each other's practice.

Executive coaching, life coaching and personal coaching—all prevalent in the literature today—are at times conducted by coaches with little, if any, experience of working within the context of the person they are coaching. In this book, coaching is seen as a reciprocal process, conducted by partners who are from—or who have come from—similar positions or roles, and who are, to all intents, equal within the coaching relationship. Coaching partners bring to the relationship not only knowledge of the context in question and different strengths, expertise and wisdom, but also, and more importantly, different perspectives on and an outside (albeit perhaps less subjective) view of a leadership situation.

The coaching relationship is dynamic and constantly changing to meet the needs of the people involved. And even though a coaching relationship may not always be truly reciprocal, it can be bi-directional because both partners gain in different ways, especially if they're engaged in different roles, such as leadership coach, education consultant, facilitator or adviser, or principal. Such a relationship can also be effective in terms of critiquing the coaching practice if it's established on the principles set out in this book.

"Although coaching can make you feel extremely uncomfortable at times, I truly believe it leads to a high level of personal growth for both the parties. It's great for encouraging a higher level of thinking, enhances connections and leads to a feeling of self-satisfaction, through effective questioning and listening."

The development of the coaching model

The model of leadership coaching in this book has evolved over more than two decades of my research and development in this field. Other research literature has also influenced the model's development in the field. However, the three major pieces of research that had the greatest impact on the developing model are described in the following sections. The model is still evolving as I continue to research coaching practice (see, for example, Robertson & Earl, 2014) and participate with professional colleagues here and overseas in critical reflection focused on the process of coaching.

The first research study

A naturalistic qualitative study involving primary, intermediate and secondary school leaders during the first year of the Tomorrow's Schools' reforms to educational administration in New Zealand (Lange, 1988) was considered an important precursor to first understanding the role and needs of these leaders and second to identifying the most effective professional development for them during a time of major administrative and curriculum change. I spent one year shadowing 11 leaders from across the school system (primary, intermediate, secondary), in a cluster of schools in an urban environment. I interviewed each leader on at least three occasions, organised professional development activities for them, and then evaluated these experiences with them. The aim of this study was to develop some substantive theory about appropriate and effective educational leadership development.

The findings indicated that site-based professional development, which included outside perspectives (i.e., another person's observation and views) on the concerns these leaders were experiencing at that time, was most valuable. This and other related research led me to conclude (Robertson, 1991a, p. 130) that leaders' professional development should:

- acknowledge the realities of leaders' daily practice;
- acknowledge the philosophic, values and visionary elements in leaders' work;
- offer opportunities for values awareness and resolving dilemmas;
- have a strong emphasis on educational leadership, that is, leadership centred on the quality of teaching and learning;
- encourage critical reflective practice and experiential learning rather than offer *a priori* theoretical or prescribed models;
- be needs-based, participatory and collaborative;
- focus on problem posing as well as problem resolution;
- be developmental over time, with that process leading to completed action;
- emphasise interpersonal skills, such as communication, presentation skills and stress and time management;
- acknowledge the needs of individuals for stimulation, freedom, creativity and fun;
- offer a variety of delivery modes; and
- be provided by people (often practitioners and consultants in partnership) who are credible within the field of education.

Two recommendations from this study had had a direct influence on the development of the coaching model:

1. Leaders need to experience professional development in critically reflective practice, and this practice needs to be formalised and structured through such initiatives as professional partnerships, learning and research communities, study groups and action learning sets.

2. Scholar–practitioners need to be made available as consultants to leaders to assist them with their professional development, to help them with problem posing, managing change and critiquing practice and political context, and to support them with education development generally. Consultants can come from the teaching profession—the untapped source of leadership development that Wadsworth (1990) described as a "pot of gold" in his article on the School Leaders Project.

Conversations that I had with two of the leaders who participated in the study were another major contributor to my thinking at this time. The first stated that there was nothing new in the professional development offerings and that during his career he'd been to everything available, or at least some form of it. He also said if the development didn't correspond with a "hurt" or a need being experienced by leaders, then no matter how good it looked, or was, other more pressing factors within the institution would take precedence. It seemed obvious, then, that any professional development had to focus on leaders' current leadership experience(s). The second leader had this to say: "What I would really like to do is … buddy with someone. They'd spend a day or two with me, and then I'd say, 'Okay, warts and all, what can you see in here that I'm doing wrong? Tell me. What things do you like? What things am I doing that I could do better?'"

I realised that this type of coaching practice was generally missing from leadership development initiatives and that I needed to carry out a second study if I was to pursue this line of thought. However, it also seemed to me that I needed to move this second leader's thinking away from having somebody else telling him what was wrong, to having him reflect on what might be wrong and what he might be able to do to improve the situation. This reflection and subsequent critical dialogue between the two leaders would allow him to engage more effectively in the vicarious learning he described.

The second research study

A national curriculum leadership development contract provided opportunity to trial the use of peer-assisted learning, of the type exemplified by Barnett (1990). This time round, 44 leaders from primary and secondary schools were selected from their individual applications to take part. Each participant was asked to "partner" another leader during a first group session, to set goals, engage in deep reflection and dialogue and focus on their leadership role when leading learning required by curriculum and programmes.

During each of four group sessions, conducted by a development team of 15 consultants and extending over an 18-month period, the partners worked together in pairs, using the skills of listening, reflective questioning and goal setting. (Strachan & Robertson, 1992, provide a fuller description of this process.) We asked the partners to think of ways of contacting each other and working together between these formal meeting times, which they did, to varying degrees. During these "in-between" times, the consultants also worked with each leader in his or her school and with the other teachers there.

The study involved over 50 hours of face-to-face data-gathering sessions (individual and group interviews and surveys) with the 44 leaders. During the study, the leaders also completed two individual surveys designed to monitor and evaluate the issues and successes the leaders personally experienced when working in their professional partnerships. Each leader also received five letters across the 18 months reminding them of goals set from group sessions and prompting them to initiate further action and reflection with their partner.

Data from the interviews, observation and surveys were shared with the leaders at the group sessions. This action research process assisted with clarification and validation of emerging findings, and it also intentionally influenced the continuing development process. At the end of the trial period, all data were further analysed for grounded theory development—a process described by Strauss and Corbin (1997)—to ascertain how the leaders had established and maintained successful professional partnerships throughout this time. In-depth interviews were then conducted with five volunteer participants whose coaching experiences had been relatively fulfilling but not without issues. The aim here was to further saturate the emerging themes from the data that would influence the selection and maintenance of the coaching partnerships in the third research study. This analysis took just over 60 hours.

The findings from this part of the study set the direction for the ensuing action research of the third study and firmed the principles of the coaching model presented in this book. The findings were as follows:

1. Leaders viewed the concept of learning partnerships favourably.
2. Leaders needed improved skill development to carry out the coaching processes effectively.
3. One year was insufficient for the coaching partnerships to develop fully.
4. Respect, honesty and trust were important elements of a successful partnership relationship.
5. Leaders needed more in-depth outside support to assist with critical reflection on leadership practice during the coaching process.
6. Regular, sustained contact between coaching partners was necessary.
7. Leaders considered lack of time for coaching an inhibiting factor.
8. Partnerships involving leaders from institutions of similar size and type benefited problem solving.
9. Engagement in group sharing and problem posing alongside the coaching processes benefited the participants' leadership development by giving them a wider variety of perspectives and ideas.

The third research study

This third study was again qualitative, involving an action-researching community of 12 leaders and an academic researcher (myself). Over a period of three years, the leaders met regularly in their peer partnerships and as a group. I worked with them not only individually but also in their learning partnerships and when they were all together as a group. The 12 leaders began by setting goals. They then used their newly developed skills to observe, reflect on and provide evaluative feedback on their own and each other's leadership practice.

A continuing influence on the development of the research and the eventual coaching model at this time was the exciting work in peer-assisted leadership development being conducted by Bruce Barnett, Ginny Lee and colleagues at the Far West Laboratory in San Francisco. Their earlier research (e.g., Barnett, 1990; Bossert, Dwyer, Rowan, & Lee, 1982; G. Lee, 1991, 1993; Lee & Barnett, 1994) also had a strong influence on my developing ideas, as did Kolb's (1984) seminal work in experiential learning conducted several years previously on adult learning theory. Ginny Lee came to New Zealand and worked with the leaders during the early stages of the coaching in the third study.

By the mid-1990s, educational institutions had assumed even more responsibility for their own management. My aim in this third major study was to encapsulate in the coaching model a strategy of professional development that would assist educational leaders to:

- conceptualise and implement new ideas and practices;
- achieve strategic goals;
- deal effectively with current issues and problems;
- gain skills for deep reflection on practice;
- develop strategies to cope with challenges; and
- receive both support and challenge.

A coaching model was the obvious answer.

The research was therefore designed as a conscious effort not only to develop a theory of professional development for leaders but also, in so doing, to provide professional development that would help them understand and then change their situation at the time of the research. The underlying theoretical principle of praxis was embedded in and interwoven through my and the leaders' methods: the developing findings influenced our practice at the time of the research and, consequently, how we worked with one another. The research was practical and based on the needs and concerns of the leaders involved. It was thus both a research and a development model.

The study comprised 18 months of data gathering and employed oral and written reflections, interactive interviewing, observations and examination of records. The findings were analysed using grounded theory techniques within the methodology of action research. The processes of action research accordingly became methods for both collecting and analysing data, with the leaders and me jointly involved in this process as a community of researchers (after Carr & Kemmis, 1986). During the data collection and analysis, the leaders helped me explain their situation and the dilemmas and tensions they faced during coaching and in their leadership practice.

All 12 leaders testified that the coaching assisted their professional and personal development in many ways. In the words of one of them: "This research has made me focus on my own educational leadership. It has led me through a series of processes, which have enabled me to reflect on and analyse my own actions. The research has made me take an in-depth look at my own leadership style and has given me the opportunity to observe others."

The particular ways in which these leaders believed their involvement in the research had advantaged them fell into four major categories:

1. assisted educational leadership development—a focus on teaching and learning;
2. enabled critical reflection on practice;
3. increased professional interactions; and
4. established a structure (action research) for educational review and development.

Chapter 4 describes these findings in greater detail.

Main conclusion drawn from the research

The thesis that is presented in this book thus rests on learning gained from engagement with the educational leaders involved in the above and other research over the past two and a half decades as well as with many other leaders involved in development work. Their collective perception is that a model of professional development involving leadership coaching, set within a critical learning community and including support and challenge from an outside facilitator, can successfully provide the essential components of professional development in which praxis and transformative practice are the desired outcomes.

As an example of this approach, the leaders in the third study, when working together, created a mild disruption to their everyday practice, which led to opportunities for reflection on leadership practices. I (as a practitioner-scholar/researcher) also assisted in this intervention process. The combination of the two—support *and* challenge—was effective in enabling critical reflection on practice and subsequent changes in practice and systems.

Are the benefits ongoing?

Research on this model of coaching has produced empirical evidence time and time again that the participants find long-term benefit from it (see, for example, T. Lee, 2002; Robertson, 2004a, 2004b; Sutton, 2005, 2004b; Winters, 1996). The case studies in Chapter 11 of this book help to illustrate these benefits. They feature leaders who were introduced to the coaching model before 2005 and who have since continued work with and on it in their schools.

For leaders, coaching through professional partnerships is (in the short and long term):

- an effective form of professional learning for transformative change in schools and education systems;
- suitable for anyone in any educational sector;
- practice based on sound research and development;
- carried out "on site" and dealing with current leadership issues and concerns;
- a chance to gain outside perspectives and feedback on practice;
- an excellent role model for education learning in any institution;
- a way of receiving affirmation for work well done;
- an effective model for formative appraisal and the improvement of practice;
- a way of seeing how leaders' many tasks and interactions link together to form the "big picture"; and
- a framework for all other professional development activities because it is ongoing.

The research also indicates that "one-off " professional development sessions (e.g., a course or a conference) do little *by themselves* to change practice back at the workplace. Coaching provides a foundation for new growth and helps solidify ideas gained from other sources such as conferences, workshops and seminars.

When leaders are asked directly at the end of their coaching experience if they intend to continue with their present coach or to establish a different coaching relationship in the future, they give these types of response:

> My present partnership will continue, as I believe we have both found it to our advantage. I've begun establishing another partnership with another leader in a much larger institution than mine and have found already that many issues are the same; [they] just involve differing numbers.

> Yes, I will continue if my partner is willing ... I will also seek other partners for different areas of expertise.

Probably not with the same one. Personalities are very different. I hold different values.

Yes, until the end of the year [as I retire then]. Next year, if it is at all possible, I would very much like to be able to do something similar—if only in a one-way manner, perhaps with a newly appointed leader somewhere!

I hope to keep working with [partner]. My [audit] is next term, and I have invited [partner] to join me.

Yes, we will! We've not only gained professionally but also get on well together—and like the same wines!

Comments like these indicate that the practice of coaching—even the idea of multiple coaches—can be well and truly *institutionalised* (Fullan, 1985) as an important part of leadership practice. If leaders don't continue with formal regular coaching once their coaching facilitator is no longer working with them, they'll still have in place the skills that enable them to be more reflective about their ongoing practice. Also, as a final point, leaders who experience coaching with their professional colleagues are generally no longer satisfied with less in-depth relationships with other colleagues and so are more likely to try to establish professional coaching relationships with them.

Summary of main points

- Today's education requires innovation and new approaches to learning.
- The concept of leadership and its development continues to be debated internationally.
- Coaching focuses on professional practice in context.
- Coaching is a relationship between two (or more) people committed to establishing and implementing goals and working together to achieve them.
- Coaching is most effective when coaches take a facilitative approach to learning and are open to new learning through the process.
- Coaching supports the principles of lifelong learning, capacity building, and continual improvement.
- Coaching is a dynamic process that develops uniquely to meet the changing needs of educational leaders.
- Coaching equips leaders with new professional ways of working with colleagues.
- The coaching model presented in this book is based on empirical research with leaders in many educational contexts and across many cultures and sectors. It continues to evolve.

This progression, from a relatively orderly to a far more fluid formation, can be seen as a paradigm for the interaction between two great principles of form and energy—and the resultant complexity.

Chapter 2

The concept and role of educational leadership

Chapter overview

This chapter highlights the importance that the educational leadership role has in terms of providing effective teaching and learning. Effective learning opportunities for students and for adults must be the number one focus and reason for leadership coaching. Many people think they're educational leaders but in actuality they merely hold a management or leadership position. This chapter endeavours to shed some light on the concept of educational leadership and just who can exercise it in order to transform professional practice. The qualities deemed important are set out and considered within the reality of the education context. The reasons why coaching is an important intervention in an educator's daily life and ideas on how coaching can help educators think about and respond to today's educational context are also explored.

Developing educational leadership
A transformative process

This book is not just about the process of leadership coaching but also about developing *educational leadership*—first in ourselves and then in others—through coaching leadership. Educational leadership encompasses the *informed actions that influence the continuous improvement of learning and teaching*—with an emphasis on "informed actions" and "learning and teaching". The primary focus is on the relationship between the two.

Caldwell (2003, p. 26) states that "educational leadership refers to a capacity to nurture a learning community." He goes on to say that a learning community is not necessarily a comfortable place in which to work because there is a "hard edge to the concept" and the "stakes are high" if every student's learning needs are to be met (see also the first case study in Chapter 11 of this current book). For Gunter (2001, p. *vii*), "Leadership is not an 'it' from which we can abstract behaviours and tasks, but is a relationship … highly political and is a struggle within practice, theory and research. Furthermore, leadership is not located in job descriptions but in the professionality of working for teaching and learning." The word *leadership*, as used in this book, signals the energy, impetus and collective action needed for change and improvement to occur; it therefore denotes *transformative* practice. Educational leadership is not about the position one holds but rather about the actions taken within practice to improve opportunities for learning. Most importantly, leadership is a *relationship* with others (Kouses & Posner, 2012).

Leadership for all

All members of an education community can contribute to the leadership energy and relationships needed to achieve shared visions and goals. This concept of leadership as that which can be contributed to and constructed by, between and among many "leaders" in the institution (Lambert, 1998) is synergistic because it's developed by those who choose to take up leadership. Many teachers do not view themselves as "educational leaders", even though they guide and facilitate the growth of learning for large groups of students on a daily basis. Providing effectively for learning needs, and exercising the knowledge management and creativity it entails, requires educational leadership!

Caldwell (2002, p. 831) stresses that "Knowledge management involves … developing a deep capacity … to be at the forefront of knowledge and skill in learning and teaching and the support of learning and teaching … This is a systematic, continuous and purposeful approach that starts with knowing what people know, don't know and ought to know." Even those holding positions of responsibility do not always place sufficient emphasis on the educational leadership aspect of their role; that is, knowing what people know, don't know, and ought to know. One of the most important roles for effective leaders, therefore, is developing leadership in others— encouraging them to take on responsibility for improving learning and achieving goals (Fullan, 2001; Fullan & Langworthy, 2014). Developing leadership in others is how leadership capacity is built. A "key notion in this definition of leadership is that leadership is about learning together and constructing meaning and knowledge collectively and collaboratively" (Harris & Lambert, 2003, p. 17). Accordingly, educational leadership is not about having all the answers. Rather, it is about asking the hard questions, putting a stake in the ground in terms of a desired future and "learning the way", together with the people whom that future will affect. Leadership capacity is built through these learning relationships.

Effective use of coaching practices for the development of such educational leadership practice is, of course, the focus of this book. It is for leaders in education who are committed to improving pedagogy and learning for themselves and for others. By using coaching as part of their daily practice—as a way of being—leaders can promote continuous leadership development and improvement of practice and, from there, effective learning in their institutions.

An underlying premise here is that education institutions that establish coaching relationships are more likely to form democratic communities of learners and therefore a special type of education culture that focuses on the continual improvement of learning. These "coaching cultures" may thus be better suited for meeting the needs of students and leaders in this knowledge age, where flexibility, creativity, innovation and ability to adapt to change and take on new learning are essential skills.

The qualities of the educational leader
Many qualities but one goal

Educational leaders are leaders who, no matter at what level in the institution they reside, focus on improving learning opportunities as their main function. They are also people who work to develop their own educational leadership capacity and that of their institution by developing the leadership capacity of others, within and across institutions. This type of leader is wanted more than ever in education today. We need leaders who can work in a complex, ever-changing educational context, who are aware of the social and political influences on their work and who can draw on this knowledge when working with others to create necessary changes to systems and practices.

Effective educational leadership requires much more than any individual leader can attempt to do alone, and so has the potential to be greater than the sum of the individual leaders in an institution or across communities and networks. Coaching practices drive the development of a leadership culture that produces educational leaders able to contribute collectively to the sustained and ongoing improvement of their respective institutions (Leithwood, Jantzi, & Steinback, 1999). Contributing collectively also includes working with other leaders outside of the school. This type of capacity-building among leaders engenders the development of an education culture of *system leaders* (Caldwell, 2011) who care just as much about the students in the school down the road as they care about the students in their own school. They understand that if their actions impair opportunities for others in an education system, they are compromising their own moral purpose with respect to education. Education leaders are thus the people in educational institutions who:

- work collaboratively and in partnerships to search for more effective ways of facilitating learning opportunities;
- are not content with the status quo and will act *on* as often as they act *within* the system so as to redesign education to address quality and equity;
- see the importance of being transformative and innovative and encourage their colleagues to take considered risks in the pursuit of changed practice;

- have a strong set of values and beliefs that focuses them firmly on social justice, so facilitating their critique of policies and practices within their educational communities;
- stand out (and up) from others as people who want to make a positive difference in the lives of others, and who still believe they can;
- are enthusiastic, energetic and believe that enhancing the learning opportunities of others is central to their work and that of others;
- lead by example and model the types of practices they believe are important in the education community; and
- have developed the ability to critically reflect on their practice and know how to seek out opportunities to develop this skill with others.

Educational leaders constantly strive for the ideal of democratic communities, where all community members assume responsibility for learning. This process is distinguished, in part, by leaders critically reflecting on the role and effect of their educational leadership, particularly in terms of building learning communities for themselves, their colleagues, students and local business and parent communities (Apple & Beane, 1995). They value diversity yet have a sense of shared purpose. While critical reflection and thinking can be developed to some extent through the institution's learning curriculum, these practices need to be modelled in the institution's *culture*. Democracy, too, needs to be learned through day-to-day *experiences* as Maxine Greene (1985, p. 3) has stated: "[D]emocracy is neither a possession nor a guaranteed achievement. It is forever in the making … For surely it has to do with the ways persons attend to one another, and interact with one another. It has to do with choices and alternatives, with … the capacity to look at things as if they could be otherwise." Coaching maximises the effect of these experiences by enhancing the learning gained from them and enabling leaders to repeat Greene's words, "to look at things as if they could be otherwise."

Statesperson, connoisseur and entrepreneur

Studies conducted in the late 1980s and early 1990s (see, for example, Marshall & Duignan, 1987; Robertson, 1992) grouped the qualities of educational leaders into three areas: those of the statesperson, who lobbies in the wider community for the education in their institution; those of the connoisseur, who is learned about research and committed to lifelong learning and inquiry into pedagogy; and those of the entrepreneur, who always looks for new ways of working more effectively and innovatively both inside and outside of the school gates, so as to facilitate continual improvement of the learning experiences offered.

Leaders who are *statespeople* focus on relationships because they know their work is with and through other people. The learning relationship is one of the most important of all relationships within an education institution, and leaders fluent in coaching practices usually have had first-hand experience of developing effective learning relationships. Teachers talk of how they approach their teaching differently after the experience of being coached. They say they hear themselves using the skills of coaching with their students in order to facilitate their learning processes rather than simply teaching content and telling students what to do. They become learning partners, learning from and with their students as they create new knowledge together.

As *connoisseurs*, educational leaders focus on pedagogy—their own as a leader and that of others in the institution. Conversant with current research practices, they work to develop continual improvement in their own teaching and that of colleagues. They use evidence-based leadership (Earl & Katz, 2002; Muijs et al., 2014) to encourage commitment among the people they work with. They also encourage these people to take ownership of issues related to improving learning opportunities within the institution. The process in this latter regard is one of "rich accountability".

As *entrepreneurs*, educational leaders research their own work and that of others. They gain outside perspectives and feedback to confront their thinking, and they seek out new ideas, challenges and opportunities to improve what they do. As inventors and innovators, they like coaching because it gets them beyond the usual façade of leadership to the "nitty-gritty" of their work. They focus on problem posing as well as problem solving and work collaboratively so that they are challenged and enriched by diverse perspectives in rich networks of learning.

Coaching and the present-day reality of leadership

Barriers to effective leadership

As early as the mid-1980s, Apple (1986) pointed to the increasing complexity of the role of the educational leader in modern society, a situation that has intensified rather than diminished over time. The world over, reforms to educational administration and national curricula have seen educational leaders endeavouring to negotiate multiple demands on their time and to cope with being pulled in many different directions. As Robertson (1995) has observed, leaders often feel they are in reactive mode, responding within a context of ambiguity, paradox and change and to a plethora of tasks characterised by brevity, complexity and fragmentation. Although principals and teachers continue to gain enjoyment from their jobs, many of them feel over-stretched (Wylie & Bonne, 2014). Every day, they find themselves having to make choices between conflicting options raised by various issues.

According to commentators writing nearly 30 years ago, such as Marshall and Duignan (1987) and Robertson (1991b), the dilemmas causing the greatest conflict for leaders were between

- the administrative and educational leadership aspects of their role;
- being accessible and being efficient; and
- decreasing authority and increasing responsibility.

Many, me included, would argue they still are. Resourcing for schools is often stretched (Wylie & Bonne, 2014). Many of those in positions of leadership feel the administrative demands of their daily work limit them from exercising their leadership role within learning, yet learning is what they see as their most important focus (Robertson, 1999). Wylie (1997) and Wylie & Bonne (2014) have identified funding and property (building maintenance) as the two major concerns facing leaders in self-managing schools even though the institutions' educational leaders should have, as their main focus, quality provision of learning opportunities.

One leader, a newly appointed principal who participated in the research informing the development of the coaching model, voiced his frustration in this regard: "I've really wasted a year. I've looked more at the administration side rather than at the education in the school, and I haven't pushed that side enough. That's why I'm a bit nervous that I've wasted this year." His lament continues to be one of the most frequently voiced among educational leaders internationally; it is here that coaching can help leaders bring their focus back to their educational leadership role of improving teaching and learning.

Although it is imperative within self-managing institutions that educational leaders are available and accessible to their communities, consulting with them over the formulation and implementation of educational goals (within nationally prescribed managerial and curricular guidelines), most leaders can achieve this facet of their work only by putting in very long hours, in their own time (Robertson, 1995). For these leaders, self-responsibility and autonomy can feel like a sham as they struggle to cope with an increasing raft of centrally imposed policies, innovations and practices, a situation at seeming variance with the devolution intent of educational reforms and a product of what Codd (1990) refers to as government's centrally imposed managerialist ideology. Indeed, some educational leaders liken their role to that of a "middle manager", implementing, at the behest of others, policies for which they feel no ownership (Robertson, 1995).

This ideology also negates the intention of education policies developed to celebrate and encourage the diverse nature of the communities that schools serve. Educational leaders work with wide-ranging and ever-changing educational communities that singly and together reflect multiple values and beliefs. Conditions in these communities' educational institutions are therefore not linear. They do not allow for clear inputs and outputs, as in, say, factories producing baked beans. Educational leaders deal constantly with the many issues, decisions, changes and concerns that reflect the communities they serve. Implementation of a potentially transformative policy, whether nationally or locally directed, can lead to divisiveness in the community, given the multiple values and beliefs that preside there (Robertson, 1995). Building learning partnerships with key leaders in the community is accordingly vital to the ongoing process of leading transformative change.

The importance of critical thinking

The coaching model provides a structure whereby leaders can "learn the way" of dealing with these pressures because it allows them to think critically and regularly about the issues as *they* experience them and then to adapt their practice accordingly. Coaching helps them determine if their leadership practice is little more than a façade—if it merely encompasses activities or ways of talking with colleagues that give the impression the institution is being well managed and is highly effective when it may not be, as the following leader articulated:

> They were waxing loud on this—"In my institution this and in my staff … that," and "We do this," and "We've got that," and "I've got this," and "I've got that"—and I used to think, "Holy cat fish, how will I ever become as good as they are?" And then I discovered … what I call the "whited sepulchre syndrome" … a biblical allegory. The sepulchre is a raised tomb which you whitewash every year in memory of the death. So, on the outside, everything is beautiful, but on the inside it is all corruption.

Coaching helps leaders develop special relationships with their professional colleagues, a process which, as a matter of course, significantly improves professional communication within and across institutions. In the conflicts occasioned by central imposition on the one hand and localised autonomy on the other, and by the market-driven imperatives of competition and choice, such dialogue and collaboration among leaders of different institutions can only be advantageous in terms of rebuilding collaboration and maximising the strengths of each educational institution in a community as its members create new knowledge together. Leaders, moreover, can become more aware of the external influences on their work and, through this understanding and the collegiality that develops, find strategies to manage stress. They develop confidence and self-efficacy through the coaching process, affirmation of their work, self-awareness and recognition that the role of educational leadership is complex. The support that professional colleagues offer is also vital in helping leaders to bed in the changes to practice they make as an outcome of coaching and to strive for ongoing reflection about and improvement of their practice.

"You tend now to really look. You really are looking for some of the things that are occurring, and when you're doing that, you're thinking to yourself all the time, 'Would I do this?'"

The need for more relevant professional development

For many leaders, attendance at their association's annual conference, the monthly meeting of the regional association or executive group, and perhaps a professional development seminar or workshop slotted in here and there when a brochure catches their attention typifies their professional-development activities. Leaders state that they seldom, if ever, have to confront their own leadership on such occasions, and so have no impetus to change their practice when back on site. A disruption, an intervention, is often needed before transformative change can take place. Leaders who assume the role of professional coaching partner provide this challenge for one another, as does the facilitator developing the coaching processes between teachers and leaders. The same can be said of the members of the institution's learning community or their local network or the consortium of institutions established to support the innovation being implemented.

In similar vein, leaders rarely have opportunity to discuss educational leadership with one another or to *observe* each other in practice. The term "reflective practitioner" is often more rhetoric than reality in leaders' lives unless time is set aside and structured for the process. Coaching provides an ongoing venue wherein leaders can talk about and observe one another in action in the workplace, be it a departmental meeting, a classroom, a community or business meeting, a meeting of the executive team, or time spent working on students' issues or with the board of trustees.

Over the years of my research, many people have asked what competencies, standards and/or attributes of leadership I've been intent on developing through the coaching model. My answer has always been: "This is not a recipe approach. The model develops critically reflective leaders, with a strong moral purpose for equity, committed to the continual improvement of their leadership practice." The coaching model approach is therefore the antithesis of many of the recent and current leadership development trends, which Gronn (2003, p. 7) describes as "production of leaders by design or the idea of designer-leadership". Here, sets of competencies, which are often culture-, context-, and gender-neutral, determine the quality or readiness of the practitioner for management positions. This preoccupation with competencies is integral to the aforementioned managerial ideology of the New Right exercised in many countries around the world, and it is at variance with the approach to leadership development researched first in Australia and then extended to New Zealand (Wildy, Louden, & Robertson, 2000)—an approach that highlights the importance of context in leadership development and practice.

I'm also asked at conferences what motivated the leaders who participated in my research to take on coaching partnerships. I often answer by referring to the old adage: "You can lead a horse to water, but you can't make it drink." The answer revolves around not only how to get leaders *to* the water, given that job conditions often prevent them from making the journey, but *how* to get them to drink once they're there. (I cover this "how to" aspect in depth in the next chapter.)

"My coach has been truly amazing. He is professional, challenging, purposeful, and seems genuinely interested in my inquiry and my progress as a leader. It's the best professional development I've had."

Coaching educational leadership provides an answer to these questions. Educational leaders who keep education at the centre of their work by critically reflecting on their practice are aware of the influence of managerialism on their work. They are consequently able to hold fast to their educational leadership role and so do not become mere managers (Robertson, 1999). I believe that without this perspective, Goodlad's words, written over 35 years ago in the USA, could become a portent for leaders in education across the world.

> We corrupted the educational process through over cultivation of the system. And now as we reflect on all this—and reflection is a luxury in which we too little indulge—we become dimly aware of something missing. That something is what motivated most of us to become teachers or educators in the first place … to put education at the centre again, [to] want to become educational leaders again, not mere managers. (Goodlad, 1978, p. 324)

I also fear that unless this perspective comes to pervade professional learning and leaders' mindsets in the near future, Goodlad's words could well be the lament of educational leaders 25 years hence.

We have yielded to the pressures and temptations of becoming experts in fiscal and personnel management, public relations, collective bargaining, and the political process. Few of us are trained or experienced in any of these, even though we must take responsibility for them. What we are trained and experienced in, most of us, is education—its traditional and emerging goals, its historical roots, alternatives, curriculum, counselling, instruction. (Goodlad, 1978, p. 331)

Summary of main points

- Effective educational leadership can be developed through professional coaching.
- Coaching can be a reciprocal practice between peers and/or involve a learning community with or between schools.
- Important qualities of an educational leader are the statespersonship of developing relationships, the knowledge of education, and the entrepreneurship necessary to see opportunities for innovation.
- The work of an educational leader is complex, varied and context specific.
- Coaching, as professional development, acknowledges the reality of leaders' work.
- Support and challenge are essential in leaders' professional development. Coaching offers this.
- Coaching allows leaders to critically reflect on and respond to the realities and demands of today's educational context.

With the formation of the river systems *li* there is a certain paradox of priority: rivers shape the landscape and the landscape contains the river.

Chapter 3

Learning for leadership

Chapter overview[1]

Coaching is about seeing leadership practice as opportunities for learning. The new education context requires lifelong learning as we struggle to keep abreast of new technologies, new programmes and curriculum, new ideas and new ways of working. This chapter therefore highlights the importance that lifelong learning and theories related to adult learning hold for the process of coaching. Also emphasised here is the importance of leaders' values and beliefs. These provide the "educational platform" upon which leaders base their leadership decisions. The notion that coaching helps close the gap between espoused theories of practice and leadership practice in action is also discussed here. So, too, is the idea that coaching challenges leaders to think about the theory of learning in different ways, and to recognise that if new leadership learning is to take place, leaders must cross the boundaries of their comfort zones, into the zones of critical

---

1   For this second edition, much of this chapter has been taken, with permission, from the following journal article: Jan Robertson (2013), Learning leadership, *Leading & Managing*, 19(2), 54–69.

thinking and possibilising, an experience that can be constructed through the process of coaching.

The importance of lifelong learning

The professional learning of school leaders has been at the forefront of education policy development internationally for well over a decade now. Recent syntheses of research on educational leadership and student achievement show that quality school leadership and teacher quality is inextricably linked to improved student achievement (Dempster, 2009; Hattie, 2009; Robinson, Hohepa, & Lloyd, 2009; Timperley, Wilson, Barrar, & Fung, 2007; Wiliam, 2011). Despite their best efforts to find otherwise, a group of researchers in the United States reported that "To date we have not found a single case of a school improving its student achievement record in the absence of talented leadership" (Seashore Lewis et al., 2010, p. 9). Not only is the link between effective leadership and improved student learning outcomes strong but, as research has found, "The principal is the single biggest determinant of whether or not teachers want to stay in their schools, which suggests that better leadership may be a highly cost-effective way to improve teaching and learning throughout schools" (Wallace Foundation, 2012, p. 25).

Current international discourse in the leadership field includes a focus on reflection, shared leadership, equity and social justice, and professional learning communities. However, there is more rhetoric about reflection than ever occurs in school settings, more talk by leaders about shared leadership and learning than is seen in practice, and more discussion of equity and social justice than is addressed in practice. Resnick, Spillane, Goldman, and Rangel (2010, p. 287) concur that "The vocabulary of 'distributed leadership', or 'professional learning communities', can be heard at professional meetings but is more rarely found in practice."

Leaders who elect to use the coaching model can develop a greater awareness of themselves in practice and be supported and challenged to develop their practices in a manner that exemplifies the principles of lifelong learning. Learning leadership is not simply about getting more knowledge; it is also about embracing opportunities for more *thinking about that knowledge*—for more sense-making. The metacognitive skill of self-regulated learning from practice of how *to be* and *to become* in

leadership practice and what the new knowledge means for one's identity as an educational leader are fundamental elements of this process.
By adapting the coaching model to their context, experience, culture and
situation, leaders take responsibility for their learning and therefore ownership of the process. Coaching is a valuable model for formative appraisal
because it focuses on improving learning experiences and opportunities
over time.

Effective leadership is thus learned through experience and by leaders
with the innate qualities that allow them to learn effectively from that
experience, which is why coaching through partnership relationships is
crucial to ensuring *ongoing* learning of effective leadership practice. Thus,
learning *in* leadership and leadership *as* learning is paramount to effective
engagement and ownership of the change process facilitated by developing and achieving shared visions.

Seeing their leadership *as* practice, and learning effectively from it, on
a daily basis is an important skill for leaders. Leadership learning of this
kind is based on the real experiences and actions that constitute leaders'
daily work. It's also based on reflective observation of those experiences as
well as opportunities to question, pose and solve problems, opportunities
to analyse and develop new ways of thinking and leading, and opportunities to try out new ideas. In essence, this type of leadership learning is an
essential part of the ideal of professionalism.

Experiential learning

The exercise of educational leadership requires leaders to act intentionally—to strive to improve the teaching and learning experiences of those
in their education communities. This desire is at the heart of praxis, which
must be governed, as Duignan (1988, p. 5) reminds us, by "conscious,
reflective, intentional action … [which] is the bridge between theory and
practice—between reflection, analysis and action." For leaders, opportunities to engage in this form of action are best engendered through dialogue,
observation, experimentation and reflection on practice; in short, through
experiential learning, another vital component of the coaching model.

Kolb (1984, p. 40) describes the process of experiential learning as "a
four stage cycle involving four adaptive modes: concrete experience; reflective observation; abstract conceptualisation; and active experimentation."

Kolb stresses that when all four stages are given an equal weighting (see Figure 3.1), the (desired) outcome is effective praxis.

Experiences

Leaders' everyday work experiences, the tasks and activities they undertake, are pivotal for new learning (Kolb, 1984). But many leaders are not effective adult learners and do not necessarily have "the higher order skills … [and] the ability to stand back and take control of their own learning" that Lucas and Claxton (2010, p. 138) deem so important. In his syntheses of research on metacognition, Dawson (2008, p. 3) argues that "Adults whose metacognitive skills are well developed are better problem-solvers, decision makers and critical thinkers, are more able and more motivated to learn, and are more likely to be able to regulate their emotions (even in difficult situations), handle complexity, and cope with conflict." De Corte (2010) refers to these attributes as "adaptive expertise" (p. 45), and she lists "meta-cognitive knowledge" and "knowledge about one's motivations and emotions" (p. 46) as underpinning adaptive leadership. Metacognitive skill is thus a fundamental component of emotional and social intelligence (Goleman, 2006).

Within the coaching model, professional leadership development begins when leaders make the most of an experience by carefully considering it, conducting a self-assessment and then combining this information with feedback from the coach and others they work with to develop new principles, concepts and theories to use on the job. Learning through challenging leadership contexts, with due depth of reflection, leads to improved leadership practice. For Lucas and Claxton (2010, p. 175), "… real-world intelligence has to do with how people respond to the challenges that matter to them. As Jean Piaget said, being smart is not about 'knowing lots'; it is how you think, feel and behave at the moments when your accumulated store of knowledge and skill *doesn't* give you a ready answer, and you have to 'think on your feet.'"

Metacognitive capability is the high-level capability of intelligent leaders who can learn in their leadership practice. However, the double and triple-loop learning from professional practice that Argyris (2008) describes is not necessarily part of leaders' leadership learning experiences. Leaders accordingly don't always see this reflective skill as part of their leadership practice and are often heard lamenting they're too busy to reflect. For them, reflection is not part *of* practice but something *additional* to practice, and if they can find the time.

The learning that arises out of experience not only assists with the construction of learning but also enhances intellectual independence and reinforces self-directed professional development. Self-directed learning is "a form of study in which learners have primary responsibility for planning, carrying out, and evaluating their own learning experiences … and is the way most adults, including professional educators, go about acquiring new ideas, skills, and attitudes" (Caffarella, 1993, p. 30).

Figure 3.1 presents a summative depiction of Kolb's seminal work (1984) on adult learning theory. Kolb maintains that the most *effective* learning for adults takes place when they progress through all four of his identified adult learning stages. However, what is often missing from adult learning in school leaders' professional practice is the *how* of Kolb's reflective-observation and abstract-conceptualization stages. Many leaders get caught between the concrete experience and active experimentation parts of the cycle, by simply trying out different strategies to resolve the same problems and challenges they face on a daily basis. Their approach is reactive rather than proactive. As Hallinger (2011, p. 137) puts it: "Leaders who possess a single set of tools will find themselves bouncing around

Figure 3.1: Adult learning theory (after Kolb, 1984)

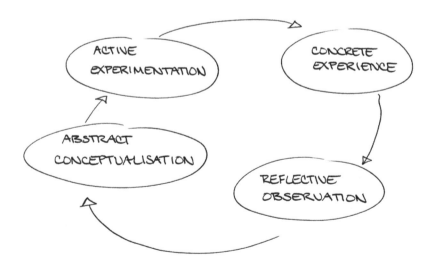

from success to failure without understanding why. The capacity to read your context correctly and adapt *your* leadership to the needs largely determines your success" (emphasis in the original).

Argyris (2008, pp. 2–3) states the concern this way:

> Most people define learning too narrowly as mere "problem solving," so they focus on identifying and correcting errors in the external environment. Solving problems is important. But if learning is to persist, [they] must also look inward. They need to reflect critically on their own behavior, identify the ways they often inadvertently contribute to the organization's problems, and then change how they act. In particular, they must learn how the very way they go about defining and solving problems can be a source of problems in its own right.

Leaders who are not metacognitive typically default to a problem-solving, single-loop reactive style of leadership in their practice, which means they are unable to improve that practice in ways that benefit student achievement. They are also unlikely to challenge teachers in ways that will improve teachers' professional practice and encourage their ongoing learning. Leaders therefore require opportunities to investigate themselves and their own values and beliefs in the learning process.

Reflective observation

Reflecting on experiences and the actions related to those experiences helps leaders become more receptive to trying out new strategies and behaviours. This practice can also see them changing a value or a belief and, from there, their actions. Sometimes, however, leaders don't find it easy to reflect adequately on a particular experience, and this is where coaches are so useful. Through careful questioning and prompting—direct challenge even, where warranted—coaches can help leaders more readily relive an experience or look at it differently (Barnett, O'Mahoney, & Matthews, 2004). They can help leaders see what attitudes and values might have made them act in a certain way at a certain time and to consider whether that way would be appropriate in future.

Figure 3.2 shows the levels of confronting questions that educational leaders can ask of themselves and their colleagues when pursuing improved professional practice. So often professional questioning stays at the level of the "what" and "how" of strategies and activities. The real learning and change occurs in the zones of "Why?" and "What might be?" This type of questioning "requires reciprocity and dialogue in a relationship of trust to get beyond the bluff exterior and impression management" (Robertson, 2010, p. 56) that leaders usually maintain with respect to their professional practice. In this instance, leaders must be willing to admit to and to anticipate vulnerability. They must also, of course, be willing to learn.

Figure 3.2: Deeper learning from professional practice

Argyris's (2008) claim that other people and their different perspectives on issues and practices are an essential component of the process of deep adult thinking and learning in organisations is important here because meaning-making is enhanced when perspectives are challenged. In order to move from the *how* of professional practice (Figure 3.2), learners must engage with the second loop of learning, which considers the *why* and the justifications and purposes of that practice. The third loop of learning—the *what might be*—requires learners to explore transformative possibilities for future practice and indeed, possibly transform themselves. Earlier research called this important third loop "possibilising" (Robertson & Webber, 2002). These "why" and "what might be" questions are generative in that they help leaders access new ways of seeing ideas that challenge their existing paradigms and the belief and value systems that inform those paradigms.

Conceptualisation

Once leaders free themselves from their taken-for-granted ways of viewing the world, they can start "seriously entertaining and evaluating alternative possibilities" (Berlak & Berlak, 1987, p. 169). This process involves a type of conceptualisation wherein leaders are able to psychologically distance themselves from the issues under reflection. Working this process through with others, notably the coach, helps leaders deconstruct the dominant, prevalent discourses relating to these issues and the effect they are having on their leadership role (Foucault, 1977). As leaders become aware they're not the only ones experiencing the same difficulties and dilemmas, they gain the confidence to find solutions to the problems collaboratively rather than to expend energy blaming themselves for some perceived lack of ability.

Research knowledge and best and next-practice knowledge are important aspects of the conceptualising process. Observing how different practice looks in action can be a necessary precursor to someone trying the next practices. Throughout my work, many leaders and teachers have told me that their seeming reluctance to change is more about a lack of understanding of what that change actually means to their everyday practice. Coaches modelling quality practice can be a very powerful link in the change process (see the case studies in Chapter 11).

Experimentation

Conceptualisation works best when it gives leaders confidence to actively experiment with different concepts and ideas in their practice. Experimentation becomes the new concrete experience as the learning cycle begins again. This cycle of active experimentation is therefore not uninformed action but praxis: "It is this whole process of reflection-in-action which is central to the 'art' by which practitioners sometimes deal with situations of uncertainty, instability, uniqueness, and value conflicts" (Schön, 1983, p. 50). Reflection-in-action, Schön explains, "consists of on-the-spot surfacing, criticising, restructuring, and testing of intuitive understandings of experienced phenomena; often it takes the form of a reflective conversation with the situation" (1983, p. 242). If done properly, reflection-in-action becomes "knowing-in-action" because it allows people to act with confidence on the basis of informed decisions arising out of reflection on their experiences. A professional coaching partner assists leaders to be reflective *in* action, *on* action and *for* future action, a level of engagement which results in a knowledge *of* practice. This process moves leadership inquiry into a new paradigm, that of leadership *as* learning.

Thinking about learning

When educational leaders become involved in systematic inquiry about their practice, whether in coaching partnerships or in professional learning communities, they gain knowledge of practice that facilitates effective leadership. This process, as described by Cochran-Smith and Lytle (1999), rests on a way of thinking about learning in order to improve leadership that is new for many educational leaders (see Table 3.1). This mode of thinking requires leaders to think about their work in terms of problems to be solved—to problem pose rather than just problem solve—and to be systematic about that enquiry by establishing support structures such as coaching.

Table 3.1: New conceptions of learning

New conceptions of learning	Differing assumptions	Implications for professional development
Knowledge for practice	Research generates formal knowledge for use.	Dissemination of knowledge.
Knowledge in practice	Knowledge embedded in exemplary practice and reflection.	Focus on experience-based projects and practical knowledge.
Knowledge of practice	Learn by making leadership, learning and research problematic.	Systematic and critical enquiry in communities.

Source: Adapted from descriptions given by M. Cochran-Smith & S. Lytle (1999), Relationships of knowledge and practice: Teacher learning in communities, in A. Iran-Nejad & C. D. Pearson (Eds.), *Review of research in education* (Vol. 24, pp. 251–307), Washington, DC, American Educational Research Association.

Grossman, Wineburg, and Woolworth (2000) write that leaders who work together in these ways differ from other gatherings of leaders in terms of three factors important for systematic collaborative enquiry on leadership practice:

1. Commitment to colleagues' growth.
2. Recognition that participation is expected.
3. Recognition that colleagues are resources for one's own learning.

The thinking that supports these factors places leaders at the centre of their own learning and the responsibility for learning firmly in their court. Leadership coaching endeavours to exemplify this stance on learning responsibility.

Increasingly, most of the important challenges currently facing educators require leadership practice that examines and challenges usual modes of practice and what currently underpins that practice (Hannon, 2011). The solutions to the complex challenges being faced in education today often require a change of mindset and a change of paradigm—a new cognitive frame of learning—and not just incremental changes and improvement to the current context. It is thus the leaders themselves who must change.

Figure 3.3 illustrates the transition from entering into and being part of the change (in) to actively participating in the change (in deeper) to finally being transformed by the change process in a new cognitive frame

Figure 3.3: Positioning oneself in the change process

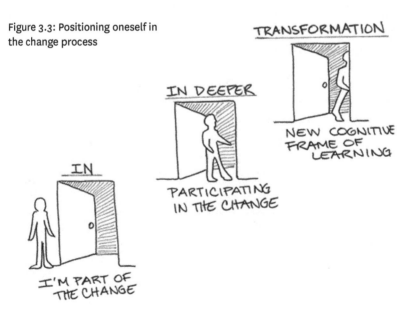

TRANSFORMATION

IN DEEPER

NEW COGNITIVE FRAME OF LEARNING

IN

PARTICIPATING IN THE CHANGE

I'M PART OF THE CHANGE

of learning transformation). Garvey Berger (2012) also believes that such transformation growth involves a "qualitative shift, not just in knowledge, but in perspective or way of thinking" (p. 17). Once again, it is the double-loop learning of meaning-making that leads leaders to a reframing of practice and rethinking, of asking why things are as they are and what they might be instead. And it is the triple-loop learning—of examining one's own values, beliefs and assumptions—that leads to the transformative leadership practice which changes systems, structures and paradigms in these complex contexts.

Developing within one's leadership is part of this process. It is worth reiterating here that metacognitive learning within leadership practice moves leaders from thinking about *what is* and *how*, to thinking about *why* and *what might be*, and how their own transformation might then be part of the solution for change. Educational leadership necessitates being able to step into the change process and transform oneself through the leadership practice that is evolving through changed mindsets. Garvey Berger (2012) calls this development stage the "self-transforming mind" and considers it vital for leadership for a complex world. A shared moral purpose then becomes the compass of the change process.

Uncovering the educational platform

One of the most important aspects of coaching is that of the coach and the educational leader together clarifying the values and beliefs about education and learning on which their leadership practice and decision making rest. These values and beliefs underpin the decisions that leaders make within their institutions and so are referred to within the context of the coaching model as the *educational platform*.

Educational leadership within the context of the coaching model requires leaders to make their values, beliefs and interests overt to others, a process that sees them having to identify and articulate their educational platforms (see Chapter 7). Leaders need to make transparent their respective educational platforms for both educative and ethical reasons. For them, ability to draw understanding from the many actions they carry out daily depends on knowledge of these platforms and recognition of the size of the gap between their rhetoric of espoused theories and their actual "leadership in action".

"You're developing very independent leaders by causing them to reflect and do their own learning, and since learning is change, [to] change themselves ... I think the strength of the system is the expectation that each leader is responsible for her own development. We don't want clones."

When people are asked what they would do in a certain situation, the answers they give are their espoused theories of action, which presumably govern their theories in use (Schön, 1983, 1987). However, the two don't always match, and leaders who are not aware of the discrepancies or gaps between their theories and actions may not see the necessity for or be open to new learning. Coaching helps close the gap between espoused theories and theories in action. It creates the essential conditions for the double and triple-loop learning that, as noted earlier, Argyris (1999, 2008) claims is so essential for effective professional development. It is worth emphasising again Argyris's (2008) argument that double and triple-loop learning happens only when learners invite other people to observe and comment on their behaviour (actions), so providing the catalyst that allows the learners to confront the views and values influencing their behaviour. The catalyst that outside perspectives provide explains why the coaching partner is necessarily at the core of the leadership learning process.

Opportunities for leaders to examine why they think in the way they do and what values, beliefs and assumptions underpin this thinking are fundamental to this learning. Such opportunities help leaders understand how their own cultural context, their social, spiritual and emotional beliefs and their own educational experiences are influencing their thinking and their actions. Those understandings provide the starting points for transformation of mindset.

Figure 3.4 illustrates two leaders standing on a firm educational platform. The platform is made up of the values, beliefs and assumptions that underpin their mental models and which therefore influence their decision making and are evident in their leadership practice (pertaining, in the figure, to parental involvement in the leaders' schools).

Senge (1990, p. 12) identifies five disciplines that leaders need to undertake to successfully introduce learning into organisations. One of these requires leaders to examine their own and other's mental models,

Figure 3.4: The platform underpinning decisionmaking in educational leadership

and then, through deep self-reflection, gain understanding of how these models can not only prevent insights and innovation being implemented but also influence all of the leadership decisions that are made. Senge (1990) goes so far as to state that unless these mental models are identified, surfaced and examined, no changes of any importance will occur in leadership practice. Kouzes and Posner (2011, p. 36) express this aspect of leadership practice as follows: "To be credible as a leader you must clarify your own values, the principles that guide your decisions and actions and the standards by which you choose to live your life. Values guide how you feel, what you say, what you think, how you make choices, and how you act." These words also encapsulate the essence of a leader's leadership.

Because metacognitive leaders reflect publicly on their thinking and inquire into different perspectives in order to make an informed decision, and thus ensure they're truly learning from the process, they seek different points of view from across cultures and contexts and from those individuals who are most dissonant about a change process. This diversity of viewpoint and values constantly forces leaders to examine their own values, beliefs and assumptions, practice that is integral to triple-loop learning and the metacognitive process. Dawson (2008, p. 3), however, offers a caution in this regard: "Although metacognitive skills, once they are well-learned, can become habits of mind that are applied in a wide variety of contexts, it is important for even the most advanced adult learners to 'flex their cognitive muscles' by consciously applying appropriate metacognitive skills to new knowledge and in new situations.'

Effective metacognitive leaders are able to be part of a situation and yet at the same time willing to stand back from the same situation in order to critique it and to think about what is happening and why. Such leaders, positioned on the left-hand side of Figure 3.5, are part of the change process. They demonstrate what Garvey Berger (2012) calls a *self-transforming* mind because they seek out and see other perspectives and use them to transform their own understanding. Less effective leaders, depicted on the right-hand side of the figure, are those leaders who don't have this level of metacognitive skill. Their conception of change is that it is the responsibility of others. They're consequently outside the change process.

Figure 3.5: Positioning inside or outside the change process

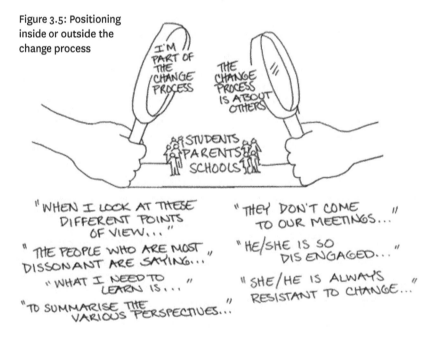

These two opposite perspectives, exemplified by typical statements in the figure, lead to either the effective, transformational, metacognitive leadership style (left side) or to the less effective, single-loop-learning leadership style (right side) of situating oneself outside of the change process and blaming others. The statements in Figure 3.5 also make apparent the need for leaders to be cognisant of how language highlights positioning in educational practice. This awareness is another key leadership skill.

All of this leads us to the important question of how leaders learn and develop quality leadership practice in their organisations. First and foremost, they must focus on themselves as active participants in the leadership practice and change process. As Duignan (1989) points out, discontinuity between espoused theories and professional educative goals, principles and values can lead to stress and tensions within daily practice. Awareness of discontinuity, however, directs attention to the possibility for positive transformation.

My 20-plus years of development and research on educational leadership in combination with insights gained from my coaching of leadership practices with school leaders has continued to confirm for me that leaders who pursue this focus become ever more self-aware, more cognisant of and thoughtful about the learning process, starting with their own. This mindset enables them to enter and continue to participate in a type of *coaching leadership* that I define as goal-oriented reflective inquiry. This form of coaching is reciprocal and collaborative, and the coached leaders are self-regulated and metacognitive in their learning, which at all times is directed towards achieving desired outcomes. Throughout, the coach's support as well as his or her challenging (through critically reflective questioning) of the leader provides the means of driving the learning process on.

It's important to remember that this model of coaching leadership encourages the *coach* to be a learner in the process. This "learning in partnership", or reciprocal learning (ako, in Māori) takes leaders' professional practice from operating according to a threatened or defensive mode to practice that reflects openness to new learning and new knowledge. As trust builds in the coaching relationship, leaders become willing to approach the spaces of vulnerability and new learning. *Both* leaders learn as together they challenge each other's thinking and co-construct new ways of being, knowing and doing in leadership practice (Robertson, 2008). This new learning usually involves a measure of emotional engagement, which is not surprising given the challenging of values, beliefs and assumptions brought about by the examination of counter-cultures and the crossing of different boundaries that coaching stimulates (Robertson & Webber, 2002).

In essence, the true path of transformative leadership begins with the leaders' own transformation—of seeing things differently, of wanting to explore new frontiers, of being in a different place, of knowing more than they had known previously. These new ways of seeing, doing and knowing create possibilities for changed practices. As shown in Figure 3.6, the path of transformation in educational leadership thus becomes a shared meta-cognitive practice of co-constructing knowledge, challenging the thinking behind that knowledge and being transformed by the process of that new learning.

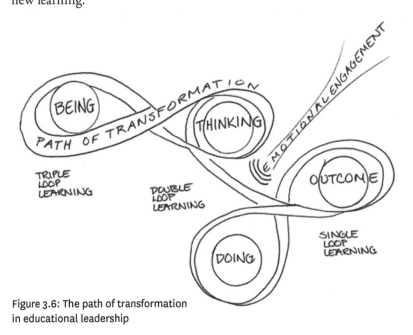

Figure 3.6: The path of transformation in educational leadership

Within educational contexts, coaching is most effective when it assists leaders to understand their values and beliefs about how people learn best and what their true interests as leaders of their institutions are. Coaching should also assist leaders to develop the ability to articulate their educational leadership platform in dialogue with their colleagues. Argyris (2008) found that many leaders, particularly those in senior consultant positions, are generally willing to look outside of themselves for the reasons for poor practice. He posited that those leaders able to critique their own practice and the role they play in leadership practice in general enter a virtuous cycle of self-awareness. Self-awareness leads to greater learning about one's own and others' leadership, and that learning in turn leads to improved leadership practice. Because capable metacognitive leaders are positioned very clearly inside the change process, they have the wherewithal to constantly seek ways to examine and challenge their own thinking and thus to rethink and to see the influence of leadership practice from different and agentic perspectives.

Sergiovanni and Starratt (2002, p. 71) summarise the importance of this process as "knowing *what* the platform position is, understanding the relationship between … practices and platform elements, perceiving inconsistencies between the spoken platform and the platform in practice, [and] appreciating differences between one's own platform and that of another" (emphasis original). They give examples of the types of platforms commonly found among educators. There is the basic competency platform, the democratic socialisation platform, the urban teacher platform and the ecological platform. Most of the values and beliefs making up these platforms could belong to teachers, principals, academics and so on, but the platforms become particularly cogent when senior leaders add in the values and beliefs they have about their role in monitoring the quality of the teaching and learning within the institution. (For detail on how to uncover leadership platforms, see Chapter 7.)

"Through the coaching and talking through my inquiry, I was enabled to see a different perspective and to think about different approaches. It allowed me to be productively critical, reflective and to think of different aspects that I hadn't thought about."

Creating opportunities for other leaders to uncover their educational platforms is another important role for educational leaders in positions of responsibility, and they can realise it by engaging in collaborative "storying" during the coaching process (Sutton, 2005). This type of collaboration requires leaders to be particularly mindful of, and to be prepared to reflect on and critique, how they work daily with others; coaching allows this. It assists leaders to solve the dilemmas in their leadership practice and, where necessary, change it to the advantage of those with whom they work. Metacognitive leaders see their leadership as *opportunities* for learning, and herein lies the true meaning of "leader as learner". Such a leader is willing, ready and able to learn *from* their leadership in ways that enable them to develop the adaptive capabilities necessary for successful leadership.

A leader of single-loop learning is concerned with "more of the same": improving practice (doing) and looking at fast results (outcome) rather than participating in processes that lead to real transformation in the long run and at all levels—individual, group, organisation and system. Leaders of double-loop learning are more motivated. They engage in the change process by thinking and reflecting on the *path of transformation* (thinking) so that they themselves change through the *process of transformation* (being). They live and practise the change, which means they move beyond espoused theory to theory in use (Schön, 1987). To put this change more colloquially, they walk the talk, thus modelling, as triple-loop learners and leaders, the way forward for others: "The ability to effectively make meaning in a rapidly changing world requires collaboration and constructivism" (Robertson, 2010, p. 58). (Read more in Ch. 13.)

Co-constructing knowledge

While coaching requires leaders to engage in learning partnerships with one another, the partners need not have the same values, beliefs and ways of operating. As Elbaz-Luwisch (2001, p. 86) points out, "encounters with others who define themselves differently [allows] one ... [to] participate in dialogue with many voices, a dialogue in which the self can engage in ongoing definition and redefinition." Coaching develops learning communities of leaders whose diverse perspectives on issues challenge leaders to move beyond self to a bigger, more critical perspective on their own practice in particular and educational leadership in general (Webber & Robertson, 1998). Fullan and Stiegelbauer's (1991) belief that leaders are constrained in their learning by a ceiling effect if they keep to themselves highlights the value of the dialogic encounters brought about by coaching relationships.

If we believe that knowledge is socially and culturally constructed— as well as *deconstructed* and *reconstructed*—by people at both personal and group levels, a model of leadership coaching must rest on social-constructivist principles. Bell and Gilbert (1996, p. 57) support a view of learning for preservice and inservice teacher education that takes account of how the individual contributes to the construction of socially agreed knowledge (i.e., shared knowledge developed by the group for that particular context) and of how those who have contributed to that construction then use it to reconstruct and transform the culture of the workplace and this social knowledge itself. Knowledge of empirical research and theory is important in regard to this process.

Bell and Gilbert (1996) consider that the process involves what they term "human agency"—the ability of individuals to feel they can transform their beliefs into actions that make a difference (for a more detailed consideration of agency, see Chapter 12 of this book). Their premise is very much in line with the view of leadership learning espoused in the coaching model, wherein learners experience scaffolded learning in new leadership practices in supported, authentic contexts, most notably their own institutions. The effectiveness of this learning context relies on a generative, constructivist approach to leadership learning, such as coaching, because it encourages leaders to focus on their own issues, as they occur, and then to relate the research theory and co-constructed knowledge to their developing practice. This "sustained interaction produces wisdom" (Fullan, 2003b, p. 47) not only about leadership but also about the institution and education.

"To be honest, I think I'm a lot more relaxed because I know there is at least one other [person] out there who has got the same problems as me, the same hassles, the same worries, and I know that I am not unique, not the only person who has got everybody doing the wrong thing at the wrong time ... some days are like that, and it's something you can ring up and laugh about."

Crossing borders

Reciprocal coaching, involving shadowing (observation in the workplace) and experiences in different educational contexts, obliges learners to cross over their own professionally formed "borders" and boundaries of knowledge to view how others work. Giroux (1992, p. 26) calls this crossing over "border pedagogy" and defines it as "challenging, remapping, and renegotiating those boundaries of knowledge that claim the status of master narratives, fixed identities, and an objective representation of reality ... [and] recognizing the situated nature of knowledge ... and the shifting, multiple and often contradictory nature of identity." Giroux argues that effective border pedagogy requires "pedagogical conditions in which students become border-crossers in order to understand otherness in its own terms" (p. 28).

Leadership coaching establishes opportunities for leaders to cross borders in order to understand otherness, different ways of being and knowing, and how the situated nature of leadership knowledge is created. For Robertson and Webber (2000, 2002; see also Webber and Robertson, 1998), Giroux's notion of border pedagogy is an essential component of effective leadership-learning methodology because it creates the conditions for "boundary-breaking leadership development" (their terminology). In a reciprocal learning relationship, these places of innovation are often found *in the spaces between.*

Clandinin and Connelly's (1995) belief that "teachers' professional knowledge landscapes" are made up of shared stories aligns well with the concept of border crossing. Each leadership context, even within the same institution, has its own stories, its own culture of rites, artefacts and taken-for-granted practices. It is not until leaders cross borders and share these narratives with others that they are challenged to critique their own leadership practices, identities and stories.

Support for this claim comes from Jasman's (2002) findings from her five research studies involving participants in a variety of border-crossing practices. Taking the border-crossing metaphor further, she identified several types of traveller: tourist, migrant, tour guide, trekker and explorer. The various travellers journey within a new knowledge territory in different ways, revealing how their amount of familiarity with, respect for and trust, experience and knowledge of the new context affects the ease with which they engage with it and construct new knowledge from it:

> Not only are there different borders to cross but the visa under which we travel in the other territory is an important factor in the ease of access, familiarity with, understanding of and comfort within the other territory. As with border-crossing there are rites of passage, [and] gate-keepers may subvert or ease the passage from one professional knowledge context to another. (Jasman, 2002, p. 44)

Educational institutions have many boundaries: between teachers and students, theory and practice, roles, departments, neighbouring institutions, institutions and communities, cultures, genders, ages, ranks and so on. Leaders' ability to cross these borders is therefore extremely important. Coaching facilitates this ability because it creates opportunities and experiences wherein leaders develop the professional skills and ways of working together in partnership that assist them to cross over boundaries. In short, the skills that arise out of coaching contexts become passports for crossing borders (Jasman, 2002) and securing boundary-breaking leadership development (Robertson & Webber, 2002).

Professional development considerations

Effective coaching is based not only on theories related to adult learning but also on four elements that Fullan and Stiegelbauer (1991) identify as important for effective professional development programmes. They are:
1. Active initiation and participation within the process.
2. Pressure and support to maintain the process long term.
3. Changing behaviour and beliefs in a manner that leads not only to appropriate changes to behaviour but also to those changes becoming institutionalised.
4. Ownership of the change process.

Change of this kind, which leads to new learning and practices, rarely occurs by chance in an institution. It's for this reason that coaching practices need to be initiated as a professional development initiative, either by one of the educational leaders or by an outside leader who has experience in coaching. When this initiation does not occur, or when it does and leaders still fail to participate, there are likely to be several reasons why.

First, people in educational institutions tend to work in relative isolation from one another. The education profession is a lonely one when compared with other professions such as medicine and law where collegial interactions and a culture of shared experience and observation of practice is commonplace. Second, leaders become so enmeshed in the "dailiness" (Griffin, 1987), routine and habit of their everyday tasks that they rarely, if ever, have time for quality reflection (i.e., to think critically about their actions). Third, there is the need for others to participate in the process if critical reflection is to occur (Argyris, 2008). Collegial exchange and dialogue is paramount in the adult learning process.

Senge (1990, p. 59) defines dialogue as "a sharing of thoughts, feelings, and beliefs, and a suspension of commitment to a particular perspective until all available information and positions have been heard." It is this suspension of commitment that Isaacs (1999) believes is also an important component of the process of dialogue. (This is especially so in education, where there seems to be a culture of judgement in the critique of practice. Many teachers are fearful of opening their practice to observation for this very reason.) For Isaacs, effective dialogue entails four skills: listening, respecting, suspending and voicing.

Isaacs' (1999) paradigm leads to the fourth reason why critical reflection on practice is not initiated, and that is lack of skill. Many leaders don't have the interpersonal or coaching skills necessary to provide quality feedback to their peers or to reflect critically on their own practice. Educators are rarely taught how to engage in this type of reflection at any stage of their career development. Coaching tends to fail in educational cultures where skill development focused on enabling educators not only to reflect but also to work with one another in ways that differ from their usual practice has not been prioritised. Deep learning conversations are enabled through coaching relationships (Robertson, 2015).

Changing leaders' habits so that they become reflective practitioners is difficult. Critical reflection cannot be achieved by reading about it. Rather, it must become a habit through use, and through reflection on that use. If critical reflection is to occur, the structures that support it, the time needed for it, and the expectation that leaders will engage in it must be in place first. Coaching provides this support and challenge on an ongoing basis. It also emphasises critical reflection as one of its most important outcomes.

Summary of main points

- Coaching is about seeing leadership practice as opportunities for leadership learning.
- The information/knowledge age education context requires lifelong learning.
- Articulating and understanding one's educational platform is important to leadership development.
- Espoused theories are not always leaders' theories-in-action.
- Coaching is based on maximising experiential learning.
- Coaching provides opportunities for affirmation and validation of practice.
- A knowledge *of* practice is important for effective leadership.
- Coaching is based on a social constructivist theory of professional learning.
- Vicarious learning, through observation of others, is a very important aspect of leadership development because it breaks down barriers between and within institutions so allowing leaders to "cross borders".
- Coaching can provide all of the elements necessary for effective professional development to occur.

Branching *li* systems may gather 'inwardly' or distribute 'outwardly' and they may even support an energy in both directions.

Chapter 4

The value of shared learning: Confirmation from the research

Chapter overview

This chapter takes the premise that this book stands apart from many other books about coaching because its content is based on a great deal of empirical evidence gathered over 25 years of working with educational leaders in tertiary, early childhood, primary and secondary institutions, as well as leaders in other state services and corporations. The chapter accordingly builds not only on the earlier descriptions in this book of the research underpinning the coaching model but also on the work of other researchers and theorists. It does this by summarising the material according to the four main ways that the model benefits leaders. The model brings greater competency to leaders' educational leadership in terms of it positively influencing student learning outcomes. It gives leaders a greater facility to reflect critically on their practice and how it can enable transformative change. It increases and enhances leaders' professional relationships and interactions, and it helps them establish the structures for action research and development. The chapter describes and discusses these advantages.

Educational leadership capability and development

Strength is gained from the *support* and affirmation that comes from working closely with a professional colleague (or colleagues) and the subsequent lessening of feelings of isolation. Support through coaching enables leaders to *focus* more directly on the *quality* of education in their institutions and on their own leadership and its development. Leaders become increasingly open to new ideas and *growth*, which leads them to engage in further reflection on practice and, from there, to make *informed*, committed actions in leading learning. In taking *ownership* for their self-development, leaders gain greater intellectual independence and *agency*. They move from being reactive and isolated to being proactive, collaborative and politically empowered, a state of being which gives them the confidence to relentlessly improve learning opportunities in their institutions.

Support

The comment that "You're only as safe as your last board meeting" is a common one in principals' circles. "You're damned if you do, and damned if you don't" is another familiar iteration. Education systems that facilitate fierce competition across schools add to these concerns. The precarious, complex and dichotomous situations that many educational leaders experience in today's ever-changing educational climate often leave them feeling isolated and uncertain. The resultant loss of confidence lessens their ability to carry out their role effectively. Unless leaders experience the type of professional leadership development or support that enables them to cope effectively and comfortably with change, they are likely to assume more tentative and ineffectual styles of leadership, as these comments from one leader who participated in the research attest:

Before coaching: I'm always afraid—every time I stand up, just to give a few notices at meetings, or something like that. Am I going to say the right thing? Am I going to say something that someone is going to pick up on that I can't give them a good answer on?

After coaching: I've gone from one extreme to the other. If I'd known then what I know now, I wouldn't have let them push me about. I would have felt so empowered, supported and emancipated, that I would never have taken all that rubbish! I would have dealt with it quite differently.

Change of this sort is apparent not only in attitudes, feelings and confidence, but also in skills learned. As Hargreaves and Fullan (1992, p. 7) emphasise, "[T]eacher development … involves more than changing teachers' behaviour. It also involves changing the person the teacher is … Acknowledging that teacher development is also a process of personal development marks an important step forward in our improvement efforts." Personal development is a key feature of powerful professional learning (Robertson & Murrihy, 2005) because the process is one that involves challenging values and beliefs. Changes in mindset are therefore an important outcome of this process (Kaser & Halbert, 2009).

"My peer partner relationship has also been very successful and we meet regularly. I find it challenging that she is a secondary teacher where I am a primary teacher. This has certainly stretched and developed my thinking and understanding of leadership and education further."

Coaching places leaders in a position where they no longer feel isolated. It does this by making them accessible, first to their colleagues and then to other members of the profession. This accessibility provides the starting point for the development of collaborative system-related leadership—a form of leadership that engenders among the members of a system an ethic of care and moral purpose for that system as a whole.

Focus

A particular benefit accruing out of the dialogue and collaboration associated with coaching is that of leaders becoming much more willing and able to focus on their *educational leadership* role of leading student learning. In the absence of an approach typified by the coaching model, leaders find it much easier to focus on school systems, proposal development, form filling and finalising budgets than on their own educational leadership actions. "Coaching," said one leader, "focuses us into leadership issues, and we seek evaluation. Although we may wear many hats in our institutions, we are the professional leaders [even though] sometimes … other issues can take priority."

Growth

The collaborative partnership relationship that is implicit in coaching challenges leaders' existing thoughts and ideas in a way that heightens leaders' openness to new ways of knowing and thus constitutes a growth mindset (Dweck, 2006). This openness to new ideas develops over time as the trust within the coaching relationship strengthens; it is not always present in the initial stages. As trust develops, coaching can help educators approach places of vulnerability, which are the place where real professional learning can begin.

The personal development that leaders experience through coaching often involves changes of approach brought about by observing alternative ways of acting. Leaders talk of the new skills and ideas they pick up from visiting one another's institutions, of innovations they can immediately implement in their own institution, and the agency they acquire that gives them the confidence and skills to implement the transformative change that they know is essential if more effective student learning is to occur. The new approach might be a policy on restorative practices or a presentation for a board meeting, or it might involve ideas for developing a strategic plan for a paradigm shift in teaching and learning. When leaders embrace new ideas, their actions become more informed and committed. As one leader said: "I had to think about my actions ... [My coach's] questions, and especially her last question—"Would you do the same again?"—made me think that I would handle things differently."

Informed action

Opportunity to see other leaders doing things differently, or doing things in the same manner, allows leaders to set their leadership practice in a much wider educational context. They're able to view issues and problems associated with their leadership role at both the micro level of their institution, and at the macro-system level of education nationally and internationally. This perspective gives them the confidence to change their previous structures and way of working, often in a manner they may have neither expected nor envisaged. Once again, they are empowered and gain greater self-efficacy. Their actions become more informed, more committed.

Ownership of self-development

Increased confidence and receptiveness to new ideas and growth bring with them a natural ownership of responsibility for self-development, for the necessity to effect change. As self-awareness increases, leaders consciously make changes to their leadership practice in their institutions. They recognise the importance of utilising the mentoring and instruction they gain from their coaching relationship to develop and meet their own professional goals. They draw on their coach's strengths and expertise, which is why good coaches are those who model effective practices. As areas for development are highlighted, leaders naturally seek ways to make improvements. They become more proactive within the coaching relationship, seeking out opportunities to discuss and "dissect" their practice and to engage in professional development sessions that might help them in some way. Examples from the different coaching research studies include:

- attending a January course for rural school principals together;
- travelling together to a conference;
- inviting a university graduate student to facilitate dialogue among teachers in the centre;
- sharing professional learning opportunities with other schools with similar needs; and
- initiating tertiary-level study groups where participants can muse about their current research projects.

During coaching, leaders often set personal and/or professional goals and ask their coach and others for evaluative feedback on these areas of focus. Some coaching partners choose to have their coach observe them taking senior meetings or when they're teaching. Or they might ask their coaches to watch as they conduct appraisal interviews with their staff. Others may ask their coach to observe them during strategic planning sessions or at meetings of the board. Education consultants and facilitators

"I started the journey into exploring coaching as a model for developing leadership. This has had a profound impact on my leadership and I have confidence that it will be a part of my life from now on. I am looking forward to the rest of the journey!"

"I needed some honest feedback. I didn't feel the least bit threatened. I asked his opinion of how I gained co-operation from the staff and how he felt relationships were."

who are coaches but who also have coaching partners sometimes conduct consultancy projects together with their coach, setting goals for improving the facilitation of professional learning and giving specific feedback on resultant consultancy practice.

Agency

When leaders realise that they don't have to continue practising as they have previously, they experience agency; they feel sufficiently freed and empowered to take alternative and transformative actions. Agency was seen when one of the leaders (newly appointed to his position) in my research benefited from the previously learned experiences of another more experienced leader: "I was new and … fairly gullible. I would have taken it all on, but when I heard [partner] say that, I thought, 'Cripes I don't have to do that!'"

Agency also helps leaders present a united front on issues. A senior leader in one of the research studies saw this as a particular benefit of developing a professional partnership with a colleague. His presence at one of her senior staff meetings lent valuable support as she discussed with staff the issue of implementing mandated policy relating to senior staff agreements: "I could see that such a situation could be useful for a leader wanting to gain support for unpalatable policies if the leaders prepared themselves beforehand."

Critical reflection on practice

Coaching builds capable leaders by enabling them to bring critical reflection to their leadership practice. Through involvement in coaching, leaders gain practical experience of and skills in utilising reflection in, on and for practice. They come to recognise that reflection is a powerful tool for enhancing the quality of leadership actions in their work, and is a part of effective leadership practice, not an add-on.

Reflection

The importance of reflection on practice—and ensuring that it occurs—is well noted in this book. However, educators do not necessarily see this reflective skill as part of their professional practice and are often heard lamenting that they're too busy to reflect. In these cases, and as I mentioned earlier in this book, they tend to see reflection as something *additional* to practice, and only if they have time to do it. Because being reflective is an essential quality of good leadership, it is one that needs to become embedded in the culture of the institution. One leader commented that reflection arising out of her ongoing commitment to collegial coaching had become a "fully accepted … part of this institution". She now included her coach and the partner institution in activities and decisions made, and in the consultation process for future planning.

Structure

Reflection that leads to agency rarely occurs naturally in leaders' practice. While leaders may recognise that reflection is important, they find it difficult to put aside time within the day for critical reflection. Reflection time therefore needs to be structured so that it becomes formalised into the busyness of leaders' days. The coaching model teaches leaders how to take the time to reflect on their leadership performance and their proposed actions. Structured time enables leaders to become increasingly reflective about what they are doing or are planning to do. The effects of the reflection through coaching are present even when the coach is not!

Vicarious learning

Because the coaching model involves reciprocal processes, leaders gain benefit from reflecting not only on their own practice but also on their coach's leadership actions within their practice. The time that the model makes available for the coaching partners to observe each other's actions becomes enforced time for reflection on practice. Leaders are able to stand back from the demands of the day and think about their own practice as they observe their coach in action in his or her own role. Here, leaders are learning vicariously about leadership and teaching.

The leaders who participated in the research valued the shadowing aspect of coaching. Most said they had seldom, if ever, watched a leader in a similar position

"Shadowing my coach makes me think about what I'm doing, ways I could do things differently. It's just so neat for me to have the chance to watch and to think how I would act or what I would have done … I learn so much."

to their own carry out their leadership work. They spoke of "freshness" and of "taking away ideas" each time they worked with their coaches in this way, but mostly they spoke about the depth of reflection about their own practice and their ways of working in leadership.

Challenge

"He challenges my thinking and gets me looking for answers within myself and my role— exactly what effective coaching should do."

When leaders are given opportunities to observe the leadership practice of others, they're challenged by what they see. They develop doubts and questions about their own work. They begin to problem pose about it, and in so doing develop new ways of "knowing" and of "being". However, reflecting through coaching doesn't always lead leaders to change their own practice. Often, consideration of another leader's practice affirms them in the way they are operating. Leaders' styles are different in different contexts, and coaching is effective here because it's not about one leader telling another leader how they should lead, but about one leader assisting another leader to think critically about their practice, in their own context.

Perspectives

The reason why leaders are challenged by their observations of the practice of others is that the process gives them different perspectives on how leadership actions are done or might be done. One leader described the value of different perspectives as "a pair of eyes coming in from out". He felt that the fresh perspectives provided by his coaching partner would help shorten the time he'd originally set to achieve certain goals. Different perspectives help leaders become not only more critical of their own leadership practice but also more knowledgeable about the values and philosophies that underpin their practice. These perspectives, moreover, are essential for double-loop learning, where reflection and feedback on previous actions inform and perhaps change future practice, thereby creating the knowledge for action emanating from triple-loop learning (Argyris, 1999).

Praxis

Many times in the coaching process, leaders become aware that their espoused theories are not the same as their theories-in-action. Once leaders become more critically aware and informed of their actions through the receiving of feedback from their coaching partner and others, they're better able to think more carefully about the effects their actions are having on the quality of learning in their institution. They ask, according to Smyth (1991, p. *xviii*), questions such as these ones: "What am I doing? Why am I doing this? What are the effects of my actions on my students and colleagues?" It is at this point that leaders' practice moves to praxis, with their leadership, of itself, providing opportunities for learning and, in turn, enhanced professionalism.

Increased professional interactions

The many ways in which professional interactions and relationships can be enhanced through coaching depend on how the practice of coaching is established in an institution or between and across groups of leaders from different institutions. These interactions can be between peers, between institutions and other members of staff in the institutions, between the members of a group, cluster, network or community of learners, between an outside facilitator, researcher, adviser or principal–consultant, and between the leaders themselves.

"We're terribly critical people. When anyone says anything [wrong or untoward], we don't overtly do anything, but we think a lot ... we are all very critical of each other and jealous of our own patch and our own domain."

Between partners

As leaders become increasingly conversant with coaching, they begin to reflect on the differences between their interactions within their coaching partnership and/or their coaching group, and their usual interactions with colleagues at other times. These "other times", they say, are characterised by talk that is more social than professional, or by discussions that focus more on the administrative and organisation-based features of their institutions than on resolving the specific leadership dilemmas that arise within them. Leaders speak of an unspoken rule, that of not revealing personal concerns or feelings of inadequacy, thereby upholding the belief they are managing well.

Goffman (1959) described this stance as *impression management*. We might describe it as the professional façade that leaders employ both with their colleagues and with the outside world. The leaders in the research studies observed that colleagues rarely revealed anything of depth when they talked together in their usual social and professional situations (Robertson, 2010). Groups of like-minded people, such as educational leaders, maintain the façade whenever they get together because they observe the rules and rituals they've established for "usual" behaviour. The members of the group support and portray a view of themselves that they know others will find, at least temporarily, acceptable. Their message is: "We're all finding the job easy. Our institutions are running well. We're keeping up with everything." This "bluff exterior" or "veneer of consensus" is, according to Goffman (1959, p. 21), the means by which people conceal their own needs.

The coaching model research shows that with the right opportunities, leaders can get beyond the veneer of consensus to reveal their own professional needs, gain a deeper understanding of themselves and one another, and from there work towards the development of quality leadership and system leadership. Coaching gives "pause for thought"; it interrupts accepted ways of interacting with colleagues and frees the participants to engage in new and more fruitful interactions. This freedom provides leaders with the confidence to share things with their coaches that they thought they'd never share with colleagues, although sometimes the degree to which they lay themselves open to their partner's critique concerns them. For example, when one leader invited his coach to observe his visit with an audit team, he was as concerned about seeming inadequate in front of his professional colleague as he was about appearing inadequate in front of the team: "[My coach] said he was impressed with the fact that I clearly knew [his institution], knew the staff and knew the programmes that were going on within it. So that was good, because, between ourselves, that was the thing that worried me. I didn't want to look silly, not only in front of them but in front of a colleague."

"He challenges me to do my own thinking and come to the best solutions. He provides analogies which challenge and promote intelligent thought and reflection."

Feeling secure enough to display vulnerability and lack of surety with colleagues takes time, but once that point is reached, many advantages follow. Leaders who can demonstrate they're learning in their leadership lead in a much more collaborative, reciprocal manner. Receptiveness to constructive feedback, to considering and accepting the need for change, is an obvious one, but there's also the support that comes from sharing problems and concerns: of not feeling alone, of knowing that others feel the same way. With time, collegial coaching partners also give more of themselves, in terms of wanting to help their partner. They share ideas and they exchange and share resources, including teacher expertise. They note down ideas and become more enthused about what they do. Their meetings and observation visits are punctuated with these types of question: Have you seen this? Have you done that? What have you done about this? What do you think of this? Would this work?

Between institutions and within institutions

When coaching relationships are established between leaders from different institutions, there is often a flow-on effect to the other professional relationships within the institutions and between the institutions. As leaders become more familiar with one another's institutions and contexts, they begin to identify the strengths in their colleagues' practice and look for ways in which they can share this valuable resource.

The philosophy of collegiality that two principals in one research study fostered through working closely was pervasive throughout the culture of their schools. The role models they portrayed to their staff along with their belief in the value that openness to professional development and lifelong learning would have for improving education in their respective schools paved the way for increased collegial and collaborative interactions among the individual members of their respective staffs. One principal identified very early in one research study the importance of the role model he was setting: "I think it's important that the staff see that the principal is also committed to the concept of professional development and that the principal doesn't think, 'Well, I'm at the top. Now you others catch up!'" For this principal, being the principal learner in his education community was the most important facet of his educational leadership role. Coaching helps leaders establish this type of role model, that is, of being visible in terms of their learning to staff.

Within a learning community

Developing relationships with other leaders who are involved in professional coaching builds learning communities. This development is especially so when the regularity and quality of professional interactions among individual sets of coaching partners is such that a climate of trust and professionalism is engendered. The development of an ethos of trust in the group is one of the outcomes of coaching, and for the following leader was evident in a lack of hierarchy:

> There are the ones starting off, the others retiring. There is a good atmosphere of sharing, and it certainly never comes to me at any time that the experienced ones have the answers. If anything, it is some of the young ones in the less experienced positions who tend to feel they have the answers and are certainly innovative in the way they attack problems …
>
> For me, there are two distinct groups involved, and neither feels dominated by the other, and each is prepared to learn from the other.

These reciprocal learning relationships are key to the effectiveness of learning partnerships. Because trust takes time to develop, it cannot be assumed and may require careful facilitation by the members of the learning community or by someone selected to provide a facilitative role. Nonetheless, comments like the one made by the leader immediately above confirm the reciprocity that arises from a spirit of trust. Recognition that colleagues act as a learning resource and receptiveness to new learning are important principles of the coaching model. A group diverse in terms of gender, ethnicity, experience and the type of institution they work in provides the many different perspectives needed to challenge thinking about leadership issues within individual coaching partnerships.

Coaching within senior teams or within collaborative teaching teams is equally powerful in building learning communities (see the case studies in Chapter 11). Colleagues use their coaching skills in order to focus attention on particular aspects of practice. As their learning communities develop and the members of these communities gain a shared understanding of the new knowledge they're creating in relation to practice, each member has ongoing opportunity to reflect on what this new practice means for his or her own repertoire of teaching or leadership.

Between coaching partners and outside facilitators

The research on coaching partnerships that I've conducted over the years demonstrates that the presence of facilitators operating as scholar-practitioners and/or researchers in the coaching process not only is welcomed by participants but also strengthens the reflexive nature of the model. Both participant and facilitator experience an increase in useful interactions between their respective communities, something they rarely expect. Both gain from the perspective of the other and draw together in a way that sees each person contributing to and benefiting from the research process. In short, they move towards becoming a community of researchers (Carr & Kemmis, 1986). However, as various studies have shown time and again, the two parties move to what is essentially an action research process (i.e., cycles of related actions based on reflection and inquiry, evaluation and evidence) retain as their primary focus their own sphere of interest. As Somekh (1994) has put it, such collaborators generally simply inhabit each other's castles, with the educational leaders always more interested in how they can use the outcomes of the research to improve their practice and their institution, and the scholar-practitioners/researchers more interested in how practice confirms and informs theory and is driven by it.

"It will be necessary to set up some system [of] confidentiality when we talk in the larger group. I don't think there's any problem between coaching partners ... but I don't know the other participants, and I'm sure that we all need to feel secure in what we have to say."

Leaders often act differently in their coaching partnerships in the presence of an outsider, but this effect can be used to change practice. One leader thought third-party feedback should be built into the coaching model on a permanent basis: "I've begun to wonder about the value of groups of three, since skill in causing another to reflect needs careful honing and should be the highlight. A third person could give feedback on the interview."

This example also points to how the practitioners themselves help develop the professional coaching model. The model as originally conceived saw the leaders becoming autonomous through coaching. However,

"We need you here though—to keep us focused on leadership, as that is ... the hardest thing to do; systems and management are the easiest things to focus on."

it became increasingly apparent that an outside facilitator could bring to the reflection-based aspect of the model the added dimension of research theory and other relevant matters, such as the political context within which education operates. This contribution made for a very valuable modification to the model.

The coaching model is, therefore, enhanced by the input of a facilitator, by somebody who can challenge, give feedback on the developing processes, professionally supervise the coaches and keep working to extend the skills of critical reflection. The facilitator can thus improve the quality of the professional coaching relationships. He or she can also keep the practitioners "on track". Some leaders describe their coach as their "conscience and guide", as a person who keeps them working consistently towards their professional goals. Leaders frequently neglect critical reflection because of the demands of the management issues they face daily. The facilitator can challenge them in a way that returns them to their educational leadership role. An outside facilitator is often the person best suited to bring about the type of critique which leads to the professional transformation that Dempster (2001) calls for.

A framework for research and development

Coaching establishes a framework for the development of collaborative action research processes that promote personal, professional and institutional transformation. The depth of these transformations was one of the leadership developments most evident in the data gathered during the research studies. The ongoing relationship with a colleague that coaching provides helps leaders formalise a process to achieve their goals because the colleague-as-coach keeps leaders' focus firmly on their educational leadership actions and encourages them to monitor how these influence progress towards their goals. This type of focus, it seems, is the one most likely to produce consistent, reliable change. Exactly how the action research nature of the coaching model works in this regard is the subject of the next chapter.

Summary of main points

- Coaching leads to enhanced critical reflection on practice.
- Coaching emphasises the educational leadership role of focusing on the quality of teaching and learning.
- Increased professional interactions are an important outcome of coaching relationships.
- As a result of collaborative engagement with others through coaching, leaders focus on how their learning informs their educational practice. They also come to understand the impact of this process on improvement and innovation in learning in their institutions.
- Coaching establishes processes and practices for action research and education development, which helps bed in long-term transformative change in professional practice.

*Triangles are rare in nature, but as in every other, energetic forces engage
with formative principles to create a distinctive li.*

Chapter 5

Action research and coaching

Chapter overview

When educators set long-term goals and begin to work surely and consistently towards those goals by monitoring progress, reflecting on and
evaluating actions, and developing new plans of action in the light of
that reconnaissance, they have moved into cycles of action research. This
chapter outlines the close alignment of action research with the process
of coaching. It begins with a brief definition of action research. The definition is followed by a look at the theoretical construction, principles
and methodology of action research and then an outline of how action
research operates within the framework of the leadership coaching model.
The chapter ends with a case study focused on two principals who aligned
action research and coaching to achieve a shared vision for their schools.

Action research defined

Action research is a process involving cycles of action that are based on
reflection, feedback, evidence and evaluation of previous actions and the
current situation. The data gathered during this process inform future
decisions and actions. This type of research is favoured by people who

want their research findings to have an impact on the situation or context as the intervention takes place, and it sees the practitioner as researcher. The process of research and action thus results in people using the "findings" of the action research—the theory—at the time of the research. "Action learning" is closely aligned to, and is indeed part of, action research. However, with action research (or "theory of practice"), close links are made between theory and practice, and the findings are often shared in a written form.

Theoretical constructs

Action research can be traced back to the sociological work of Kurt Lewin (1948). Lewin believed that it was not only important but also ethical for emancipation and change to be the direct and immediate outcomes of research processes. He observed that although people are often very clear about the "what" outcome they hope to achieve when conducting research or development projects, they tend not to be so clear about *how* to reach that point or to examine *why* it is important to do so. The action research process is extremely powerful in helping and allowing them to do both.

The process begins, according to Lewin (1948), with the researcher setting down a "general idea" of what he or she wants to achieve. Examples might include:

- "Develop a community of learning,"
- "Develop an inclusive education philosophy," or
- "Develop a coaching culture."

The next step involves gathering information about the present situation, which allows the researcher to formulate "an 'overall plan' of how to reach the objective, and [to make] a decision in regard to the first step of action" (Lewin, 1948, p. 205). This stage is followed by a series of phases, each involving "circles" of action, evaluation, feedback, reflection, fact finding, modification of the original plan and planning the next action. The process delineates how effective educators work to the meet the individual and unique needs of different students. Lewin likens the process to a spiral staircase, where the steps ultimately lead to achievement of the desired outcome.

Lewin's (1948) description of action research has particular resonance with the coaching processes used to facilitate effective leadership.

Zuber-Skerritt (2011, p. 33) argues that "since action research is characterized by creativity and flexibility, its greatest utility in the workplace is that of dealing with complex social and organisational issues/problems that arise in unprecedented situations." Many other theorists and researchers propound action research as a powerful means of building communities of learners and of influencing and changing practice (see, for example, Dick, 2009; Fullan & Stiegelbauer, 1991; Kemmis & McTaggart, 1988; Nofke & Somekh, 2009). One of the major benefits of action research is that the practitioners not only pose the research questions but also search for and try out their own answers to those questions by engaging in reflective iterative inquiry cycles. Because the research is practitioner driven, it promotes the development of professionals and the body of knowledge on which they base their actions. In today's rapidly changing educational climate, it is important that leaders study and inquire into their own practice and construct the new knowledge needed to answer their current questions and solve their own problems.

Guiding principles

The guiding principles of action research appear over and over in the literature. These principles posit action research as an intervention, as self-evaluative and collaborative, as site based and concerns based, and as transformative and as agentic (i.e., acting with agency). Another principle resides in the link that action research provides between theory and practice.

Intervention

Like action research, coaching is an intervention because it requires people to stop and look critically at the reality of their worlds. For Cohen and Manion (1980), seminal writers in the field, the benefits of action research come from "a close examination of the effects of ... intervention", of reflecting on the information "thrown up" by the intervention, and then determining how understandings elicited from that reflection can be used to advantage personal and professional development and practice (p. 174). They go on to say that action research as intervention involves several key components:

[It is] ... *situational* ... concerned with identifying a problem in a specific context and attempting to solve it in that context; it is usually ... *col-laborative*—teams of researchers and practitioners work together on a project; it is *participatory*—team members themselves take part directly or indirectly in implementing the research; and it is *self-evaluative*—modifications are continuously evaluated within the on-going situation, the ultimate objective being to improve practice in some way or other. (p. 186, emphasis original)

There is some dissension in the literature as to whether the intervention aspect of the action research process should focus on an issue, problem or assessment of current practice (see, for example, Alcorn, 1986; Kemmis, 1985) or on a desired goal (e.g., Lewin, 1948). As Winter (1989, p. 13), asks: "Do you start by implementing a change? Or do you start by analysing current practice in order to formulate a desirable change?" He answers these questions with another: "Does it matter which comes first?" My research has demonstrated that when educational leaders undertake action research as part of the coaching process, they generally start with the vision they wish to achieve for the development of their institution or the inquiry they wish to explore with respect to classroom teaching.

Self-evaluation and collaboration

The practitioner-as-researcher aspect of action research is deemed an intrinsic *part* of the "general ideal of professionalism" (Winter, 1989, p. 4) for educational leaders rather than as an addition to it. There is an assumption here that leaders, during their research role, become "capable of determining their own performance on the basis of self-reflection" (Elliott, 1991, p. 27). They also contribute to the development of a critical learning community when they come together to explore their new learning and understandings and to share their experiences (Robertson, 2000). "The possibilities for critical self-reflection and critical collaboration should not be bypassed ... if those involved truly wish to initiate change and sustain improvement" (Cardno, 2003, p. 25).

Site based and concerns based

Action research is site based because it is carried out where the leader is actually working rather than on an island of professional development some place removed. It is concerns-based because it focuses on the issues and difficulties that arise in everyday practice.

Transformative and agentic

Action research is a particularly powerful tool for professional and institutional development because it leads people to a point where their actions are informed by new understandings (their transformation) and a desire to improve the conditions in which they are working or living (their agency). As they come to see that they can act otherwise, they gain a heightened sense of self-efficacy. Action research fulfils Fullan's (1993) call for educationists not only to base their practice on a strong value system but also to be change agents within their institutions. This approach, he says, sees them become transformative rather than reproductive agents of existing social patterns. Carr and Kemmis (1986), in focusing on the emancipatory power of action research, take a similar stance. They stress the need to "develop a systematic understanding of the conditions which shape, limit and determine action so that these constraints can be taken into account" (p. 152).

The words of these researchers have particular implications for educational leaders who undertake action research. For them, such research must involve critiquing the societal and political contexts in which their leadership is being carried out (Zuber-Skerritt, 2011). The research must also allow them to view matters from a variety of perspectives—to have "the capacity to look at things as if they could be otherwise" (Greene, 1985, p. 3). In this regard, leaders engaged in action research designed to bring about change in their institutions need to seek out diverse opinion so that not only the most dissonant voices are *heard* but the responses are actively *sought* (Fullan, 2001).

Link between theory and practice

The coaching model outlined in this book is based on the precept of theory informing practice and practice informing theory. This link between theory and practice is important for the development of an education theory that "fits" the complex, constantly evolving context in which educational leaders work. It also aligns well with the development process in action research, which endeavours to lessen the gap between espoused theories and theories-in-action—to "transform ... the situation from what is, to something … better" (Schön, 1983, p. 147). This consideration does not imply a rejection of all *a priori* theory but rather an understanding that theory and practice must be linked for "both the advancement of science and for the improvement of human welfare" (Whyte, 1991, p. 8). This appreciation is the basis for "leader as learner" praxis. Zuber-Skerritt (2011) names this this type of praxis "action leadership" and states that "theory can be formulated by practitioners as practical theory, i.e. theory generated from the concretized reality of their practice and professional or leadership experiences, and thus, more relevant and practical to the people at whom it is aimed and who will be affected by the results of the action research" (p. 71).

There is some disagreement in the literature over the question of whether action research as described thus far constitutes real action research. According to Stenhouse (1975), research can only be called research if its findings are made public. Ebbutt (1985, p. 157) concurs, stating that "if action research is to be considered legitimately as research, then participants in it must be prepared to produce written reports of their activities." Kemmis and McTaggart (1988) take a contrary view. They argue that because action research assists participants to improve what they do, there is no need for them to write up and disseminate their work: "… action research provides a way of working which links theory and practice into the one whole: ideas-in-action" (p. 6). Oliver (1980) also sits on this side of the debate, claiming that the purpose of action research is "to promote a continuing process of professional development" (p. 395). Robertson (2000) holds more to the middle ground, demonstrating in her research that there can be action research for theory and action research for practice, and often they are part of the same process.

Another facet of the theory versus practice debate is whether practitioners can develop theory. The answer to this question rests on the belief in the credibility and importance of the co-construction of professional knowledge—the theory—that practitioners create through their collaborative practice. It is this type of professional theory and knowledge—or, more particularly, co-constructed knowledge developed through critical reflection on practice and related information—that is essential in a rapidly changing leadership context. Coaching validates practitioner theory development as part of adaptive leadership

Action research in action

Within the framework of leadership coaching, action research involves several cyclical steps:

1. Identifying the needs to be met or a vision and the related goal setting or an area of practice to inquire into.
2. Gathering data, including feedback from students and colleagues.
3. Developing an initial action plan.
4. Implementing action.
5. Undertaking reconnaissance on that action.
6. Modifying the action plan.
7. Taking further agreed action.

The last step provides the beginning step for a new cycle of research, and the process continues in this cyclical way until the leader achieves the desired outcome. The role that the coach (as critical friend) plays in this process is detailed on the following pages.

The cycle is presented in diagrammatic form in Figure 5.1. The representation draws on the conception of action research that developed out of the coaching research studies. It's also premised on the action research processes described originally by Lewin (1948), particularly his claim that although practitioner-researchers start with a perceived outcome, they cannot necessarily identify how they will get there. Within the coaching framework, it is the reconnaissance after each action that helps leaders decide what step(s) to take next.

(a) Needs identification and goal setting

This step begins with leaders identifying a vision or need or inquiry arising out of their practice and then articulating that need or vision in terms of a goal they wish to achieve or articulating why that line of inquiry is important to pursue. The goal should be stated as a succinct statement that provides direction for the action research. When setting research goals, educational leaders need sufficient time to think about and define exactly what it is they want to achieve with their coach. Here are some examples of goals that leaders have set:

- To lead the staff positively through the upcoming review.
- To standardise formative assessment throughout the institution.

- To develop a five-year education plan.
- To establish resource-based learning across all rooms.
- To develop the institution's profile so that there is ownership by faculty, council and senior management.
- To lead staff into data gathering and classroom observation in a non-threatening way.
- To develop a performance growth culture.
- To set a better system of teacher appraisal in place.

(b) The initial plan

"At the end of this session I find myself thinking about the next step, the goals I want to achieve ..."

Setting a goal is one thing. Reaching it is another. The initial plan allows leaders to bridge the gap by setting out the means and methods whereby they will carry out their actions. The plan usually requires leaders to gather data in order to gain a better understanding of any issues relating to the achievement of goals or to help point out future directions for action. Here are some examples of first steps leaders might take:

- Have coaching partner observe me taking a staff meeting and then assist me in getting all staff on board.
- Look at areas such as organisation of time (class, staff, administration, secretarial, cleaning, environment).
- Interview each staff member separately to get agreement on performance agreement contracts.
- Hold one-day workshop for deans to develop initial ideas for profile document.
- Month 1: Set up meeting. Involve board and community members.

(c) First action and reconnaissance

Having identified the first action they want to take, leaders carry it out. (In the coaching situation, this may occur with or without the coach's observation and feedback on the leader.) Leaders then reflect (often through dialogue with their coach) on the outcomes of the action and decide what direction(s) to take from there (reconnaissance). The direction decided on may require modification of the ensuing steps in the initial plan.

Figure 5.1: The action research process

A NEW REALITY

A GENERAL IDEA OF A DESIRED CHANGE ... BUT UNSURE HOW? ➤ ACHIEVEMENT OF A CERTAIN GOAL

DATA GATHERING

A MODIFIED IDEA

AN OVERALL PLAN

ACTION STEP 1

RECONNAISSANCE
• EVALUATE ACTION
• LEARN – GATHER NEW INSIGHT
• PLAN NEXT STEP
• MODIFY OVERALL PLAN

ACTION STEP 2

RECONNAISSANCE

ACTION STEP 3

RECONNAISSANCE

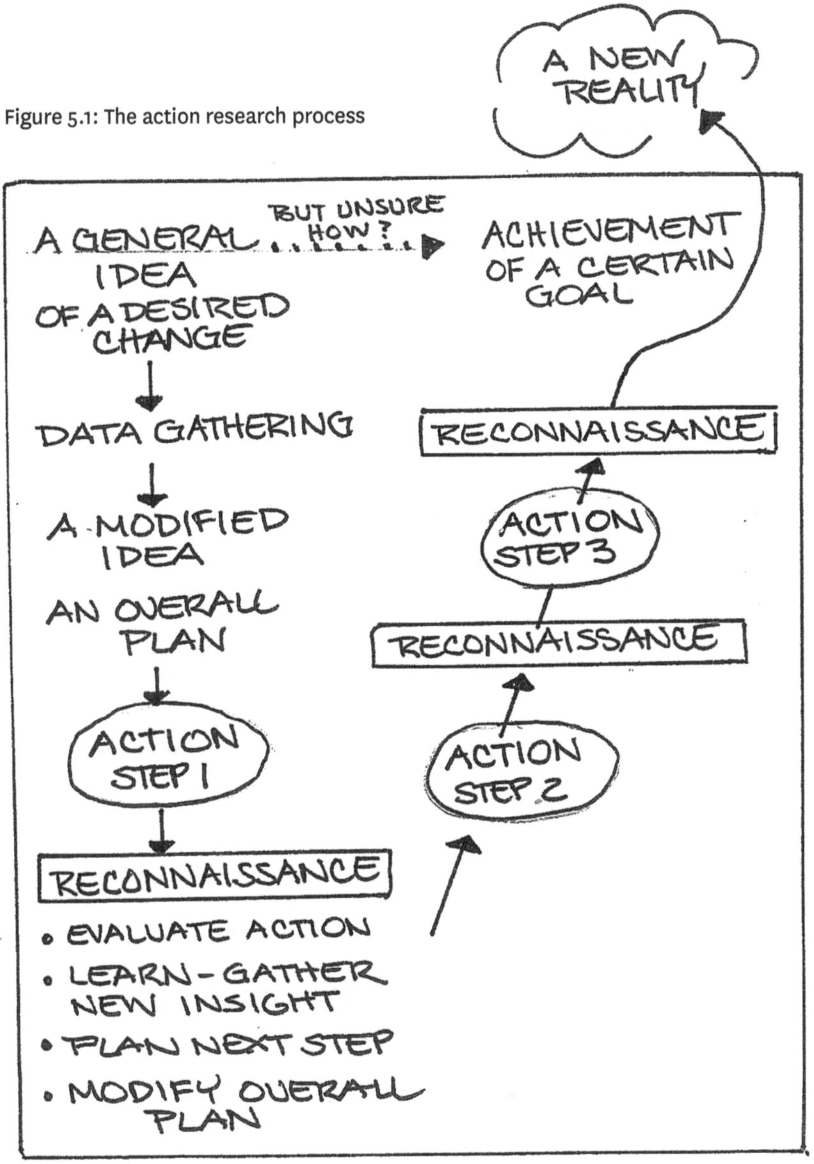

Note: Developed through Robertson's coaching research and development studies from Lewin's (1948) conceptual framework for action research.

(d) Second and subsequent actions

Leaders now move on to their second action and period of reconnaissance and plan modification. The coach can become part of some of these circles of reconnaissance. Leaders continue this process until they are close to achieving the desired outcome. If leaders are truly learning the way through an action research process with their colleagues, the "outcome" will almost surely *not* be the outcome they envisioned all those months before.

Coaching action research

The collaborative nature of coaching is a key feature in leading leaders into action research processes. Coaches, as critical friends, help to keep their partners focused and moving systematically ahead to achieve their goals. Leaders can all too easily get side-tracked by the minutiae of their everyday work, which limits their ability to assess progress towards goals. Coaching reminds leaders to monitor their action plans and related time-frames. Coaches also keep their partners firmly focused on the bigger picture of education and leadership, rather than on the management tasks that make up much of their day.

The leaders involved in the research studies were quite specific about how their respective coaches could assist them with feedback. Examples include the following:

- Monitor the introductory process and see if goals are clear.
- Evaluate the degree of change.
- Assist with evaluation through reflective interviews with staff.
- Observe an executive team meeting.

One leader said the best way her coach could assist her was to act as her conscience. The goal she had set herself was a personal one: "To see something through to the end."

An action research case study: Coaching towards a shared vision

The following case study describes the collaborative, consistent approach that two principals took to achieve the same outcomes for their individual schools in rural communities. They regarded their coaching partnership as equal give and take at all times and felt that they both benefited from the processes of collaborative action research. The two principals continued their coaching relationship over a four-year period. The case study as presented here has been adapted and abridged for this publication so that only Mary's story is told. For the full version, see Robertson (1995).

Year 1

The developing partnership

Mary was moving into her first year of principalship at Cloverleaf School (a pseudonym) when she saw advertised a one-year programme offering support for and development of school leaders. She applied and was selected. At the first session, the 42 leaders present were each paired with another leader in the group. This person would be their "partner and coach" for the professional development throughout the year. (Leaders were given as much personal choice of partner as was possible within the constraints of pairing up the members of a large group.) Mary had not met her partner Laura before this meeting, and she later said of it: "Very surface-level sharing took place. Very safe territory; factual sharing of information only."

Over the next three months, Mary commented on the process of developing a professional working relationship with her partner: "Slowly and unobtrusively a partnership and trust is developing." As the trust developed, so too did the pair's desire to work together on professional issues such as appraisal of themselves and their staff, and as the two principals began to recognise the value of sharing ideas and issues with a professional colleague, the sharing became more productive.

The beginnings of action research

Mary began by reflecting on her school. "I started spending time at the course thinking: 'Is our school effective? How do we know this? How can we show this?'" She developed a general idea of a goal that she wished to achieve: "I wanted a shared vision for the school—to develop an education plan owned by staff, children and community." At this stage, she was not clear as to the specific steps she would take to realise this aim.

Year 2

Data gathering

Mary began gathering data relevant to her area of interest. She spent time looking at other schools' long-term plans and discussing her developing ideas with Laura. She re-read previous course notes on development plans and talked informally with staff and her board of trustees. Mary had four excellent staff members, but she sometimes felt that they were all working in different directions. If they could all work together towards a common goal and vision, she was sure the whole school would then be so much greater than the sum of its five individual parts. Mary located an article on shared vision and total-quality management principles that echoed her sentiments and gave her ideas.

Goal refinement

Mary refined her original series of questions to include these questions: "What type of children should leave Cloverleaf School? What knowledge, skills, attitudes, ideas, values, should they have? Are we all working to the same end? "

Establishment of the overall plan

Mary's next step was to prepare a one-year plan of action towards her goal of developing a shared vision for the school. Her plan identified curriculum areas that the whole school could focus on, as well as other aspects affecting the school. The plan included professional development, staff meetings and community surveys. The first action Mary put down on her plan was to hold a full staff meeting.

Action

During the staff meeting, discussion centred on methods of monitoring assessment in the school. Questions such as "What are we doing? How do we know our children are being successful?" were beginning to be asked.

Reconnaissance (evaluating the action)

On evaluating the outcomes of her first action (the staff meeting), Mary quickly realised that none of the teachers at Cloverleaf School had the whole picture of a child's progress at and through the school. Each teacher was focusing on the one small part they individually played in the process and had no particular conception of the desired outcome for the graduating student or real accountability for it. This lack of clarity meant that the whole school had no clear accountability for the children's learning journeys.

New insights

On the basis of her reflections, Mary and the teachers collaboratively decided that they all needed to become far more aware not only of what was happening in one another's rooms but also of the beliefs and philosophies that each of them held. Mary talked to each teacher separately and tried to understand more fully herself what was happening in each classroom. She talked to Laura about whether she felt the teachers at her school were also working in relative isolation. As her coach, Laura was a constant source of outside perspectives and support. She also acted as a facilitator of the review and development process throughout this time.

Mary and Laura continued to practise the skills of observation of leadership actions, giving feedback and conducting reflective interviews. They also spent one week of their first school-term holiday break together and attended a rural school principals' conference. Mary found herself still reviewing previous notes on developing a shared school vision and school achievement, and discussing these ideas with Laura and other colleagues.

Modification of the initial plan

Mary then decided that the next step would be that of allocating one entire day to the professional development of her teachers. She modified her original plan to include this day of consultation and sharing.

Action

For the teachers-only development day, Mary set up an individual folder for each staff member. The material in the folders outlined and summarised the main points she'd taken down during each of the principals' courses she'd attended. It also included ideas for developments in the school. Mary invited the mathematics advisers and an academic researcher to spend different parts of the day with the teachers and to provide them with outside perspectives on their discussions. Laura and her teachers also came and joined this day of professional learning. Staff shared with one another their own assessment and evaluation systems for the different curriculum areas. Mary introduced the idea of a portfolio for each child that could follow the child through each of their years at the school and that highlighted their development in each curriculum area. Much debate and discussion on the issues followed.

Reconnaissance

The development day led Mary into another period of reconnaissance and refinement of the overall goal. She decided that the key question arising out of this day should set the wording of it: "What do we want children leaving Cloverleaf School to have achieved?" She then decided to gather more data, and to this end asked each staff member to answer the question in relation to each of the school's curriculum areas. Mary typed up their responses and then talked to Laura, other principals and the school advisers to obtain ideas about what other schools were doing in regard to developing curriculum objectives.

Action

Mary took the collated results of the questionnaire along to the next staff meeting, where they were discussed with considerable interest. "Discussions were held on some items identified, some we wanted removed, and some we hadn't thought about and had overlooked." One of the key questions that arose at this meeting started the next phase of reconnaissance: "What do parents want for their children? Are our goals and perceptions the same?"

Reconnaissance

During this period of reconnaissance, Mary spent time talking with Laura about future actions and past actions. The two women then approached another school leader in the coaching group for advice and assistance. He invited them to visit his school to view how the staff there were conducting and recording evaluations in the junior school. Mary began to reflect that the one-year plan she'd initially set down would not be long enough to achieve the objective she desired. Her original idea of a five-year plan would be much more realistic. She again modified her plan, having decided that her next action step would be to send the same questionnaire, with supporting explanations, home to the parents to gauge their views.

Input from observing researcher

It was at this point that the researcher observing Mary and Laura's coaching partnership stepped in. The researcher considered that although action research was occurring, very little in the way of action plans was actually being written down. She initiated a discussion with the two women about the action research processes taking place. Both were very interested to see how the theory of the process and the principles of action research matched what they were currently doing, as neither of them had realised they were "action researchers". Mary then wrote down the next six months' worth of actions and put an asterisk besides the items where she felt her coach could best assist by shadowing (observing) her and giving her evaluative feedback. "I wanted my partner's help to achieve my goals by keeping me on track, checking dates [were] being met, watching a staff meeting to see if I'm selling the overall idea to the staff, that they have ownership too, [and] observ[ing] board of trustees' reaction to the ideas at a meeting."

Further modification

Mary and Laura then worked together to collate the community survey returns and typed a summary to present to the staff at the next meeting. Once again, as a result of evaluating previous actions, learning new insights, planning future actions and all the time discussing matters with her coach and the researcher, Mary modified her original plan.

Postscript

This coaching partnership went on for another year, during which Mary continued to develop, in accordance with her five-year plan, her vision of two and a half years previously. Throughout the third year, Mary and Laura's professional coaching partnership helped them support each other in their personal, professional and school development processes, and allowed them to gain sound skills to help each other reflect on their leadership practice in their schools.

During their time together, the two leaders were able to "cross-credit" their learning of the skills of coaching and the skills of action research. For example, in learning how to conduct reflective interviews, they learned how to ask in-depth questions of each other, enabling them to reflect on what they were doing, why they were doing it and what effect their actions had had, or were having, on student learning. They each then found they were more often using these skills with the teachers in their schools. Mary and Laura were also able to refine their ability to observe leadership behaviours and describe and evaluate these as a valuable basis for reflection. Perhaps most importantly, they learned to act in the capacity of an outside facilitator, nudging each other along, challenging each other, affirming and supporting each other and, above all, helping each other to redefine goals, develop steps in the action research process and reflect upon the outcomes.

While working with Laura, Mary kept notes of the process her school was working through to achieve the desired outcome, and its progress in that regard. She also kept a detailed chronology, including the times she phoned Laura to clarify, discuss or share an idea. In addition, Mary willingly spent a day at the request of the researcher writing out the chronology of her action research as well as a narrative that was used as the basis of the case study presented here.

Lessons learned

Mary and Laura's story strongly demonstrates that change in an educational setting can be a slow and long process and that educational leaders often find it difficult to continue working systematically towards their goals over an extended period of time. The outside assistance provided through coaching helps them maintain the momentum.

The time that Mary took to document what she did and when along with the assistance that Laura gave her in this regard, highlights another important aspect of the action research process: writing up "the story" to share with other leaders. Usually, educational leaders are more interested in carrying out their next action rather than writing about their last. As a consequence, much valuable leadership theory is lost. Leaders need to build time for writing into their action research plans.

University partnerships, usually in the form of a researcher working alongside a programme of coaching, also assist leaders to write about their theory development. This type of collaborative action research between researchers and educational institutions is vital for job-embedded development. Leaders' job conditions are often inimical to in-depth reflection on practice and, in turn, to committed actions of praxis. Coaching and research collaborations help educational leaders overcome this barrier.

Summary of main points

Action research is:

- A natural outcome of an effective coaching process.
- An important theoretical framework for the change process.
- Effective for personal, professional and institutional development.
- An intervention into daily professional practice.
- Participatory, self-evaluative, site based and concerns based.
- A tool to maintain focus on improvement goals.
- Collaborative and develops communities of learners.
- An effective structure within which leaders can move consistently towards goals set.

PART TWO: **PRACTICE**

Emanating from centres, receding from these centres, occasionally forming boundaries with its neighbours, frequently overlapping them, lichen are the beautifiers of bare, inhospitable surfaces.

Chapter 6

Getting underway

Chapter overview

Establishing and maintaining the coaching process is not without problems. In most situations, it's difficult for leaders not only to initiate the process on their own but also to sustain the relationship due to the busyness and intensification of their everyday work. This chapter outlines the processes important in developing the coaching partnership, including selection of partner, regularity of contact, the development of trust and respect, building skills and bringing commitment and stringency to the coaching process. The chapter also sets out the format for a first coaching session, outlines a typical coaching programme over a year and aligns the coaching process with Fullan's (2007) model of the change process. The chapter concludes with a case study that documents how two principals developed a coaching relationship.

Developing the partnership
Selecting a coaching partner

The first step in initiating coaching between colleagues is determining who should partner whom. This is a question I am always asked. In line with the principles of coaching and self-directed professional learning, my answer is this: "It's important that the leaders themselves have some say in who their coaching partner will be; that person should not be arbitrarily allocated by someone else." However, it's not always easy to find a suitable coach. Impression management (i.e., management focused on maintaining a positive reputation) and competition across institutions and among leaders within institutions often mean that leaders consider colleagues in neighbouring institutions or departments to be unsuitable candidates. This, despite the fact that, as research studies have shown, coaching can actually improve relationships between and among leaders to the extent that collaboration, collegiality and knowledge creation prevail. Within an educational institution, lack of "choice" can also be an issue. Those leaders working with an outside facilitator to establish the coaching partnership (see Chapter 10) might suggest two or three people they consider appropriate coaches and will then leave the facilitator to make the necessary approaches.

During the leadership coaching research studies, leaders often commented that they thought the coaching relationship most benefited them when they could work with leaders from institutions or departments of similar size and type to their own, or from similar positions within an institution. The findings from the research confirmed that this was indeed the case. It does not matter if the two partners in the coaching relationship hold disparate goals and visions, or even that their education communities are quite different, as long as the leaders feel able to relate fully to the experiences of their coaching partner. When this is the case, leaders are able to ask questions of one another that are appropriate in terms of assisting deep reflection on leadership. As one leader said, "Similar size means facing similar sorts of problems." However, it can be argued that a coach not as familiar with the leader's context has the opportunity to ask the more challenging or perhaps more naïve questions that encourage leaders to question their current ways of practice.

Facilitating trust, respect and confidentiality

Selection of coaching partners must be based on honesty and a respect for difference. Leaders willing to debate ideas and listen carefully to their partner make valuable coaches, as this leader attested: "An open and receptive mind is important. Not a wholesale acceptance of anything and everything, but a willingness to consider multiple options and ideas. Sound self-esteem is helpful in this as in all aspects of life. Honesty, reciprocal trust and respect are essential. Philosophical similarity is not paramount, in my view."

Trust is as vital in relation to those facilitating the coaching process as it is for the coaching partners themselves. But for all parties to the process, trust takes time to develop, and this time must be allowed for during the initiation phase of the partnership development. At first, the partners will be tentative, testing the extent to which they can trust one another. However, with time, they will become more and more open with each other in direct relation to the degree of trust engendered. Confidentiality of information shared is paramount to the developing trust, and a coach's personal integrity and professional ethics must be the ultimate guide here.

Leaders often fear that being too open with a coaching partner will lead to a lack of respect, especially if they conduct the operations in their institutions in quite different ways. One leader, early in one research study, said after his first shadow visit with his coach that he was concerned the relationship would not develop successfully because his coach didn't seem to respect the way he did things in his institution: "I found [coach] difficult to understand at times and was a little concerned that during his time to discuss things with me he seemed to be a little judgemental about what we discussed. I feel a bit apprehensive about the partnership at this stage." It's therefore important that coaches are not judgemental about their partner's practice, but rather assume the role of critical friend in the reflection process.

> "That confidentiality is so important. We share a lot of things. He knows I wouldn't tell ... anything. It's a privileged position, and you can never betray that trust, and you have to know that."

In a context such as education, judgement is often a part of the culture, and it is therefore one of the biggest areas of challenge for leaders. During the early stages of coaching, the coaching partner may look for appraisal according to the judgemental dichotomies of good/bad and right/wrong, but once they develop the inquiry mindedness and self-directed learning that coaching supports, the need for this type of judgement dissipates. But judgement can also be leaders' greatest source of fulfilment, as long as the judgement is exercised not in terms of "good or bad" or "right or wrong" but in terms of critical reflection and evaluative feedback based on a specific focus set by the leaders themselves. It is this practice that allows both coach and coached to see how powerful coaching can be.

Effective coaching partners realise that it is the critical reflection on their practice that is most important. Coaching personalises professional learning in this way. The more that trust is built up, the more open partners will be to sharing their most challenging aspects or weakest aspects of practice. For change to occur, and real learning to take place, trust is essential.

Agreeing on regularity of contact

Regular contact at the beginning of the coaching relationship enhances the development of rapport and the relationship between the partners. The coaching research indicates that four to six-weekly intervals between coaching sessions are viable, depending on the specificity or intensity of the particular project or issue under focus, and that a two to three-hour session is often more beneficial than a one hour, particularly if it involves shadowing. However, any coaching session—even the 10 minutes over coffee at morning tea—is an important part of maintaining the relationship and regularity.

The longer the period of time between meetings, the more likely it is that the two colleagues will lose the continuity and the more difficult they will find it to build the intimacy and trust necessary to engage in open and deep dialogue about the issues facing them in their institutions. Irregular contact also lessens the "conscience-based" imperative of coaching that ensures the systematic carrying out of action plans and reviewing and monitoring of goals set. And, of course, coaching that becomes little more than a "one-off" visit or session can never be as professionally fulfilling as coaching that continues over time.

Another reason why regular contact is important is that partners accrue greater benefit from the coaching relationship when they work together regularly over a sustained period of time (Robertson, 2013). As my research studies showed, leaders tended not to experience or realise the full benefits of the coaching until they had worked together for approximately one year. A further point relating to regularity of contact over time is that coaching is then more likely to become institutionalised into the partners' daily practice.

Making a commitment

The many demands on leaders' time mean that the processes of coaching can easily be superseded by other events. To prevent this happening, those participating in coaching must be firmly and equally committed to their own professional development and to that of a colleague. It is, as one leader stressed, a matter of priority as well as commitment: "Time! It's important to see the coaching as a vital part of professional development and make time for it."

When the coaching partners are as committed as each other to establishing and building a professional partnership, the coaching relationship is more likely to succeed. When partners are not equally committed to the coaching process, and when they do not plan ahead by scheduling in, at an early stage (and thus prioritising), the times when they will meet with each other over a year or so, disappointment and disillusionment are the outcomes.

"Time factors [are the greatest barrier]— fitting in times to visit/ be visited, balancing this with all the other aspects of the day/ job. Realising the importance and benefits of visits has made it easier to prioritise these times."

Exercising stringency

The small amount of time that leaders generally have available for their own leadership development (including through coaching) means that they must make the most of that time. Leaders need to agree in advance to conduct their meetings with one another with stringent adherence to the coaching skills. This interaction is therefore a different kind of interaction from what they normally experience. Stringency relies on leaders agreeing to bring a formal, structured approach to each meeting, to use their skills of active listening and reflective interviewing, and to record descriptive accounts of behaviours during observations. Without this degree of formality (stringency), leaders are likely to lapse into a general conversation that, while possibly providing each other with support, is likely to offer very little in the way of challenge that coaching focused on going deeper into a colleague's practice will provide.

Building skills

No simple formula can guarantee the success of the coaching process, but spending time getting the basics right during its early stage does appear to have a marked effect on whether the coaching develops into a relationship where the partners are equally committed to each other's ongoing leadership development. However, getting the basics right is one thing. The other is ensuring that leaders build into their sessions, across the period of coaching, opportunity to practise and extend those early attributes, skills and procedures so the partners can participate ever more effectively in their leadership development. This is where the outside facilitator is particularly useful in coaching supervision. The facilitator's knowledge of the processes of coaching and the theory of leadership helps leaders determine what they need to do and know in this regard, and how to go about achieving these aims. An effective facilitator will help coaches deepen their coaching skill repertoire.

The more leaders work together, the more skills they'll develop, and the more they'll be able to work in different ways within their coaching relationships. The skills for effective coaching are many and varied. The following are some of the most important ones for improving professional practice:
- active listening;
- reflective interviewing;
- self-assessment;
- goal-setting;
- developing action plans;
- setting time-frames;
- observing and describing practice;
- giving effective feedback; and
- acquiring knowledge of the change process by understanding and engaging in action research.

These skills, described in detail in the next two chapters, help leaders develop new ways of thinking about learning. They are predicated on the principle of the importance of deep reflection, firstly for developing greater self-awareness and ultimately for self-efficacy and agency for transformative change, brought about by a greater understanding of the leadership role and the social, cultural and political influences on education. These skills lead coaches, through dialogue, towards praxis and are thus an intentional bridge between theory and practice.

Setting up a coaching folder

Reflection is aided by keeping records of the coaching process. Early in the relationship, coaching partners need to determine what type of records will be kept and who will keep them. A chronology of time spent together along with the outcomes of sessions provides one important set of records, as do self-assessment, goal-setting and action plans. These sets of materials should all be carefully filed for future reference. Some form of reflection, either field notes or a short reflective statement written during or immediately after each session, can also benefit the ongoing leadership development. It's important this reflection is on the leadership learning that has accrued through the deep, critical thinking. The reflective exercises in the next chapter can also be kept in the coaching folder and referred to over time.

The coaching sessions

The "getting started" considerations just outlined form part of the content of the first meetings between the partners. From there, partners can ease themselves into the skills and procedures of coaching by setting up sessions that follow the steps below. (These are presented at this time in summary form only. Chapters 7 and 8 provide greater detail on the development of skills.) Throughout the entire process, coaches need to keep in mind these points:

- The process takes time to work.
- The process should never be hurried.
- Every encounter is valuable.
- Each partner will at times be the coach and on different times the coached.
- Just as good leaders know how to lead and to follow, good coaches know how to coach and be coached.

The main point to remember at this juncture is that coaches enter the

EXAMPLE OF A YEAR'S COACHING PROGRAMME

February

- The first professional development coaching skills and theory workshop
- Followed by context interview in each partner's leadership context

March

- The first shadow observation in Context A
- Followed by a reflective interview and goal setting

April

- The first shadow observation in Context B
- Followed by a reflective interview and goal setting
- Meet with other coaches in workshop for ideas, debriefing and further skill development

May

- The second shadow observation in Context A, with related feedback and goal-setting
- Action planning and self-assessment

June

- The second shadow observation in Context B, with related feedback and goal-setting

August–October

- Implementation of action plans with coaching support as negotiated

October

- The third shadow observation in Context A, with related feedback and goal setting
- The third shadow observation in Context B, with related feedback and goal-setting

November

- Reviewing the year
- Reviewing goals
- Resetting goals

Note: If the coaching is integrated with the performance management systems in the institution, the formal appraisal interview may be conducted and recorded during the November session. This report can be co-constructed on agreed frameworks. Also, while three shadow observations/reflective interviews a year for each person is minimal, this number is perhaps realistic given the demands on leaders of their educational contexts. In keeping with the vicarious learning through reflection on another's practice that occurs during the reciprocal coaching process, each partner would thus be involved in six in-depth coaching conversations focused on professional practice during the year. This formative process will support the changing practice.

relationship as a learner, inquiring deeply into professional practice in order to learn from their coaching practice.

First sessions

1. Complete a coaching development workshop in order to learn the principles of coaching and to practise the essential skills of active listening and reflective interviewing (see Chapter 7).

2. Browse through this book again to ensure familiarity with the principles and processes of coaching.

3. Confirm the date for a first coaching meeting. (Ideally, as noted above, partners will have set out meeting dates during their very earliest meetings.)

4. Meet in Partner A's context (whether institution, classroom or office) to carry out a context and/or self-assessment interview (see Chapter 7), make notes and confirm the date of the next meeting.

5. Meet in Partner B's context (if a reciprocal coaching relationship), carry out a context and/or self-assessment interview, make notes and confirm plans for a shadow (observation) visit.

Subsequent sessions

1. Complete a coaching development workshop to revisit the skills of observing and describing practice, self-assessment and goal setting.

2. Confirm the date for Partner B to do a shadow observation of Partner A.

3. Carry out the observation. This should not be too formal; the idea is just to let it flow.

4. Give descriptive feedback, seek self-assessment and carry out a reflective interview and goal setting as soon as possible after the observation.

5. Confirm plans for Partner A to do a shadow observation of Partner B (if reciprocal coaching).

6. Carry out a reflective interview and goal setting as soon as possible after the observation.

Further sessions

1. Complete a coaching development workshop to deepen all skills and to practise the skill of giving evaluative feedback.

2. Include feedback and all other skills in future sessions as necessary.

A typical session

An acronym often used in coaching books to guide the format of coaching meetings is GROW (Eaton & Johnson, 2001; Landsberg, 2003; Whitmore, 2002). G stands for Goal, R stands for Reality, and O for Options. As for W, Eaton and Johnson use WHEN, Whitmore uses WHAT (will you do?), and Landsberg uses WRAP-UP. The latter, "wrap-up", is perhaps the most useful expression, as it can incorporate the when and the what, as in "What will you do from here on? When shall we have our next meeting?"

However, before following through with the steps dictated by the acronym, the coaching partners can "warm up" by having the person assuming the role of coach ask the coached partner such bridging questions as:

- What's been happening since my last visit with you?
- What have you learned from some of the leadership actions and incidents?
- What have you been thinking about lately?

The coach must remember to listen *actively* to the answers, to what is said and not said, and to follow up with questions accordingly. At any one session, one person takes the role of coach throughout. If the coaching relationship is a reciprocal one, the partner assumes the role of coach in the leader's own context during the next session.

From here, the partners follow through with reflective interviewing and self-assessment in a professional goal-setting session structured by the acronyms GROW and SMART (Eaton & Johnson, 2001; Landsberg, 2003). (See the chart on the next page.)

GROW AND SMART

- **GOAL**—Review the major goal(s) set at previous meeting(s) and discuss the focus for this coaching session.

  Questions to ask (**S**pecific, **M**easured): What progress have you made towards your goals? What evidence do you have? Why is this goal so important to addressing student achievement needs? Specifically, what will you be doing when you've achieved the goal? What will the students be doing more of? What will it look like in this classroom if you achieve your goal? How will you measure achievement of the goal? What would you like to achieve from this coaching session today?

- **REALITY**—the partners together discuss and examine contextual issues relating to achievement or non-achievement of goals and the situation as it currently is. The coach endeavours to ask further questions of the partner that relate directly to and elicit further reflection on these considerations.

  Questions to ask (**A**chievable): What has worked in previous similar situations? What might hinder you in this process? What was the outcome from what you have already done? What did you learn from this? What issues were there? What resources can you call on? What was successful in moving you towards your goal(s)? What is the current state of play? What is worrying you most? Who feels as strongly about this as you? Who will help you as you move forward?

- **OPTIONS**—the partners decide, as an outcome of their discussion and reflection, on the options the coached leader could take regarding his or her goals. At this stage, the partners need to explore every possibility, to think laterally and outside the square. It's at this point that the coach is particularly valuable in terms of providing outside challenges to the partner's thinking and offering suggestions and expertise after the coached leader has exhausted their own ideas..

  Questions to ask (**R**elevant): What options are available? What would [someone else] think to do in this situation? What is the most outlandish thing you can think of to do? If you could just work with these students alone, what would you do? What do you think the parents would want you to do in this situation? Have you thought about … ? Is this an option you might try? What is the most important option at this time? What will work against these options being successful? What will facilitate your progress? What would you specifically like feedback on?

- **WRAP-UP**—Discuss which actions, based on a selection from the options generated above, will follow from here. Set goals and confirm the time of the next session.

Questions to ask (**T**ime): When do you think you will achieve this goal? What will be your first step, and when? Is there any support the coach, a colleague or a consultant could give during this process? Is there any other learning you need to do? When will you meet to review progress?

Note: If the meeting between the two partners involves a shadow observation, the coach will need to include the following steps in the goal-setting session described above:

- Observe the action.
- Take careful, descriptive notes.
- Select one pre-determined focus for reflective interview.
- Each take a quiet 5 to 10 minutes for self-assessment and reflection:
  - Fill in notes from observation/ and or thoughts about the session
  - Prepare questions for reflective interview.
- Resume meeting with coaching partner.
- Describe the leadership actions observed.
- Seek self-assessment on focus set
- Give feedback.
- Carry out the reflective interview.

(See Chapter 8 for more detail on these processes.)

Group-coaching and team-coaching sessions

When teachers teach or plan collaboratively, many naturally occurring opportunities for group coaching arise, which means there is no need to look for additional "time" in the busy schedule. The same can be said for senior leaders in team meetings, or for departmental heads and colleagues in regular team meetings. Leaders who are skilled in coaching and facilitative leadership practice will lead dialogue directed towards developing ideas that facilitate collaborative co-construction of new knowledge together. As part of this process, they'll be encouraging active listening and reflective questioning from the group.

These approaches should all be established as norms during these collegial meeting times. Over time, leaders will become skilled at asking the hard questions of one another. They'll find themselves focusing on specific areas of practice. They'll ask "why" and "what if" and "what might be" as they seek new ways of understanding the challenges they're facing.

This type of practice helps build rich accountability for student outcomes—rich because all members of the school management and teaching team share the accountability as they coach one another in practice-shifting conversations. Deep inquiry and critical reflection on collaborative teaching practice provides teachers in particular with opportunities to ask themselves such questions as: What do I bring to this practice? What do I still need to learn? What will I try in our work together tomorrow? They may ask these questions silently or, preferably, in my view, feel safe enough to sound out their thinking and questions publicly. When teachers share in this way, everyone involved is a *learner*.

Colleagues working in these ways know how to build their own leadership capacity and that of others as they support and challenge one another through effective coaching practices (see Case Study 1 in Chapter 11). These situations can often lead to even more robust coaching conversations because stories and contexts are shared and a level of trust has already been established. It's still vital, though, that everyone involved sees the requisite skills as an important part of developing and benefiting from these deep learning conversations.

The developing relationship

The coaching relationship that develops over time represents a process of change in leaders' professional ways of working. Leaders therefore need to understand how this process works, not only in terms of actual coaching processes but also in terms of developing the coaching relationship.

Fullan's (2007) model of the change process is particularly useful in this regard because it provides an easy description of the development stages of any change process and the development of any successful coaching relationship. Fullan holds that all change involves an initiation phase followed by an implementation phase. If the implementation phase is successful, it leads to an institutionalisation phase where new ways of working become embedded in the culture of individuals and, therefore, organisations.

During the *initiation phase* of the coaching relationship, time must be allowed for trust and confidence to develop. There's no rush to move into observation of practice at this stage. Leaders should be given as many opportunities as possible to talk about their practice, their values and beliefs, and the vision for what they're trying to achieve. Coaching partners need to understand each other's role and the context for the professional practice under scrutiny. They also need to learn what is important to their partner and that person's practice. The coach must keep this in mind as she or he facilitates the process with the leader. If an outside facilitator or consultant is working with pairs of leaders to develop the peer-coaching relationships, that they too must demonstrate integrity to the process by recognising, as trust develops, the importance of process and relationship versus task achievement.

"Formal structured interviews have to be planned for. That's the only way, because otherwise you don't let it happen ... [You have to say,] 'We will start our interview now.' ... [T]hey are very worthwhile."

The *implementation phase* begins when leaders are comfortable enough to focus on deeper educational issues and are open to new ideas and ways of working. They'll bring a more formal focus to their meetings, be ready to observe each other in practice and to give and receive constructive evaluative feedback on their leadership. The facilitator's critique of and feedback about the developing coaching relationship (shadowing the leaders as they coach in their institutions or classrooms) is invaluable at this stage. The leaders begin to recognise the leadership strengths they both bring to the coaching partnership and to utilise these more fully in the developing relationship.

During an effective coaching partnership, the partners will find using each other's expertise is a valuable way to support the changing practice. The partners will start to act as consultant to each other at times in the coaching relationship. The mindset is not the "coach as expert and knower" but the coach "as learner with expertise" who is able to acknowledge that both partners bring strengths to the relationship that both can learn from. Even if the partners are an experienced teacher with a first-year teacher, the same mindset is important in a strong coaching and mentoring partnership. The first-year teacher has much expertise that the mentor coach can gain benefit from but only if he or she approaches the relationship as a learning partner.

During the *institutionalisation phase*, leaders become more autonomous and authoritative in their coaching relationship. Their reliance on the input of the outside facilitator (if they've used one) to sustain the process lessens, and they'll have a sound appreciation of how coaching practices support their continuing leadership development, which they will initiate themselves. The leaders may be prepared at this stage to take on a new partner or partners in the process. They may wish to teach other leaders the skills of coaching and to work as an outside facilitator with these people in order to widen the developing community of learning, or to build leadership capacity in their institutions. The point at which coaching practices become an accepted and integrated way of working for both adults and students in these leaders' institutions is the point at which the practices have become institutionalised and a coaching culture has developed as a way of being in terms of learning partnership.

Case study: Snapshots of a developing relationship

The story below traces the coaching relationship that developed between Sue (an experienced principal) and Rawiri (a first-time principal), both of whom participated in the leadership research. The study is set out according to Fullan's (2007) model and is told mainly through Sue's and Rawiri's voices, and through quotes taken out of guided written reflections or the transcripts of interviews conducted throughout the two years of research. My field notes and other comments (in italics) provide the linking narrative. Please note that the following is not drawn from coaching sessions between Sue and Rawiri, but rather from Sue and Rawiri reflecting (with the researcher) throughout the two years on the developing coaching relationship.

INITIATION: First six months
Establishing the partnership
First meeting

Sue: Although we are in the same district and teach within three kilometres of each other, our schools are quite different. Although we have differing visions and priorities, the end result is the same—to provide the best possible educational outcomes for our children.

Rawiri : We talked for another two hours after you [the facilitator] had left, and we found it extremely valuable. We've set a future shadowing date in each other's schools and look positively towards working together in the research.

First professional development meeting: Moving through lack of surety

9 a.m.

Rawiri: I arrived with things on my mind—the community worker at school; the employment service worker starting next term; transport for tomorrow's trip; forgot my reflective diary [for researcher].

Sue: I'm not yet fully clear about this partnership. My expectations are developing as we go along.

3 p.m.

Sue: [We've been] getting to know each other's communities and problems and realising that perhaps problems weren't as great as originally thought. Good to hear different approaches to same or similar jobs, and important to have a partner with same or similar needs.

Rawiri: I feel I have a little more idea of what I'm supposed to be doing. I'm lucky to have Sue as my partner. I feel very comfortable with her, and I'm sure it won't be long before we'll share almost anything.

Sue: We have set some objectives and times [to meet] and are happy to continue with the partnership. Personally, I am much clearer about where we go from here.

IMPLEMENTATION: Second six months
Developing and maintaining the partnership

Sue: Rawiri and I have been slow to get our shadowing done this term because of other commitments. I know we're meant to prioritise these tasks, but the following is a typical example of what happens to teaching principals. Just as I was leaving school at 3 p.m., a distressed? concerned? parent arrived determined to see one of my teachers. My teacher requested that I stay for the interview.

The shadowing that Sue referred to was a staff meeting being conducted by Rawiri. Sue did eventually attend a staff meeting that Rawiri was leading so that she could observe and provide feedback on how he worked with his staff. She described her first experience of shadow-coaching as follows.

Sue: It was interesting to hear another principal promoting visions, policies, positive attitudes and involvement to a staff who, like all staff, have individual and varying attitudes. I came away deciding that, as principals, we have to be constantly motivating children, staff and communities.

Goal-setting session

Sue: GOAL: to set a better system of appraisal in place. ... [Rawiri can help me with this by being] able to first observe and then assist me in getting *all* staff on board. [This session] made me consider carefully preferred outcomes.

Rawiri: Kia ora. I've just come out of a really stressful period from about the last five or six weeks—school, and union and principals—it's been a really hard time, and it has placed pressure on my family. I notice that a lot of smaller things upset me that normally I wouldn't worry about. It really does affect your home life. So I've just got my head above water— just this week—and now I feel really tired. I'm looking forward to just keeping the school running—just doing the day-to-day things … I was just thinking about board of trustee meetings and writing the report and how stressful it can be prior to a board of trustees meeting—basically, because you never know what's going to hit you when you get there.

Sue: I think you have to come to terms with the fact that you're going to make mistakes, but the important thing is not repeating those mistakes.

Rawiri: I find that I'm not always sure when I've made mistakes 'cause I haven't had the kickback yet. So I tell people when they ask, that "Things seem to be going all right," but I'm waiting for the letter to say, "Why haven't you done this?" … It will probably come quite a long while after … [My goal is] to lead my staff into the area of data gathering in a non-threatening way—to delegate jobs to the board of trustees and not do them all myself. [Sue's role as coach will be] to monitor my progress; share her first steps in this area.

Sue and Rawiri then went on in this coaching session that I was observing to talk further about their boards of trustees. Sue had worked hard to get hers to take far more responsibility and was pleased with the amount of work they had carried out. Sue shared with Rawiri the view that the members of her board should take responsibility for their portfolios and should get the work done. Rawiri said he had to do most of the work and that his board looked to him for all the answers, which he was finding a huge responsibility. The two compared how their boards operated, and Rawiri agreed to shadow-observe Sue at her next board meeting.

Meeting after the shadow observation

Rawiri: I really admired you, Sue, when you told them that about the health issue. In my [board] meetings from then on, I just kept writing down that they were responsible, until one day there was a close accident and I was able to say, "You guys are responsible for this." That really helped me.

Sue and Rawiri's discussion then turned to the amount of money budgeted for curriculum and the deferred maintenance in their schools.

Rawiri: One thing that really scares me is that you can go and get money to reseal the tennis court, and if you tried to get the same amount of money to put into science, you wouldn't get it! ... I want to have a staff meeting on this next week—just to get the wheels rolling before next term. I'm quite excited about it actually.

Sue: I remember being so taken aback when one of the staff members questioned me on measurement and evaluation. I was so fired up; I just imagined that everyone else would be too.

Rawiri: I've thought about that, too, and thought about a couple of questions I could ask them (they may be the wrong questions), but I know I could say, "You know Johnny Smith—what year is he reading at?" I know that would pull the rugs from right under their feet and the defences would come up straight away, and it wouldn't work, so I've really been trying to think about this.

Sue: You'll find that the enthusiastic ones will help to bring on the other ones because they'll start bringing things of theirs and say, "Look at this," and things get left lying around and others pick them up.

Rawiri: The enormity of the task has just come home. The quality of the school and where it is all at is right here in the classrooms where the work is done. It's hard work. So I expect I've just answered my own question, then, that I have to lead the way by lifting my own standards. By doing that, I can actually begin to raise theirs.

INSTITUTIONALISATION: Second year
Reflecting on the coaching

Rawiri: I've found a principal that I can confide in. I trust her and enjoy listening to her views. And, yes, I do enjoy working with her. Problems? Sometimes we talk too much. We need to set an action research plan.

Sue: I think these things take time to make them work. I needed the year before I could see how valuable working like this with a colleague could be. We got to know each other and what we wanted to achieve. I think, then, that after an interview you could come in and keep going back to our objectives rather than just chatting, which we did quite well ... we've had time to develop respect and trust. I didn't know Rawiri very well until this. I had just met him.

Rawiri: I sort of take this for granted now really. Like I said, it would be a shame if we didn't have our [coaching] partnership.

Advice to others starting out ...

Rawiri: Find a partnership that suits your style. It helps if you're not in competition with one another. If the first [partner] doesn't work, at least try one other. Have some open talking sessions about whatever comes up. This is more difficult ... make formal sessions to observe and reflect on them. If you're a teaching principal and, depending on the success of the partnership, you may or may not meet regularly out of school. Two heads can be better than one.

Sue: Developing a partnership has proved to be a very supportive way of working professionally with another leader ... my present partnership will continue, as I believe we've both found it to our advantage.

Summary of main points

To develop successfully, coaching relationships need:

- trust, confidentiality and respect;
- commitment to ongoing professional learning;
- time to develop effectively;
- regularity of contact;
- ongoing practice in and building of coaching skills;
- sessions conducted with stringency (i.e., with structure and purpose);
- initiation, implementation and institutionalisation phases; and
- consideration of each leader's unique professional learning needs.

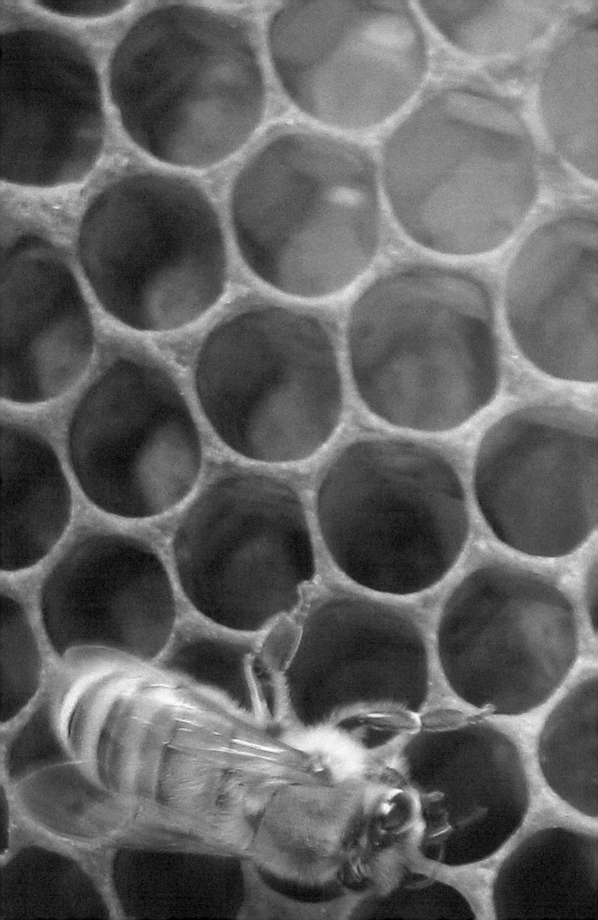

The realisation of a geometric ideal is rare in nature. The appearance of disturbances is the distinguishing work of *li*.

Chapter 7

Coaching the skills that build trust and understanding

Chapter overview

It's most important that any coaching partnership maintains the principle that, first and foremost, coaches are effective learners and enter the coaching relationship willing to learn—about coaching and about professional practice. To be effective, coaches need to be equipped with specific skills. This chapter looks at the skills required for the initiation phase of coaching, where the main emphasis is on building trust and understanding between the partners in an unhurried manner. The skills of listening and reflective interviewing are outlined and then followed by a description of the skills required in the context interview. This important interview is conducted during a visit to the partner's workplace to observe the realities of the day-to-day leadership practice for that person. The descriptions of each of the skills are complemented by activities that you can work through individually or with a coach, or in a workshop session.

Active listening

Active listening is one of the most important of the coaching skills and is one of the first requirements of effective dialogue (Isaacs, 1999). To listen for even three or four minutes without interrupting and without sharing one's own stories or giving advice is something that leaders often find difficult. Within the coaching relationship, active listening gives each leader, in turn, the freedom to articulate their practice, to justify why they're doing what they're doing, and to reflect on the impact they believe their actions have. When first given opportunity to speak uninterrupted, leaders often comment on how seldom this happens and of how strange, yet liberating, it feels. They state that having the responsibility to articulate and justify their professional practice while a coach listens is extremely challenging at first. Leaders also talk about the effect that this one small skill-development session has on their everyday work. They find themselves "listening first, in order to learn" (Covey, 1989) and not interrupting others when they're telling their stories.

When coaches actively listen, they're modelling their coach-as-learner role and building trust and respect because they're conveying to their partner that "what you are saying is worth listening to". Suspension of judgement is also an important aspect of dialogue that involves active listening (Isaacs, 1999). Great coaches listen for at least 80 percent of the time and ensure that the responsibility for improving professional practice is kept firmly in the hands of the coaching partner.

Listening guidelines and process

To be effective active listeners, coaches should:

- give the speaker full attention;
- encourage that person to keep talking;
- not break into the conversation by sharing "war stories" or their own experience;
- not give advice;
- suspend judgement;
- take careful note of what is said, in writing if necessary;
- not ask questions;
- focus in particular on what is said about leadership practice; and
- listen as well for what is *not* said and for what is important to the speaker.

Activities to build the skill

The following short reflective activities give leaders opportunities to talk about their practice and give their coach opportunities to practise active listening. The activities can be structured into workshops or you can use them to reflect individually on your leadership as your read this book and in preparation for working with a coach in the future.

Reflective activity 1

A. On a sheet of paper, write down three situations that you've been involved in recently and that have involved other people. Such situations might include a departmental meeting or senior management team meeting, strategic planning sessions, talking with parents about the placement of their child, engaging students in their learning, speaking with an incompetent staff member or working on induction with new staff. The situations might be positive events or involve issues that have been worrying you.

B. Put an asterisk (*) by the situation that you'd find valuable to talk about in a coaching situation.

C. Share this situation with your coach, telling him or her as much as you can about the situation, what happened, what you were thinking about then and are thinking about now, the issues you face, what might happen from here on—in fact, anything that comes to mind. Spend three to four minutes doing this, during which time your coach will be required to actively listen to you without interruption.

D. Take time with your partner to reflect on the listening process. What was the experience as the listener? What was it like for the speaker? What mental processes were occurring as you listened/spoke? This metacognitive means of reviewing your thinking and assessing the impact of the active listening and speaking uninterrupted is an important part of the adult learning process. It needs to be one that you've practised and feel confident to enact before you move into the next session.

E. Repeat the activity, with a different issue, or swap roles, again focusing on the reflective processes.

Extension: Your leadership is in the multitude of tasks and actions that you perform each day—even if you feel at the end of a day that you've not "done anything". Talk about, analyse and reflect on some of the things you do in your daily practice and how these might influence how others see you in your leadership.

Reflective activity 2

What are three things important to you in your professional practice? If your coach came and shadowed you for a week, what might be some of the things that he or she would see you doing on a regular basis? (This activity links to the extension exercise above.) For example, are you visible in the institution? Do you hold your meetings in different venues? Do you analyse data to provide evidence at meetings focused on future action?

A. Write down three things of importance to you in your practice and then jot down why you do them and what impact you think they have on the quality of learning in your institution.

B. For each item, write your answers under these headings:
    – What I do.
    – Why I do it.
    – Impact on learning.

Extension: Take your listed items and consider them according to this schema (after Smyth, 1993):

What do I do?	(Describe)
What does this mean?	(Inform)
How did I come to be like this?	(Construct)
How might I do things differently?	(Reconstruct)

Reflective activity 3

Your educational platform is the "soapbox" you stand on when you make a decision about educational issues. You could call this your philosophy of education. All educators have an educational platform, formed from their educational, social, cultural and religious histories. It's important to be clear about you what you and your colleagues' platforms are and how they affect the quality of education is a school or classroom. Self-awareness is an essential component of changing mindset and practice. This activity allows you to identify your educational platform, to surface your values, beliefs and assumptions, and then to use this understanding in another active listening session with your coaching partner or colleagues as you engage in further thinking together (Activity 4).

A. Copy and then fill out the questionnaire (adapted from work by Sergiovanni & Starratt, 2002) on the next pages. Work right through the questionnaire without stopping. In other words, write down what immediately comes into your head. You'll have a chance to revisit what you've written later on.

B. Work through this surfacing process on your own.

C. When you've done that, take your answers from those sections of the questionnaire that you believe have particular significance for your own work and reflect on each independently. If you're in a workshop or in a collaborative-teaching or senior-team situation, you can listen to how other educational leaders respond to each aspect of the platform. If you wish to add anything to your answers as a result of your reflection, place this in the "afterthoughts" sections. You may wish to add other parts of the platform that are of particular concern to your cultural and educational contexts.

Reflective activity 4

A. After you've worked right through the platform, share your ideas with your coach or other leaders. There should be no debate or discussion, just active listening. Add any more ideas you gain as a result of this activity in the afterthoughts. When you've completed all commentary on the educational platforms to your satisfaction, open up the session to questioning and discussion. There's no need to try to reach consensus. The most important thing is to learn and so understand why people believe the things they do and how these beliefs inform their leadership practice.

B. At this point you should also be able to identify your own "pedagogy of leadership practice", that is, what you believe is important in the *way* that you work with people. Do you believe in, for example:
   - consultation and partnerships;
   - pastoral care of colleagues;
   - culturally responsive practice;
   - learning communities;

Questionnaire

1. Aims of education
- If you had to give one overall general aim of education, what would it be?
- Extrapolating from that, what, in order of priority, are the three most important aims of education for the students in your institution?
- Afterthoughts?

2. View of knowledge
- What is knowledge? How do people become "knowledge-able"? What does it mean to be knowledgeable?
- Afterthoughts?

3. Major achievements
- What are your major achievements over the past year, particularly as they relate to your students' achievement or colleagues' work? List those that relate specifically to your leadership influence.
- Afterthoughts?

4. Social and cultural significance of what students learn
- What do you think this is? Can you give examples?
- Afterthoughts?

5. Image of the learner
- What are your assumptions about how one learns? How do you view the learner in the learning relationship?
- Afterthoughts?

6. Image of the curriculum
- What are your attitudes about the value of the curriculum or the programmes offered?
- Afterthoughts?

7. Image of the teacher

- What is your view about the changing role of the teacher?
- Afterthoughts?

8. Pedagogy

- What is your preferred mode of teaching and learning (and/or leadership)?
- Afterthoughts?

9. Language used in learning situations

- Describe the type of language you use when working with groups.
- Can you give any examples of actual phrases you hear yourself saying?
- Afterthoughts?

10. Teacher–student and working relationships

- What is your preferred type of teacher–student relationship? Why is this important to you?
- Afterthoughts?

11. Institutional climate

- What are the three most important qualities, norms or values for you in a workplace for you to be working at your highest potential?
- Afterthoughts?

12. Image of parents and/or community consultation

- What is your image of the "place" and role of parents and/or community consultation in education? What is your definition of "community"? How far does it extend?
- Afterthoughts?

- new ideas and innovation;
- risk taking;
- shared decision-making;
- developing leadership in others?

Make your own list, and then talk with your partner/coach about what each item means in terms of your work.

Reflective activity 5

This activity requires you to think about the values and beliefs that form your educational platform, which in turn underpins the decisions that you make. Would others you work with be able to articulate your educational platform? Do the people you work with know what is important to you and why you do the things you do? In other words, do you "speak the language of educational leadership" in your work?

A. Take the situations and items you listed in Activities 1 and 2, and think about them in relation to these questions:

–   Which of your values, beliefs and assumptions about education do these relate to?

–   How do you believe the values, beliefs and assumptions you hold make a difference to the quality of learning offered in your institution?

–   What have you identified about your values, beliefs and assumptions?

B. Now consider what you deem to be particularly important in terms of education:

–   What are you *not* willing to compromise on?

–   How does your viewpoint affect the decisions you make?

–   How does your viewpoint affect the way you work with others when setting your institutional goals?

–   How do you learn from the viewpoints of the other people you work with?

Reflective interviewing

Questioning partners in a way that encourages them to critically and deeply reflect on their professional practice is the essential skill of coaching, and it's the one that leaders are most likely to have to learn and practise over a reasonable period of time in order to build their repertoire of skill and confidence. This technique provides opportunities for those being questioned to explore their knowledge, skills, experiences, attitudes, beliefs and values (G. Lee, 1993), and it leaves ownership of the reflection—and any judgement arising out of it—in their hands.

It's important that leaders do not feel that coaching involves a colleague coming in and telling them how to lead their school/department/institution/centre or teach their class. Instead, they should see this person as someone who will help facilitate understanding of their practice. Such an approach is more powerful than telling or giving advice because it's empowering and encourages self-direction in learning. The person being asked the questions must come up with answers that will work for them and their particular context. This approach facilitates ownership of the outcomes and the process of change. A telling or controlling approach leads to either dependency or resistance, neither of which is conducive to rich professional learning.

Leaders shouldn't rush to move onto other coaching-related skills until reflective interviewing or questioning has become a comfortable, established skill. As leaders look back on their developing coaching relationship, it's likely they'll recognise that their ability to dialogue about their leadership practice is commensurate with their ability to employ the skill of reflective interviewing.

Question levels

Leaders can use at least three types or levels of questions to assist their coaching partner reflect critically on their practice. These questions are based on those formulated by G. Lee (1993) but have been further developed through the research on coaching leadership. For an example of how these three levels work within the context of a reflective interview, see the example on the next page.

Level 1

Level 1 questions are designed to clarify thinking about events, situations, actions and feelings. Such questions often start with: "Tell me ... what, when, if, whether, who, how and why." They're used to make sure that leaders in the coaching role have all needed information about an observation they've just made or are quite clear about the details of an incident that their partner has just described. Examples might be:

- "Tell me how often you have these meetings?"
- "Who sets the agenda?"
- "How many members attend the planning meetings?"

These Level 1 questions can sometimes provide leaders with insight as they reflect on the answers they give.

Level 2

The "coach as learner" is very important at this point. The questions are used to clarify purpose, reasons and intended consequences of the professional practice. They help the coach understand context, practice and the professional partner. Level 2 questions often start with how, why, who and which, and are concerned with probing the reasons why a leader has taken a particular action and what that person sees as the intended outcomes of that action. Examples include:

- "What is the purpose of these meetings?"
- "What do you hope will develop from them?"
- "How do (or will) they affect learning and teaching?"

Level 3

This third level of questions should move leaders into exploring the basis or outcomes of their actions. These "linking" questions are often called "So what/how …?" questions. Examples are:

- "So what evidence do you have?"
- "So what will happen next?"
- "So what might you do differently?"
- "So what impact will this have on the culture of this institution?"
- "So how does this link with your goal of shared decision making?"
- "So what does the evidence say the needs are here?"
- "So how does this support your improvement plan?"
- "So how does this lead towards achieving your vision?"
- "So why might this be important for students' futures?"

Example of a reflective interview

The coach in the following scenario has employed the three levels of questioning, with the aim of facilitating in-depth reflection on the part of her partner.

COMMENT: This morning I observed you carrying out a planning session.

Level 1 questions

- How often do you carry these out?
- Who is usually present?
- What are the goals of the institution?
- How were they developed?

Level 2 questions

- Why did you carry out this session at this point of time?
- How did you structure your session? Why did you structure it this way?
- What is the purpose or goal of the planning sessions? Why?
- How will you know you've achieved your goals?
- What might facilitate progress towards your institutional goals?
- What might hinder your progress?
- Why do you believe these sessions are important?
- What do you think are the most important benefits for those concerned? For the institution?

Level 3 questions

- How do you believe this planning session will affect learning and teaching and the programmes in this institution in the future?
- How do these meetings assist you in your work as a senior leader in this institution?
- So what effect do these sessions have on your overall leadership-development programme?
- How might you do this type of planning differently?
- So what is the most effective way of developing ownership and shared vision?
- What specifically helped you move towards achieving your goals?

Reflective interviewing guidelines and process

Coaches need to follow quite specific guidelines when conducting reflective interviews. They also need to consider afterwards how effective the interview sessions were in stimulating their coaching partner to think critically about their leadership practice. In order to encourage critical reflection, coaches need to:

- Base questions on the experiences of the respondent (not "What if …" situations).
- Use non-judgemental wording.
- Maintain a neutral tone of voice.
- Be prepared to follow up initial questions, but also note down a few questions applicable to each of the three question levels before you start the interview, if possible.
- Use active listening skills, such as nodding, looking at the person, perhaps using a short question prompt such as "What happened then?" or "Tell me more." Don't break into the flow of talk or ask questions that might change the speaker's direction of focus.
- Refrain from giving advice disguised as questions.
- Don't break into general dialogue until the reflective interview is officially over.

Another skill that can be used here is *placement* (Rock, 2007), which requires coaches to simply relate to their partners what they're hearing and understanding from what their partners are saying. This approach is not paraphrasing. It is a matter of coaches taking the time to clarify the situation in their own minds and the minds of their partners. Whether the coach is right or wrong doesn't matter. Placement provides both partners in the coaching relationship with opportunity to sound out their thinking and thereby gain a shared understanding of the situation and context. Coaches typically start this approach with these types of statement:

- "What I'm hearing is that …"
- "What I'm thinking at this stage is that you …"

Opportunity to practise reflective interviewing must be an integral part of the coaching process. Time must also be set aside for leaders to discuss with their coaches their experiences of the *process* so that they can use the insights gained to develop advanced reflective interviewing techniques.

After an observation or active listening session, leaders in the coaching role should take 5 to 10 minutes to note down some questions—perhaps two at each level—that they could ask their partner about this leadership incident. However, the number of questions asked should be kept as few as possible. This is not a game of 20 questions; the aim is for coaches to listen actively for 80 percent of the time. Their partners know the rules and how to play the game (good coaches make their processes overt), so will probably start off and work through the reflections to many of the questions listed before their coach has a chance to ask them!

An activity to build the skill
Reflective activity 6
A. Take the leadership situation you described in Reflective Activity 1.
B. Revisit it now in the light of the three levels of questions. Tell your coach what your intended outcome was and how it relates to or has influenced your leadership in your institution.
C. Follow through with an active listening session in which your coach should also employ careful questioning, using the three different levels, to help you critically reflect on your leadership practice and goals for your institution.
D. A prompt that your coach might employ here is this one: "Think back to the leadership experience that you were just interviewed about. In the light of the reflective questioning and discussion, and in relation to a similar future incident, consider these questions:
   - What would you do differently?
   - What would you do the same?
   - Did the reflective interviewing highlight anything for you?
   - What other questions should have been asked?
   - Was the reflective interviewing useful?
   - In what ways?
   - How could the reflective interviewing be improved?"

Context interviewing
The context interview is generally the first field-based reflective interview that leaders carry out with their coaches. This interview is most effective when the partners have practised the skills of active listening

> *"My leadership inquiry has been about coaching other leaders within my school, so all of what I have 'experienced' myself (e.g., being coached, being reflective myself, researching, discussing, etcetera)— has been highly practical in what I have led within my school, as I've been able to 'apply' the coaching."*

and reflective interviewing in a workshop coaching situation. The interview is called a context interview because it refers to the context(s) in which the leader works, whether the classroom, the department, the office and/or the meeting-room. The observation should involve a type of "show and tell" session in which coaches look at their respective partner's rooms, resources, displays, files and programmes, and perhaps meet other staff with whom the leader works.

The aim of this exercise is for coaches to become thoroughly familiar with the context in which their partners conduct their actions. This degree of familiarity is important and should not be assumed prior to the observation, even if the partners feel they know each other's context. The way individual leaders perceive their context is unique to their leadership, because each leader's values, beliefs and experiences are unique.

The basis of the context interview employed in the coaching model is the first part of the Leadership Framework (see Table 7.1), adapted from Bossert, Dwyer, Rowan, and Lee (1982). This first section of the framework sets out the main areas and associated examples of topics to be covered during the interview, namely the institutional context, the educational community, the governing bodies, and the leader's own beliefs and experiences. Table 7.2 outlines the content of the full framework.

Context interviewing guidelines and process

The interview is carried out on site relatively early in the coaching relationship and is linked directly to leaders' reflection on the Leadership Framework. The context observation and interview is more valuable if the leaders being observed have had opportunity for individual reflection on the framework and discussion with their coach on their educational platform (see Reflective Activity 4). It's important that the observation and subsequent interview help leaders become aware of how each and every leadership action influences their leadership framework.

Table 7.1: Items guiding the context interview within the context of the Leadership Framework

Institutional context	Community	Governing bodies	Beliefs and experiences
Regional	Locale	Human resources	Professional experiences
National	Socioeconomic status	Community partners	Personal history— education and social
Professional affiliations	Partnerships	Ministry of Education	Philosophy and vision
Charter/Policies/Codes	Ethnic composition and diversity	Review Office	Cultural perspectives
Profile	Expectations	Board	Religious or spiritual influences
Staffing	Values	Associations	
Strengths	Transiency	Committees	
Experiences	Resources	Religious bodies	
Issues	Support	Legislation	
	Internal/external politics	Tertiary Education Commission	

Note: Adapted from S. T. Bossert, D. C. Dwyer, B. Rowan, and G. V. Lee (1982), The instructional management role of the principal, *Educational Administration Quarterly*, 18(3), 34–64.

Table 7.2: The full Leadership Framework

Background/Context	Leadership activities	Resources	Instructional organisation	Outcomes
Institutional context	Routine behaviours	Instructional climate	Curriculum delivery	Programmes
Community	Goal setting	Collegial relationships	Instructional programmes	Professional practices
Governance context	Planned behaviours	Policy	Pedagogy	Achievements
Beliefs and experiences		Values	Student groupings	
		Institutional culture	Assessment	
			Feedback and appraisal	
			Quality assurance	

Note: Adapted from S.T. Bossert, D. C. Dwyer, B. Rowan, and G. V. Lee (1982), The instructional management role of the principal, *Educational Administration Quarterly*, 18(3), 34–64.

The information that should be covered by the interview thus relates to leaders' own educational backgrounds, beliefs and philosophies, the political and social context influencing their leadership, the types of communities they are working in and the particular aspects of their work that make their leadership unique. The context interview process itself is quite explicit and involves these steps.

A. Leader being observed

- Reflect on each of the four aspects of the Leadership Framework and on how each affects your own leadership in the institution.
- Share your context information with your coach; walk around your areas of responsibility, showing and explaining what you do and why you do what you do in the way that you do.
- Use the notes you made prior to this session to describe yourself and your context to your coach. This description will form the basis of your *context interview*—the first in-depth discussion you'll have with your coach/partner on site.

B. Coach

- Actively listen.
- Ask reflective questions in order to clarify or procure additional information.

Activities to build the skill

Reflective activity 7

A. On your own, rule a piece of paper into five columns, and head the columns with the headings of the Leadership Framework in Table 7.2 (Background/Context, Leadership Activities, Resources, Instructional Organisation, Outcomes).

B. Assign each of the following leadership items to their appropriate columns.

- The local community holds a negative perception of the institution.
- Very little hard data are available on student enrolment and/or achievement.
- Ten percent of the budget is allocated for professional development.
- Teachers have designated reflection times built into work structures.

- Few incidences of (staff or student) bullying occur.
- Teachers meet regularly for dialogue about teaching.
- Institution receives funding from entrepreneurial contracts.
- Leaders observe teaching and give feedback.
- Fifty percent of the teaching staff are new to the institution
- Veterans resist change.
- Leader talks to students personally.
- Innovation is part of the institutional culture.
- Teachers are involved in team teaching.
- Eighty percent of the budget is allocated to salary.
- Students are bilingual.
- Performance management systems involve all staff in appraisal annually.
- Teachers are involved in allocating students to learning groups and/or classes.
- Students are interested in learning and enjoy their study.
- Portfolios are used for goal setting.
- Staff consistently research their own practice.
- Board members take a keen interest in institutional governance.

Reflective activity 8

A. With your answers to Activity 7 in hand, join with your coaching partner or a group of leaders to discuss your placement of the items.

B. When you've done this, use these questions to guide your reflection on the session.

- What discussion occurred during the session?
- What differences were there in the placement of factors in the framework by different leaders and why did this occur?
- How do these factors, designated to parts of the framework, influence educational leadership?
- What influenced your decisions?

C. Look again at your sheet of answers and identify two or three outcomes that you would like to achieve in your school/class/institution this year. Ask yourself these questions:

- What are the context factors that would influence how well you achieve these goals?

-   What will be the restraining influences? How might you work around them?
-   What resources will facilitate you meeting your goals?

Reflective activity 9

This activity gives you the opportunity to reflect on the usefulness of the skills you've learned from this chapter. Ask these questions to guide your reflection.

-   What has the reflection focused on your education context helped you identify in terms of your leadership practice?
-   How has the coach's questioning assisted in the process of reflection?
-   What part has listening played in terms of your ability to focus on and describe your leadership practice?

Summary of main points

- Initiating the coaching process and building trust and understanding about a leader's work takes a variable amount of time depending on the leader's degree of familiarity with the coach, degree of comfort with the process of critiquing his or her own practice, and his or her experience level. It also depends on the coach's skills.

- It's important not to rush the process but to assess when the time is appropriate to move the leader forward. During this time, leaders are encouraged to reflect on themselves, their institution and their leadership practices.

- The coach must take the role of "learner" to ensure that ownership of the process and responsibility for leadership development rests in the leader's hands.

- Active listening is one of the most powerful but also most underused skills of coaching.

- Effective questioning will prompt deep reflection on professional practice.

- Questioning needs to be at different levels to encourage reflection about educational values and beliefs, goals for the institution, and the social, cultural and political context.

- Reflection that focuses on one's educational platform is an important part of leadership development and change in practice.

- Knowledge of the educational context of leadership is paramount in terms of an effective coaching relationship.

Crackle and crazing networks "can be seen as force-lines, pathways, and it was this aspect that made these *li* so energising to the Chinese, with their cultural awareness of invisible energies."

Chapter 8

Coaching the skills that move leaders forward

Chapter overview[1]

Once the coaching partners have established trust and understanding, the coaching process needs to move into deeper reflection and into more formal self-assessment procedures designed to promote goal setting and action planning and to allow ongoing observation of practice leading to descriptive and evaluative feedback. This process is also the point at which links can be made to professional standards. The skills involved in the process and their relationship to the change process, with its underpinning of action research, form the topic of this chapter. The descriptions of the skills are again accompanied by activities.

---

1 Content in this chapter has been taken from or drawn on, with permission, the following journal article: Jan Robertson (2015), Deep learning conversations and how coaching relationships can enable them, *Australian Educational Leader*, 37(3), 10–15.

Deeper learning conversations

The deepest learning conversations not only focus on immediate concerns and individual needs but also arise out of deep learning relationships (Robertson, 2015). Once leaders have developed these relationships and trust through active listening, reflective interviewing and context interviewing (as described in the previous chapter), they can deepen the types of questions they ask and consider.

Deep learning relationships build trust, respect and shared commitment to the study of teaching and learning. They also involve reciprocal learning opportunities. Importantly, they're free of judgement and are therefore a place of safety—a place where it feels okay to tap into and show vulnerability. These relationships are actually *partnerships in learning* and all that this concept entails. The deeper the relationship is, the more easily coaching partners can ask each other, in a challenging but always supportive way, to question the purposes, principles and goals of their current practice. They'll probably find that the collaborative coaching conversation, arising from shared teaching environments, is a less threatening learning approach than are larger, group-based learning forums. Focusing on one aspect of shared practice with a colleague or colleagues and thoroughly critiquing that aspect in the light of shared goals and desired outcomes helps leaders stand back from their everyday practice and look more objectively at how their own teaching and learning and, in time, the learning of others, is currently playing out in the educational context of today.

As the level of trust grows within learning relationships, and coaching skills develop, colleagues feel not only better able to ask one another the more challenging critically reflective questions but also more willing to share areas needing development. They feel sufficiently safe to move away from covering up perceived areas of weakness, as is so often the case in professional development directed towards improved practice. The deepest learning occurs when partners are encouraged, through courageous, supportive and therefore effective coaching practice, to locate their own areas for development and new learning and to discuss them with each other even when they feel vulnerable doing so.

With regard to vulnerability, the power relations or conflicts of purpose that may occur if a coach is also a senior leader or an appraiser can adversely affect the relationship. But these tensions are not insurmountable if the relationship is sensitively negotiated and understood. Coaches need to be authentic and skilled, both socially and emotionally, and peers can fulfil this role if they have the right level of support and supervision of their coaching practice. Peer coaching and/or collaborative teaching develop greater levels of collegiality, a natural development of which can be group coaching.

A listening, learning school culture is also vital to the success of collegial relationships. Making coaching skills an essential part of teachers' and leaders' repertoires helps build this culture because it promotes a virtuous cycle of collegiality and robust learning in the pursuit of quality teaching and learning.

In any coaching relationship, the ability to listen deeply is just as important as asking the questions that count. Asking without listening and listening without asking produces monologue rather than dialogue. True dialogue is what facilitates the change process. Each partner needs to serve as a coach who can take the other beyond the "what and the how" of teaching and leadership practice into the metacognitive realm of critically *thinking* about that practice, and the potential for it.

Of more importance, then, than the questions about *how* a coaching partner is going to do this or that and *what* he or she is going to do next are the questions that focus on *why*. However, why questions must be asked in a way that signals not judgement but a genuine desire to learn as a coach—and that enables the partner to learn—from the answers given. Here are some examples of why questions. This is not one for a coaching session but rather a list of the types of challenging questions coaches might ask at particular points in coaching conversations:

- *Why* do you feel these students are so disengaged?
- *Why* is this important to you?
- *Why* are these particular groups not achieving as well as others?
- *Why* are you doing this in this way? At this time? In this place?
- *Why* do you think children will learn this best through these activities?
- *Why* do you think these strategies are the best ones for addressing this challenge?
- *Why* are these learning outcomes the most important ones for these students at this time?

- *Why* do you think meetings are the best places to form relationships with parents?
- *Why* do you think this is happening?
- *Why* do you think (or say) that?

Trust must be part of the relationship for these "why" questions to be asked because they could otherwise feel threatening. When educational leaders are asked questions like these, and so need to articulate and justify their practice in response, they typically begin to examine their practice more deeply and therefore reflect more deeply on the interaction between their practice and the teaching and learning outcomes (for themselves, for their students) they want to achieve. In short, hard coaching questions keep leaders firmly focused on the *relationship* between leadership, teaching and learning and owning their practice.

"Why" questions ultimately lead coaching partners to a space that I call "*what might be*". I use this phrase because responding to why questions requires leaders to critically reflect on their practice and to go on critically reflecting in the long term. It also encourages them to imagine possibilities other than those currently informing and shaping their practice. While our early answers to such questions may not yet reflect the deep learning sought, they will provide the beginnings of an ongoing coaching dialogue that takes our thinking well below surface thought and so challenges our mindsets.

The point at which *we*, as leaders, begin to change is the point at which we begin to see the new possibilities for practice. Our thinking changes and our mindsets change. Our cognitive framework changes, our belief system changes and we personally move into the transformative stage of the change process. When we change as an outcome of our new learnings and understandings, we're highly likely to have a clearer idea of and the confidence to try different things that lead to the transformative changes that matter.

A brief example illustrating these ideas

Consider a school where particular groups of students, such as indigenous students, gifted students or those students with English as a first or second language, are not achieving as well as they might. The school is working hard to support these students but is making little difference to their learning outcomes. Teachers and leaders have drawn on a few new ideas and strategies from traditional professional development and from the research literature and incorporated these in their practice, but still nothing really changes in terms of student outcomes.

A first step from a coaching context would be to ask the school's leaders and teachers why they think these students aren't achieving as well as others in the school or class or at their potential and then to listen carefully to the answers (Bishop, Berryman, Cavanagh & Teddy, 2009). If those answers are all about the students ("disengaged"; "never brings homework back"), the parents ("never come to meetings"; "never help with homework"; "not interested"), and/or the school ("not enough time"; "too many students"; "curriculum's too full"), then no matter how many new ideas or strategies come the leaders' and teachers' way, there will be no real change in desired outcomes. This is because these educators will not have placed themselves *inside* the change process, inside the learning relationship; their mindset is probably one of "It's all about others needing to change, not me."

Teachers and leaders who think this way have not recognised that *they* need to be part of the change they want to see. As such, they must be asked the hard (but respectful) questions that cannot help but make them think about what it is *they need to learn* or what *they need to change* in order to be more successful in their practice.

Wise coaches listen carefully and reflectively so they can continue to form the hard questions—whether relating to content or process—that arise out of and so are relevant to what their partner is saying. At times, bridging questions ("What is going on here today?") will be required first before reaching into some deeper concepts about education. Sometimes more direct questions ("What does the data tell you about the needs of these three students?") may be appropriate. For coaches, a sense of the colleague's readiness to engage in deep reflection and taking responsibility will guide the content and tenor of their questions, which is why a trusting, ongoing learning relationship is so important.

The questions coaches choose might be one or two out of the list that follows, but remember that the questions must only be those that arise naturally out of what the partner is saying. Again, this is *not* a coaching script.

- What is the most difficult issue for you?
- Why do the students believe they are failing?
- What could you do differently this year that might make a difference?
- Why do the parents think their children are not succeeding?
- What do you think is the role of parents in their children's schooling?
- What are the parents saying about why they're not engaging in their students' learning?
- How does your knowledge of these students and their families influence your teaching?
- Tell me about a time when you had huge success in this area.
- In what ways do students' cultures influence their learning?
- What advantages do these students bring to the classroom?
- What are you learning from the data about the needs of these students?
- What questions are you holding at the moment about these students and their learning?
- Where are you going to find the answers to the questions you have?
- What frustrates you in your work with these students?
- If you knew the answer to this problem, what would it be?
- What would be the question you'd ask yourself at this time?
- What would you advise another teacher in a similar situation?

Ultimately, when we're asked questions that delve deep into our identity of what it means to teach or lead, we come right down to the basis of our depth of accountability to the children we have in our care.

The questions that matter are therefore those that *help us surface and examine our moral purpose* against the depth of our accountability in educational terms. Here we can see the development of *rich* accountability, an accountability that comes from within, not externally, and is therefore congruent with the ideal of professionalism in education. As we engage and take ownership of the impact of our professional practice, we become more self-reflective and increase our ability to be involved in reflective self-assessment.

Self-assessment

Self-assessment is another extremely important aspect of an effective coaching relationship. The coaching partners must continually remember that responsibility for learning lies in the hands of the leader being coached. The coach must always invite the leader to first self-assess after any given observation visit or reflection on progress towards goals. Doing this helps leaders learn how to clearly identify their own strengths and their areas needing further development and to be more self-directed in this process.

Many institutions have self-assessment frameworks in place, such as those found within performance appraisal. They typically utilise professional standards or capabilities as a basis of these frameworks. The headings they use for the standards/capabilities may well be suitable for self-assessing leadership practice. Self-assessment tools can also be found in policy documents and in research evidence, while self-assessment can also be linked to external assessments involving, for example, development centres and reviews. Table 8.1 presents self-assessment topics set within five suggested frameworks, any of which can be used to guide self-assessment at the beginning of the coaching process.

Self-assessment guidelines and process

- The first self-assessment process should take place during the very beginning stages of the coaching relationship. Leaders need to set aside quiet reflection time to do this, first individually and then with their coaches.
- Self-assessment needs to occur after each shadow observation and during all subsequent coaching sessions. At these times, the leader and the coach need to take time out apart from each other to reflect on the strengths displayed and to identify areas for further development or lost opportunities for achievement of goals. In this way, self-assessment becomes part of the whole evaluative feedback process.
- Self-assessment needs to focus on leadership practices that make working towards achieving professional goals possible.

Activities to build the skill
Reflective activity 10
The self-assessment that forms this activity is important as you begin to take ownership for the areas that you do well in, for identifying when and how your leadership practice aligns with your professional goals, and for determining when you need to put more development work into certain areas.

Table 8.1: Frameworks useful for guiding self-assessment

Framework One[a]	Framework Two[b]	Framework Three	Framework Four[c]	Framework Five
Vision and leadership Building community relationships Striving for excellence Self-efficacy	**CULTURE** Provide professional leadership that focuses the school culture on enhancing learning and teaching **PEDAGOGY** Create a learning environment in which there is an expectation that all students will experience success in learning **SYSTEMS** Develop and use management systems to support and enhance student learning **PARTNERSHIPS and NETWORKS** Strengthen communication and relationships to enhance student learning	Strengths in leadership Areas for development in leadership Specific focus on student achievement Specific focus on team-building Culture-building aspects of leadership Specific goal for research Professional development goals	A conceptual job description Leading, coordinating and facilitating the learning community Managing and developing the culture Taking responsibility for communications networks Playing a figurehead in representing the institution Personal professional development	SWOT analysis (personal and professional): Strengths Weaknesses Opportunities Threats

Note. Adapted from:
[a] Hay Group (2001), *Identifying the skills, knowledge, attributes and competencies for first-time principals: Shaping the next generation of principals*, Melbourne, Hay Acquisitions Inc.
[b] Ministry of Education (2015), *Interim professional standards*, Wellington, Ministry of Education, www.education.govt.nz
[c] Stewart, D. (2000), *Tomorrow's principals today*, Palmerston North, Massey University and Kanuka Grove Press.

A. Use any one of the five frameworks given in Table 8.1, or another that your institution may use for self-assessment or that you develop, and reflect quietly for 20 to 30 minutes on your work.
B. When using the framework, focus specifically on the individual smaller goals set, or use it as an overarching assessment of your leadership practice in your institution.

Reflective activity 11

Here, you're required to set a specific focus for leadership development, teaching development or the achievement of a goal. For example, you might want to look at how to make more effective use of colleagues' strengths in group meetings, how to get colleagues to take responsibility for shared goals or how to more ably meet students' needs in particular areas.

A. After the shadow observation session, conduct your self-assessment by taking careful reflective note of anything you did during the session that moved you towards your goal. Also note missed opportunities or areas where you felt you could have done better.
B. Elicit descriptive feedback from your coach after the session, as this will provide further valuable material for your self-assessment reflection. Evaluative feedback will follow later.
C. Now review your goals individually or through a reflective interview with your coach.

Goal setting and action planning

After the coaching partners have completed (or as part of) the self-assessment and related reflective interviewing session, they can begin their goal setting followed by action planning and inquiry. Goal setting enables leaders to look ahead and determine desired outcomes. Goals can be personal or professional, individual, group or institutional, and often a combination of these. The goal-setting process establishes a framework for the professional support necessary to achieve goals. It gets leaders to become inquiry-minded in their practice and to focus on the specific leadership actions necessary to achieve long-term outcomes. Leaders need to critically reflect on what it is that they want to achieve before they can work on related action plans. They also need to understand how their daily actions ultimately influence their ability to realise desired outcomes. Inquiry into this practice is vital.

Goal setting arises most naturally out of self-assessment sessions that are effective. "Effective" means that goals are reviewed and monitored and that dialogue centres on leadership practice. Leadership goals should usually be established in more than one area of the leader's work. Just what these areas are will depend on each leader's institutional context. Some examples are:

- teaching responsibilities;
- research;
- developing a performance growth culture;
- community service and partnerships;
- curriculum responsibilities;
- pedagogical standards;
- departmental or institution-wide responsibilities;
- entrepreneurial activities; and
- contract or project outputs.

Having identified areas, leaders should take each one in turn, setting goals for it with the support of the coach before going on to the next one. The coaching partners also need to establish what indicators will help assess progress towards achievement of goals. Identifying time-frames and situations or dates where the coach can give feedback is also an important part of the process.

During goal setting, the coach acts as an outside facilitator—as a conscience and a guide who keeps the focus, inquiry and impetus firmly directed towards achievement of goals. When leaders consciously align their leadership actions with their professional goals, they naturally enhance their and others' self-efficacy, which in turn allows desired change in the institution to occur more rapidly.

Goal-setting guidelines and process

As stated in Chapter 6, the GROW model provides a particularly useful means of structuring a coaching session around goal setting. The model, which is Landsberg's (2003) version, involves four simple steps: Goal, Reality, Option, and Wrap-up. To serve as a reminder, Table 8.2 sets out how to use each of these steps during a goal-setting session.

During goal setting, the coaching partners need to:

- Set achievable but challenging outcomes.
- Keep the coaching focus on helping formalise the structure of any goal-setting session and helping the leader work consistently towards achieving the goals.
- Allow sufficient time for leaders to reflect individually on what their professional goals are for the following year or years.
- Think "behind" each goal by asking: What factors will facilitate/restrain goal attainment?
- Build self-efficacy. Popper and Lipshitz (1992) claim that the coach can facilitate this process by focusing on four processes during goal setting:
  - identifying and defining clear parameters of success;
  - building and structuring situations that have the potential for success;
  - identifying factors that lead to success; and
  - identifying inner sources of success.

"Probably giving us direction and making us more formalised; to actually get something done and achieved rather than just chatting. ... It's goal setting. I think you probably keep drawing us back to that."

Table 8.2: How to use the GROW model when goal setting

Goal	Reality	Options	Wrap-up
Agree on topic for discussion Agree on specific objective of session Set long-term aim if appropriate	Invite self-assessment Offer specific examples of feedback Avoid or check assumptions Discard irrelevant history/information	Cover range of options for future action Invite suggestions Offer suggestions carefully, by invitation Ensure choices are made for future actions	Commit to action Identify possible obstacles Make steps specific Define timing Agree on support needed from coach, others or professional development

Remember that goal setting is both an individual and a shared activity. Another useful tool for goal-setting alluded to earlier in this book is Eaton and Johnson's (2001, p. 31) SMART process. SMART requires that the goals set are:

- **Specific**
- **Measured**
- **Achievable**
- **Relevant**
- **Timed.**

Table 8.3 reminds you how SMART works and provides examples of questions that you can ask as you set goals in accordance with each of the SMART elements.

Once leaders have explored these questions with their coach, they should have a clear understanding of the goal and also of some of the

Table 8.3: Questions to elicit SMART goals

Elements of SMART	Useful questions
Specific (Make sure everyone knows about the aim.)	What will you be doing when you've achieved the goal? What do you want to do next?
Measured (Define standards to work towards.)	How will you measure achievement of the goal? What will you feel when the goal is reached?
Achievable (Ensure that the goal is realistic.)	What might facilitate or hinder you as you progress towards the goal? What resources can you call upon?
Relevant (Make sure the goal is worthwhile.)	What do/will you and others get out of this? Have other parties involved agreed to it? Is this the most important goal at this time?
Timed (Agree on a time-frame.)	When will you achieve the goal? What will be your first step?

Source: Taken from J. Eaton & R. Johnson (2001), *Coaching successfully*, London, UK, Dorling Kindersley, p. 31.

factors that will restrain or facilitate achievement. They should also have explored and discussed options for leadership actions. Goal-setting should ultimately culminate in action planning and leadership action. The overall process you and your coaching partner should follow when setting goals and attendant action plans and then assessing progress against them follows.

1. With each goal, establish indicators against which you can measure achievement and/or progress and what evidence you will need to gather. (What will the situation look like when you've achieved this goal?)
2. Prepare an initial action plan. This sets out the first key steps towards achieving the goal.
3. Set time-frames for actions and goal achievement.
4. Determine where and when your coach will fit in to provide feedback and assist with the processes in the action plan.
5. Share and discuss the goal-setting framework with your coach, using the SMART questions to identify and discuss resources and barriers.
6. Implement the first steps of the action plan.
7. Monitor achievement. Use evidence, observation and feedback to guide the process.
8. Review the action plan in the next coaching session.
9. Act.
10. Monitor …

Table 8.4 brings together the GROW and SMART tools in a way that helps you see how the two intersect. This insight assists you not only to set your goals and objectives for your coaching sessions but also to structure those sessions in the amount of time available. The plan you develop will provide you with a focus for your observation visits and performance appraisals, establish actions for your own professional learning and feed into your overall personal and institutional learning

Table 8.4: Using a combination of GROW and SMART elements to set objectives and goals for coaching sessions

Session Structure	Process	Rules	Questions
Goal setting	Define what is to be achieved Agree topics/focus for coaching session Agree objectives for coaching session Set/agree professional goals	Specific	What will you be doing when you have achieved the goal? What do you want to do next?
		Measured	How will you measure the achievement of the goal? What are the indicators of success? What will you feel when the goal is reached? What will it look like?
Reality checking	Understand the situation Invite self-assessment Offer specific examples of feedback from coaching Avoid or check assumptions Discard irrelevant history	Achievable	What might hinder you as you progress towards the goal? What resources can you call upon? What has worked in similar situations before? What will facilitate your achievement of the goal?
Option exploration	Discuss choices available Cover range of options Challenge for more options Offer suggestions and advice by invitation Ensure priorities are discussed and choices are made	Relevant	What do you and other parties get out of this? Have others agreed to it? What might someone else think to do in this situation? What is the most outlandish option you can think of? What options do you think will work best?
Wrapping up	Agree and commit to course of actions Identify possible obstacles/facilitating factors Make steps in action plans specific Define timing Agree support from coach and others	Timed	When will you achieve the goal? What will be your first step? When? What support can I give you in the process? When would you like to meet to review progress?

Source: Adapted from M. Landsberg (2003), *The Tao of coaching*, London, UK, Profile Books, and J. Eaton and R. Johnson, 2001, *Coaching successfully*, London, UK, Dorling Kindsley.

Activities to build the skills

Reflective activity 12

A. Select a template (such as the example that follows) and identify three major goal areas you'd like to focus on while working with your coach.
B. Make sure you set goals in different areas of your work.
C. Work individually through the thinking behind the goal setting (use the GROW and SMART frameworks).
D. At your next coaching session, share this process with your coach. The coach's role will be to listen, question and help you build on the SMART and GROW frameworks to develop these goals further, if necessary, and likewise the appropriate leadership action plans.

Observing and describing leadership practice

Opportunity to observe others enacting a similar role is, of course, an important predecessor of critical reflection and so must be built firmly into the coaching process. This position is a privileged one to be in and

---

TEMPLATE ONE

Goal:

Results expected: By when?
-
-
-
-

What support can the coach give to assist you to achieve this goal?
-
-
-

---

therefore needs to be treated with due respect. Observations should be authentic sessions that take place in leaders' own workplaces. If this ideal is not always possible, the observations can be construed through role plays or by demonstrating certain leadership practices via vignettes in clinical coaching sessions.

An effective observation session should be as much of a learning experience (albeit vicarious) for the coach as for the person being coached. Coaches need to give descriptive accounts of what they observe and should neither judge nor interpret the observed behaviours. However, leaders need to acknowledge that observing and describing someone else's practice is inevitably somewhat subjective in nature, and they should guard against this subjectivity when describing their partner's leadership practice. Understanding and confronting this consideration is part of the process of developing the skills of observation and giving descriptive feedback to a colleague.

Essentially, observing is not about judging whether the leadership practice in focus is good or bad, effective or ineffective. Nor is it about the coach telling their partner how they would act in a similar situation. Unfortunately, this is what colleagues most often tend to do! But it is not part of the coaching model set out in this book.

Observation guidelines and process

There is no one right way to observe practice. The coach and leader will develop what works best for them, in their context. The shadow observation may be as short as 15 minutes or involve three days in the institution. *When coaches are shadowing and observing a leader in action, they need to:*

- Gather information about the leader's practice.
- Provide a *descriptive* account of the leadership practice.
- Use this activity as a legitimate opportunity to see another leader in action.
- Remember that coaching is a privileged position, which means that the partners must take an ethical stance that encompasses trust, humility, loyalty and confidentiality.

As coaching partners, leaders need to decide together:

- How they will carry out the shadowing observation.
- What data they will gather and who will see it.

- How long the session will be.
- When the session will be.
- Where it will take place.
- What specific focus it will take.
- What feedback is necessary and from whom. (Feedback can come from other people and sources, such as student evaluations, community consultation, "360 degree" feedback and other assessment tools.)
- What the ethical implications might be. (For example, should permission be sought from staff to observe a staff meeting and take notes? How can people's anonymity be guaranteed?)

During each observation session, coaches note:
- Observable events (e.g., "Looked at watch five times"; "OHTs could not be read from back of the room"; "Students off-task").
- Key quotations and main points of conversations (e.g.., "You said, 'I am totally mortified by this!'").
- Non-verbal communication (e.g., body language, placement of chair).
- The physical environment and where people are situated.
- Time intervals, if important (e.g., "Spent three minutes in senior classroom").
- Names of people involved in interactions.
- Points that specifically relate to the goal and focus set for feedback.

After the session, coaches need to:
- Take time to fill in the notes taken during the observation.
- Do this before meeting with the partner so as to give him or her a descriptive account of what was observed.
- Follow through with the reflective interview.

At this point of the coaching, the partner can be doing some self-assessment and reflection in regard to the goals and outcomes set for the session.

Activities to build the skill

The following activities give you guidance on types of teaching or leadership practices and behaviour to look out for when observing your partner and how to describe them to him or her, without judgement. Note that facilitators can employ these activities in similar ways by using video-clips or role play in workshop sessions and then asking participants to describe the practices/ behaviour that they observe. You can then share the descriptions one by one, with the group evaluating whether each practice involves a judgement/interpretation or a straightforward description. This approach is a very powerful way of assisting leaders to see how much people's own values, beliefs and practices influence their views of the work of others in their institutions.

Reflective activity 13

A. Which of these statements contains a judgement/interpretation (J) and which is a description (D) of the observed behaviour? For each item, circle either J or D.

- Mary responded favourably to your suggestions.   J/D
- You divided the staff into four groups and set tasks for each group.   J/D
- You spoke for 10 minutes at the beginning of the meeting.   J/D
- I liked it when you asked each staff member to respond.   J/D
- You asked Peter to take notes from the discussion.   J/D
- It frustrated you when Peter took too long with the feedback section of the meeting   J/D
- You asked each group leader to provide one piece of evidence.   J/D
- You were anxious to complete the meeting.   J/D
- You dominated the meeting.   J/D
- Your PowerPoint presentation was good.   J/D
- Each person in the group contributed to the discussion.   J/D
- You were poorly prepared for the meeting.   J/D
- Your PowerPoint presentation included goals, actions and outcomes.   J/D

B. Discuss your answers with another leader, group of leaders or your coach. What sorts of ideas and thoughts do you now have about observation and description of practice?

The important aspect of doing this reflective activity is that of becoming aware of how easily judgement can become part of the feedback process. The more we're aware of this, the more we can guard against it when giving descriptive and evaluative feedback.

Reflective activity 14

This activity requires you and your coaching partner to engage in workplace shadowing. (If you think it is useful to do so, look back at "an example of a reflective interview" on page 127 of Chapter 7, which gives examples of questions related to strategic planning.)

A. Set up a workplace shadowing session.

B. Decide on the specific leadership practice that will form the focus of the session. An example might be: "Building our staff's commitment towards and ownership of our institution's education plan."

C. Conduct the session, with you, as coach, observing closely and taking careful notes.

D. Set time aside after the session so that you can give your partner descriptive feedback that will help him or her self-assess and identify the leadership practices that led towards the goal and those that did not assist in goal achievement.

E. Encourage your partner to share these thoughts with you. If it seems appropriate to do so, follow on with a reflective interviewing session.

F. Go to the "giving evaluative feedback guidelines and process" immediately below so that both of you gain a clear understanding of how observation and description of practice are important components of the full evaluative feedback process.

Giving evaluative feedback

Giving evaluative feedback is quite different from descriptive feedback, but it follows on from it and after self-assessment of the leadership practice. Evaluative feedback involves coaches giving leaders professional advice and considered judgement and critique about their leadership in terms of making effective progress towards desired goals. It's important that the coaching partners negotiate guidelines for the process. They should write these down and place a copy in the coaching folder for further reference (as discussed in Chapter 6). As with any evaluative feedback session, sufficient time must be set aside for the feedback process to occur. It can be very frustrating for leaders if there is insufficient time for their coach to give adequate feedback on the leadership practice observed.

Evaluative feedback guidelines and process

Effective feedback:

- describes leadership behaviours (that can be changed);
- is specific, descriptive, and informative;

- is related to the leadership goals and the focus set;
- makes links to the long-term goals and to how this session fits into the overall aims of the coaching partnership;
- takes into account the needs of the leader and leaves the leader's dignity intact;
- is well timed and given as close as possible to the time of the observation;
- highlights successes and is positive about the ability to improve practice;
- is understood and received in the way it was meant; and
- gives specific examples of areas for improvement or further focus.

The first step in the feedback interaction is for the leader being coached to set a specific focus *before* the observation takes place. The partner being coached must be the one who directs what is to be observed so he or she can obtain the feedback required from the coach. The focus can be quite general ("Please watch me take a staff meeting or group meeting") or specific ("I'd like you to evaluate how effectively I use the expertise of the board at the meeting next week so that they take on specific responsibilities"). The focus should also be consistent with achievement of the long-term goals set earlier.

The second step of the process is careful observation, recording and describing of behaviours as recounted previously. After the observation, the leader and the coach should each take a few minutes to reflect on the leader's actions during the session and to make brief written assessments of their thoughts. The coach's notes should include comments on positive and negative aspects of the leadership just observed and be couched in terms of progress towards goals. The leader should include in his or her summary assessment those actions and behaviours that helped achieve the set goal and those that could have be done more effectively or developed.

After approximately 5 to 10 minutes apart, the leader and coach again meet together. The coach *describes* the leadership behaviours noted during the interaction, while the leader listens. For the leader, just listening to this description—the body language noted, the words used and the leadership actions—can give a new awareness of his or her actions and so greatly enhances self-reflection and self-assessment.

When the coach has finished giving all of the descriptive feedback, the leader self-evaluates, presenting both the positive and the negative, while the coach actively listens without interrupting until all self-assessment has been completed. The coach then gives the leader *evaluative* feedback, pointing out the positive elements first and then the areas for development. The leader actively listens to the feedback in its entirety and does not interrupt, justify or explain. Finally, the two leaders discuss the session, explain and articulate reasons for comments and actions, make suggestions, bounce ideas around, set new goals together in reflective interview, and plan for the next session.

In summary, the evaluative feedback process involves this 10-step approach:

"I should have had [coach] do a reflective interview on some point, but he had to get back to [institution], and I wouldn't have had any feedback if I hadn't asked for it. There's little point in having learnt the skills to put to some useful purpose if we don't use them."

1. Leader establishes an area of focus.
2. Coach observes the leader in action (refer back to the skills of observing and describing).
3. Coach takes careful, descriptive notes.
4. Coach and leader take 5 to 10 minutes apart to prepare notes on the observation, setting these down according to:
    (a) Strengths—what worked well; progress made towards goals.
    (b) Development—what could have been done better; what were missed opportunities.
5. The pair again meets up.
6. Coach *describes* what he or she observed and the leader actively listens (refer back to skill of actively listening), without interruption.
7. Leader self-evaluates (coach actively listens without interruption), giving his or her reflection on strengths and development.
8. Coach gives evaluative feedback (leader actively listening without interruption) on strengths and development.
9. The pair open up the session for reflective dialogue, involving questioning (refer back to the skill of interviewing), discussion and putting forward ideas.
10. Coach and leader review existing goals, set new ones (refer to the skill of goal-setting) and plan out the actions needed to achieve them (action planning).

Note *after* the leader has self-evaluated (Step 7), the coach may use a shorter version of giving feedback offered by Landsberg (2003, p. 22) and identified by the acronym AID:

Actions: The coach describes the things that the leader is doing in the area under review.

Impact: The coach describes the effect these actions are having.

Desired outcome: The coach suggests how the leader could do things more effectively.

Of key importance is that the leader sets a specific focus in line with his or her professional goals for the year ahead or for the specific interaction that week. Ensure sufficient time is set aside for the feedback process to occur. Also remember, as cautioned earlier, that leaders become frustrated if coaches do not utilise, at the time of the set coaching session, the skills they have learned of providing quality feedback and assistance with critical reflection for future action.

Understanding the change process arising out of action research

The skills described in this chapter and the previous one are essential for conducting action research as it aligns with the coaching process. Earlier chapters have outlined how the coaching process leads the leader into action research, with the coach as critical friend in the process. The point of this process is to help leaders reflect on their leadership practice and the context within which it operates in a way that allows them to determine and action changes in their practice and their institutions—for the better. Leaders need to be clear from the outset that this change process—the transformation of leaders, leadership practice and institutions—is the ultimate reason for the coaching partnership.

Action research involves the self-reflective cycle described by Kolb (1984) and discussed in Chapter 3 of this book. The cycles of development that characterise action research and underpin the coaching process are observation, reflection, planning and action.

Action research guidelines and process

Leaders and their coaches need to remember that:

- action research is a change process;
- change takes place over time and is a formative learning *process*;
- leaders are *coached* into action research processes naturally because the relationship continues over a period of time;
- the change process needs to be made overt to educational leaders; and
- leaders must understand how the change process operates at the personal level and at the institutional level.

Because the action research process as it relates to coaching is detailed in Chapter 5, it doesn't need to be reiterated here. However, a couple of further comments concerning the process can be made at this point. From the outset of the coaching relationship, coaching partners need to work together to ensure they are both fully aware of the change process underlying action research and the importance of action and reflection in the process of change. When coaches encourage and help their partners to see how their many actions, small and large, work together over time to bring about achievement of long-term goals, they not only gain greater understanding of the change and development process but are also assured that progress is being made towards achieving those goals.

This understanding and assurance can be heightened when coaching partners join with other leaders engaged in coaching. Partners might find it possible to join up with another pair of coaching partners in a region, or perhaps a group of leaders in a cluster group who are also coaching partners, or even within a department or centre that has established professional coaching. Group sessions are enriching because they allow leaders to hear about the coaching projects and goals of others, to reflect on their own coaching partnerships and skills, to exchange ideas and support and to take part in group problem posing, problem solving, and action learning.

An activity to build the skill
Reflective activity 15

This activity helps leaders develop an understanding of the change process at the personal level, and also gives opportunity to review Kolb's (1984) learning cycle.

A. Individually: Think of a time when there was a huge impact on your life, either professionally or personally.

B. Jot down what happened. Was it a change of job or country? Was it the loss of a loved one? Was it the birth of a child? Was it a promotion that you were not ready for? Was it a personal grievance taken out against you?

C. Answer each of the following questions:
   - How did you feel at the time?
   - What did you then do?
   - What did you do at a later point of time?
   - How were you then different?

D. In pairs, or with your coaching partner, take turns sharing your critical incident and related thinking. Use the skills of active listening.

E. Now share another incident with each other and reflect on and answer the questions listed. Use the skills of active listening and reflective interviewing to link your incidents with values and beliefs about your institution and your vision for it.

F. After your time with your partner, self-reflect, using these questions to guide you:
   - What has this activity taught me about the change process?
   - Can I relate this to Kolb's (1984) learning cycle of concrete experience, reflective observation, abstract conceptualisation (coming up with new ideas and concepts) and active experimentation (with new ways of being)?
   - Can I relate this process to an example of institutional change?

Summary of main points

- Listening and reflective interviewing are two of the most important skills of coaching.
- Leaders must remain responsible for their own learning.
- The leader's context is unique to the leadership practices being coached.
- The skills of goal setting and giving descriptive and evaluative feedback extend the coach's repertoire.
- Ability to describe practice effectively and to give and receive feedback on practice is important in terms of effecting long-term desired change in leadership practice and in the institution.
- Coaching leads effectively and naturally into action research processes, with the coach as critical friend.
- Groups of leaders engaged in coaching partnerships heighten the sharing of ideas and theories on education innovation, thus enhancing the likelihood of forming professional learning communities.
- Knowledge and understanding of the change process and how it is promoted by action research is essential for effective coaching.

Lattice-like divisions are a feature of many li. The butterfly wing shares the same economic principles of optimal form.

Chapter 9

Troubleshooting and monitoring the coaching relationship

Chapter overview

While coaching is generally a beneficial process for all participants, problems can occur. Today's market-driven education system constantly works, in various ways, against leaders' ability to undertake the type of collegial professional development, such as coaching, that will allow them to develop the critical leadership so vital to the effective operation of their institutions. This chapter outlines key factors that can inhibit the success of the coaching relationship. These include lack of time, the guilt leaders experience in devoting time to leadership development, their perception that coaching may denote a deficit in leadership practice (or that others will think so), the fallout from loss of coaches and confidence, and the importance and difficulty of changing established practices. As a counter-measure to these difficulties, the chapter also stresses that effective reflection on and action learning regarding the coaching process (super-vision) will help partners work through problems that do arise. The most important aspect is that the relationship remains strong. Leaders must feel that the coach is genuinely committed to their work and the leadership development.

Difficulties
Lack of time

In recent years, educational leaders have had to accommodate many new and time-consuming responsibilities into their everyday leadership practice. These responsibilities have come about as a result of government policy that educational institutions should be more self-managing. Leaders involved in the leadership coaching research studies mentioned over and over again the insufficient time they had to get everything done and felt that this lack was one of the main reasons preventing them from pursuing their own ongoing professional development. One leader emphatically commented in an interview: "[It's all about] *time*—to get together; time to think reflectively. *Unforeseeable interruptions.* The exigencies of the service throw up barriers to achieving all we want to in terms of getting together." Another leader focused on the irony of time constraints, saying that the time when he most needed his coach's support was the time when he was under the most pressure and so was either unable to access that support or, if he could, to utilise it effectively or enjoy it.

Comments from other leaders involved in the leadership coaching research studies revealed that they were often in reactive rather than proactive mode, responding to the demands on them, to use Barth's (1986) analogy, like doctors in a busy accident and emergency clinic. I certainly encountered many such demands during my observations of leaders in the research studies. The following are just some of the ones that forestalled planned shadow (observation) visits:

- external deadlines;
- an angry parent arriving unannounced;
- meeting with social welfare officials;
- being caught up with the police on a suspected physical abuse case;
- taking the caretaker to the hospital because he was experiencing a heart attack;
- taking a class due to a teacher's absence and no relief staff available;
- a planned student protest; and

- the newspaper phoning to get comment on future staffing losses.

In one institution, one issue was so dominant and so volatile that the leader concerned was dealing with crisis after crisis. This situation dominated efforts to think about other matters in his institution, and he found it very difficult to concentrate on setting any professional goals or to see any value in shadowing his partner. He told me the issue was so "over-riding" that he had not been able to do his normal work. These really are the times when a coach's presence and support is paramount, because this person can assist leaders critically think through the ethical dilemmas and challenges and then respond to them in a thoughtful, considered manner. Time is an interesting phenomenon: we all have access to the same amount, but it's how we choose to use it that differs. Encouraging leaders to look for opportunities where they already meet together and to use that time more effectively for coaching is a valuable starting point to finding the time. Coaching can actually save leaders the extra time they yearn for.

Guilt

Perceived lack of time frequently sees leaders thinking they're indispensable, a perception that contributes to them feeling guilty about taking time out for their own professional development. They fear they might be letting others in their institution down while they're away or that something "bad" will occur. One of the leaders in my doctoral research study actually stated that his staff and community considered that he was away too often. He, in turn, lamented that "something always seems to happen when I'm away." For some leaders in my research, feeling guilty also related to their belief that now they'd attained a leadership position, they shouldn't require further professional training and development.

The extent to which leaders felt guilty depended on their individual personalities and circumstances. One rural principal, for example, acknowledged his feelings of guilt, but commented: "It's getting easier to leave school. I'm learning to trust my staff and realise that the place won't fall down without me." Remembering the importance of modelling the need for ongoing, lifelong learning to colleagues can also help leaders alleviate any feelings of guilt.

"This is my release day. Perhaps I should be at school working on my administration?"

The notion of deficit

The feeling of guilt aligned with the belief that leaders should not need further professional development ties in closely with the view of two leaders in one of my research studies. They considered that taking part in coaching indicated some sort of deficit or deficiency on the part of the leaders participating in this process. One of these two told me that some of the people obviously got a good deal out of coaching because of what she termed "overt personal problems". She initially felt that the openness with which these leaders talked about the issues and dilemmas facing them in their institutions was a sign of deficit, but then she later realised that it was because this group was more open and honest about their leadership concerns than were other groups of which she was a part. She stated that many principals maintained a bluff exterior and that the leaders behind the bluff exteriors were often ineffective ones. She also reflected on the lack of hierarchy in the group and how everyone listened to and learned from everyone else. She observed that it was the younger, less experienced leaders who often had the best ideas.

The other leader who held the deficit viewpoint was her coach, and he admitted that he'd discussed the coaching with his board. He told me laughingly that they'd thought it was a bit of a joke. "One of the board members," he said, "laughed and asked, 'Is [partner] developing you or are you developing [partner]?'" This type of attitude from a governing body is, of course, hardly conducive to setting the right culture for lifelong learning, and it is interesting that this leader also took the longest period of time of anyone in the group of leaders to begin to reflect on his own practice. However, he later said he valued the coaching sessions with his partner from a neighbouring school. He commented, too, on the importance of maintaining that professional sharing and collegiality within the climate of competition across schools. It is very important in this regard as to *how* coaching is introduced into a school community. If it's perceived as a method for addressing inadequacies rather than part of the ideal of professionalism and continual improvement, colleagues will probably be wary of its benefits.

Loss of partner

Given that effective coaching relationships take time to develop, the loss of a coach can be a real setback for a leader. Stress-related leave and retirement are just two of the reasons why one person may leave the relationship. Faced with the imminent retirement of his coach, the leader concerned found it difficult to maintain allegiance to the partnership and to discuss his long-term goals with the coach. This inability inevitably undermined the pair's coaching relationship during their final sessions. In one of the stress-related instances, the prolonged absences of the partner made it difficult for both partners to establish a bonding relationship. A leader who took early retirement because of stress-related illness did not share his concerns with his coach, even though they'd been working together for nearly one year. The day the leader decided that he couldn't face going on with his job was the same day he'd been to his coach's institution to carry out a shadow visit. What is important to remember in this type of context is that because every new coach has something different to bring to the learning relationship, losing a coach should be seen as an opportunity to develop a new coaching relationship that offers further learning opportunities.

Loss of confidence

In order to break established habits and confront their own leadership, leaders have to move out of the comfort zone of taking their everyday practices for granted, but doing this does have risks; loss of confidence is one of them. "Navel-gazing", to use one leader's description of in-depth reflection on practice, can initially cause leaders to lose confidence in their ability to lead, especially when, as should be the case, they confront their own leadership style rather than simply work with their partner to problem solve day-to-day issues. Any loss in confidence needs to be carefully and sensitively worked through by the coaching partners. An outside facilitator working with the two coaching partners is generally a good addition to the professional development at this point. Working through any dip in confidence and competence is an important part of the change process, and a coaching relationship comes to its fore at such times.

Loss of confidence may have been one of the triggers that caused two principals to resign from principalship during one of my research studies.

Their interview transcripts portrayed a growing disillusionment with education in general and their own inability to adjust to the changes being thrust upon them in particular. One of the principals took early retirement and allowed me to interview him three months after he'd left his school. This is what he told me:

> I just found it was taking me longer and longer to do everything, and I wasn't doing it as efficiently as I was three years ago ... I felt like I was dabbling in this and dabbling in that, and felt like I just needed to shut my office door and sit down and write ... the whole thing blew up in my face after a morning in [partner's institution]. It was a good morning. [But] I just got back and looked at the piles of paper and said, "What the hell was I doing?"

When I asked him whether he felt there was any connection between the two events—visiting his partner's workplace and then coming back to his own and feeling that he could not continue—his answer concerned me, as it indicated a loss of confidence combined with a lack of fulfilment in his new role of self-management:

> Yes, I think that is very true. I'd had a good morning in [partner's institution]. He was interacting with students, and I went back and said, "I'm not doing enough of that." I got back and just saw two monstrous piles of paper, and then my board chairperson dropped in and wanted something straight away and I thought, "This is the last straw." That was it. It put me over the top.

This leader did say, however, that he felt coaching had helped him. He said there were times when he felt he couldn't afford the time but still made the commitment and was always pleased he had. "It was very worthwhile," he said, "to get away from that paper, so it depends where you put your priorities." Coaching—especially the opportunity it gave him to observe his colleague—had helped him to see himself with greater clarity. While he didn't like what he saw and became demoralised, coaching also appears to have given him the impetus to think more clearly about his situation, both personal and professional, and to make the decision to leave. Although such a decision may not be an intended outcome of coaching, it can often be, from personal, professional and/or institutional perspectives, the right one.

Established habits

The coaching model requires leaders to work in ways that are very different to the way they usually interact with one another, and it requires them to use skills that they're not in the habit of using with their professional colleagues. New ways of operating can be a challenge for leaders, and they can easily slip back into old habits of just conversing with their coach and not carrying out the processes of reflective interviewing and giving evaluative feedback. This is the point at which the deliberate presence of a facilitator can help "institutionalise" some of these new practices between the leaders. (For more on this facilitation process, see Chapter 10.) Coaches and partners can also monitor their interactions and remind one another to "put the coaching hat back on" after phases of conversation and discussion.

"His coaching skills have been really effective. I've appreciated the many times he listened, questioned and helped me gain clarity as I process aloud my thinking. I want to coach like he does."

Outside factors

The many other events going on in leaders' lives affect the amount of time they're able to commit to coaching. These factors are those that occur over and above the day-to-day happenings of leaders' institutions. They include family commitments, secondment to other positions, community conflicts, external reviews and external deadlines. Coaching comes into its own here because effective coaches can assist leaders prioritise time and work more effectively around the unanticipated or extra events that will inevitably occur in their personal and professional lives. Dealing with interruptions and the unexpected is the very essence of the work of leadership. Helping a leader see that this is so is one of the main benefits of coaching.

Lack of attendance

While group sessions can provide near ideal conditions for the development of coaching skills, coaching partnerships and learning communities, illness or pressure of work can make it difficult to convene and develop a community of learners. The development needs to continue—but with special compensatory visits paid to the absent leaders. They, too, will feel their absence has placed them at a disadvantage. Said one leader: "At the moment I feel very lost. Why? It's a pity I didn't attend the first meeting. Result: I feel like I'm now catching up—trying to catch up." Developing expertise in coaching should also be seen as a lifelong task—the more we coach, the richer our repertoire of coaching skills and tools is. We learn to coach by coaching and reflecting on our practice of coaching.

Counter-measures: The art of critically reflecting on the coaching relationship

For all the leaders in the research studies over the years, the successes of coaching have far outweighed the problems. However, these leaders were also cognisant of the difficulties inherent in developing and then maintaining an effective coaching partnership for the purposes of their own professional development. If partners are to sustain a coaching relationship long term, they need to continually monitor and evaluate their work together. In other words, leaders improve their leadership in coaching by coaching. The following activities aim to provide leaders and their coaches with ideas on how to talk about and reflect together on the coaching process itself. The coaching partners may also find it useful to have an outside facilitator involved in critique of this kind. And they are likely to find that their learning will be greater if they can move into the double-loop learning (Argyris, 1999) that occurs as a result of encouraging outside perspectives.

Activities to build the skill
Reflective activity 16
This activity requires you to look at the depth of your professional dialogue by reflecting on your answers to these questions:
- What topics do you talk about?
- What is difficult to talk about?
- What is easy to talk about?
- What don't you talk about?
- How honest can you be?

Reflective activity 17

Now take a look at your coaching practice, and then reflect on your answers to these questions:

- How would your colleagues describe you as a coach?
- What works best for you?
- What is least helpful?
- What is the most important coaching role?
- What new learning has there been for you?
- How have you changed?

Reflective activity 18

In regard to the coaching relationship:

- How do you feel the coaching is going?
- Is it professionally fulfilling?
- What problems have you experienced?
- Have you sought feedback from your partner?
- In what ways could you improve the relationship?
- Any other comments?

Reflect on your answers to these questions.

Reflective activity 19

Now think about and reflect on your answers to these questions:

- Do you carry out a "formal" reflective interview each time?
- Why? Why not?
- What causes the most reflection on practice?
- What is the most beneficial part of time spent together?
- How useful is the reflective interview?
- How would you describe your experience of the reflective interview?

Reflective activity 20

It's important that those of you in coaching roles keep a reflective journal to support your own development as a leadership coach. The journal can form part of your professional supervision. The guidelines in the first point below are adapted and developed from those that Zeus and Skiffington (2002, p. 87) outlined in their "coach's notebook".

1. Record the following in relation to each goal set and write reflection notes in relation to these items.

    Goal: What does the leader want to achieve?

    Time-frame: When does s/he want to achieve it by?

    Steps: What steps should be taken? How can I assist?

    Results: What happened? What progress is being made?

    Issues: What new learning has there been for me?

    Reflection: Where to from here? What links can I make to anything I've read? What else could I do to assist? What sort of feedback can I get from the leader about the coaching process?

2. Include in your journal:

    - ideas from readings;
    - exploration of concepts (e.g., praxis, reciprocity);
    - chronology of contacts/correspondence with leader/s;
    - reflections on your role as coach/facilitator;
    - reflections on your new learning;
    - quotes from or communication with leader/s (e.g., an email or a comment that seems significant);
    - evaluation of the coaching sessions;
    - skills development (e.g., ability to get closure in sessions; use of GROW model);
    - session ideas for working with partner;
    - anything else you think is relevant.

Summary of main points

- Many factors, whether personal or professional, internal or external to the institution, can adversely affect the development of an effective coaching relationship.
- Awareness of these factors is the first step in countering them effectively.
- Monitoring and reflecting on the coaching process is the second important step in overcoming difficulties and strengthening the coaching relationship.
- Coaching is a relationship. The process of developing that relationship must therefore be accorded prominence throughout the coaching process.

Although the material of which they are composed is being constantly reworked, these sand *li* themselves are relatively constant.

Chapter 10

Facilitating coaching

Chapter overview

Facilitating and coaching are almost synonymous in this coaching model, given that the coaching style the model promotes is facilitative rather than instructive. Coaching partners facilitate each other's leadership development, while a third person, engaged from outside the partnership specifically to take on the work of a facilitator, coaches the coaching process. The coach and the outside facilitator take a somewhat different focus when acting as facilitators, but to be effective both must be able to facilitate learning and to assume various roles to varying degrees. This chapter describes and discusses these roles primarily from the perspective of the outside facilitator.

Facilitative roles within the context of coaching

Although peer coaching will develop effectively between two colleagues who are committed to a reciprocal coaching process, or between an external coach (e.g., a retired principal, an adviser, a consultant) and an educational leader, coaching is a process that benefits from outside facilitation. The benefit of facilitation is particularly in evidence when

> *"You [the facilitator] have had to work to get to the level the group is at now. People trust you and reveal, in the small group, small personal items related to their leadership. We trust each other."*

the coaching is between groups of leaders in social networks, such as in one department or one community of learning, or when it involves establishing a coaching relationship between a business partner and educational leader or between two different groups in networks. Because facilitating coaching is about coaching the coaching process rather than coaching leadership development, facilitators need not only to have experienced the process of coaching and to have their own coach (in order to be credible) but also to understand learning and leadership theory and to be conversant with the change process. Facilitators can come from within an institution or from outside.

People who facilitate the coaching process have the challenge of lifting the learning relationship between coaching partners to higher levels of critical thought and dialogue than is perhaps possible without this outside perspective and supervision. In the course of their work, these facilitators become involved not only in the coaching process per se but also in coaching partners' individual, partnered and group-based professional learning processes. They also, inevitably, take on many and varied roles, some of which the leaders I've worked with have colourfully termed "flea", "taskmaster", "the glue" and "devil's advocate". While the names given to the facilitator roles that follow are far more prosaic, they capture the essence of the facilitator's work and are the roles that Everard and Morris (1985) deemed important in their work on consultancy. These roles are "process facilitator", "dynamist/motivator", "exemplar/demonstrator", "pace-maker", "reminder", "learning facilitator", "coach/tutor", "consultant", "resource investigator", "co-ordinator/convenor", "catalyst/assumption challenger", "group dynamics advisor", "norm establisher", observer/note-taker/scribe" and "discussion leader/task facilitator". Two additional roles, namely "advocate" and "confidant", arising out of my own research and development work with leaders, are also pertinent here.

The different roles
Process facilitator

One of the facilitator's most important and obvious roles is that of facilitating the whole process of coaching, including the initial bringing together of the coaching partners, perhaps in learning communities. Because of the nature of their work, leaders are very unlikely to move into coaching relationships unless someone else encourages them to do so. As one leader said, "In a way, setting up … is a very difficult thing to control because of the demands of the job." It's also not their usual way of interaction.

Once the coaching relationship has been established, support is necessary to sustain it. Facilitators therefore need to keep leaders moving towards attainment of their professional goals and to help them become increasingly autonomous in the coaching process. Most leaders relatively quickly display ability to set directions and goals and work together towards these on their own, but they may still welcome the outside facilitator's "guidance—keeping us on track" and "following through" from time to time after he or she has facilitated the early sessions. Encouraging the coaching partners to stay with the process can be as simple as the facilitator asking such questions as "Tell me again, what is your goal?" "What are you going to do next?" "How will your coach assist in this process?"

Dynamist/motivator

The facilitator's own enthusiasm for coaching can be a source of dynamism, of revitalisation and refreshment, especially for educational leaders in mid-career, which is why it's important for facilitators to have their own coaching relationship as well for their own supervision of practice. Dynamism stimulates and stimulation motivates leaders to maintain their coaching relationships and work through the coaching process. Motivation of this kind can

"I've thought of you as the glue in the whole business of giving direction, encouragement, knowledge and structure to the types of contacts that we have had between each other … The most effective thing is you— that glue—because without it I don't really think it could exist. I don't think it would be as effective if you removed yourself from the situation."

also come from other leaders (whether part of cluster groups, learning communities or institutional departments) involved in the same coaching processes sharing their coaching experiences and the impact on their practice.

For leaders, stimulation often stems from the fact that somebody else is taking a keen interest in their practice. In other words, interest acts as a motivator. The interest that coaching partners show in each other and their leadership practice also acts in this way, but interest is given added impact as a motivator when it comes from an outside facilitator. While the person who ultimately takes the ongoing interest in a leader's leadership practice is that leader's coach, the interest of the outside facilitator provides the necessary impetus for leaders to carry through with their goal-setting and action plans. The impetus might take the form of providing the partners with ideas and with affirmation for things going well, or challenging them, by sharing research, professional readings and one's own experiences of being coached, questions that assist the partners to think more deeply about their leadership and the process of coaching: "What is the most fulfilling part of your coaching so far?" "What has been the biggest learning for you in your coaching leadership this year?"

> *"It's easy to just relax and forget what we should be doing next, instead of keeping just a little bit more formal. Not formal, but just thinking things through a little bit more."*

Exemplar/demonstrator

The principles of coaching serve to bind all participants in the learning community to the same processes. With facilitating, this consideration translates into "Do as I do," not just "Do as I say." Here, facilitators must model the role of a coach. They must also, as part of this activity, discuss the benefits and issues they themselves face or have faced when working through coaching processes with their own coaching partners. They might choose, for example, to share practical ideas of what works in their own coaching process, or to model how they worked through an issue of concern. Facilitators of coaching, and indeed coaches as well, should always make the principles and practices of coaching overt while they're coaching. For example: "Now I am going to move into some more formal goalsetting, using a tool called the GROW model." Facilitators who describe and discuss with others how they and their partner coach each other offer valuable practical examples of how coaching operates. Educational leaders who have established and are carrying out the coaching process for their own professional development have validity. As a consequence, their expressed and modelled belief that coaching promotes educational leaders' professional development is seen to be sincere.

Pacemaker

Facilitators and coaches take on the role of pacemaker when they help keep leaders to a time-frame for prioritising actions, set the next steps of action plans, check that skills have been practised and tasks carried out, set dates for future coaching sessions and meetings and suggest a next step or something else the coaching partners could try before the next full session. One of the leaders with whom I worked as a facilitator told me that she saw my pacemaking role as providing a support and serving as a conscience and a guide throughout the coaching process. She said: "You're obviously the facilitator. We definitely look to you for support. To some extent you're a compelling force because I know that you're going to be there, and therefore I feel, 'I must do that 'cause I'll be seeing Jan,' and I don't want to go and say that I haven't done it."

When helping set the pace of the coaching, facilitators need to nudge leaders along by, as one leader put it, "making polite suggestions" as to what they ought to be doing, "with the hope that we will take up the suggestions". She also signalled another aspect of the pacemaker role when she commented to her facilitator: "You bend over backwards to get us to do something, to change."

Reminder

At times, coaching partners slip back into previous modes of operating. For example, they may resort to discussing rather than challenging with reflective questions, use few, if any, of the coaching skills they've been taught, and neglect to reflect critically. This is where facilitators serve as reminders, by helping coaching partners refocus on the skills they need to use or ways they can work together to enhance the likelihood of achieving their professional goals and deep learning conversations. Here, a facilitator might ask the partners if they've carried out the reflective interview they planned to do, or remind them of the guiding principles of giving evaluative feedback.

Often, coaching partners' familiarity with each other works against their ability to move into the more formalized modes of interaction that coaching requires, as this leader's comments show:

We're together the whole time. You think about the time that you stopped and talked to me, and then you left me by myself, and I could stop and think about it and plan my next action, as opposed to us just talking and me responding to the moment, not stopping and thinking about it. I think that is why it wasn't happening for me, and because we talk together like that all the time, you forget the obvious things.

Reminding leaders about "the obvious things" is the essence of the reminder role, as is drawing leaders' attention to whatever they had agreed to attend to before or during their next meeting.

Learning facilitator

One of the facilitator's most important influences on the developing coaching process is that of teaching leaders about leadership learning and clarifying for them how the process contributes to it. This role presents a focus on the "why" of coaching leadership. For most leaders, working with a professional colleague within the type of coaching relationship employed in this book's model is a new experience. The facilitator consequently needs to introduce them to the principles of coaching leadership and the skills they need to carry out the process effectively. Learning these skills and then enacting them is what makes coaching such an effective means of bringing about changes in professional practice.

"In skilling us in terms of how to conduct a reflective interview, those types of things— the imparting of those abilities and skills— I think has been really, really terrific."

For those leaders who move more easily into the mode of working with a partner to set and implement professional goals and then monitor and evaluate their progress against them, the facilitator's teaching role increasingly becomes one of highlighting new and different opportunities for enhanced leadership learning to take place. At times, though, facilitators can find it difficult to know when (and when not) to intervene in this way, but skilled facilitators can usually judge when to introduce a "learning moment" and when to leave the partners to learn from their concrete experiences. Knowing the right questions to ask—and when—is also a valuable tool in the facilitator's "learning" kit.

Here is an example of how one facilitator provided coaching partners with learning opportunities. In this instance, the partners had met for a reflective interview, but instead of employing the appropriate skills, they got sidetracked in general conversation. At this point, the facilitator intervened, again rehearsed with them the skills of reflective interview, and encouraged them to proceed accordingly. Afterwards, the facilitator held a discussion about the intervention with the leaders, checking with them why they'd not utilised the reflective interviewing technique, and asking how they felt about the intervention at this point.

Coach/tutor

The role of learning facilitator inevitably encompasses the role of coaching and tutoring the skills leaders need to coach one another successfully. Facilitators take the role of coach whenever they observe leaders and assist them during that time to practise taught skills. Examples here are demonstrating how to conduct a reflective interview on a particular issue and asking leaders who have completed a reflective interview to identify the Level 3 questions (see Chapter 7) that they asked their partner.

When teaching leaders skills and then coaching them as they practise those skills, facilitators may choose to work with the leaders individually, in pairs or in groups. Leaders often need individual tuition on aspects of coaching that have not quite gelled with them or when they've missed a coaching session. At such times, the facilitator as coach is akin to a personal trainer—someone who is able to identify and target a leader's specific professional development needs.

Consultant

Educational leaders seldom have the benefit of people who are knowledgeable in both the theory and practice of education and who have the time to sit and talk with them about the larger issues in education and educational institutions. Coaches bring to the relationship a wide range of strengths and expertise. Although this model is built on the notion of "coach as learner" rather than "coach as expert", this does not mean that coaches cannot share their expertise at appropriate times, in respectful ways.

When facilitators engage with leaders in this way, they're acting in a consultative role. They bring to discussions knowledge of theory that complements leaders' practical leadership knowledge. The close association that forms between facilitators and the coaching partners with whom they work allows facilitators to gain a clear and detailed picture of each leader's professional needs and the way in which that person works towards goals. This understanding, in turn, allows facilitators to tailor their consultation to the leader's needs and chosen areas of focus. The assistance might involve professional dialogue about the day-to-day issues of leadership and relationships with staff, introducing some new perspectives about the next steps in the leader's action plan, sharing knowledge of research literature relevant to an issue at hand, or providing advice on how to run professional learning for staff. Essentially, the role of consultant is one of helping leaders help themselves, and it can be employed at individual, group and institutional level.

"I asked them to look specifically to outcomes for each of their schools for that year. One leader's reaction was to laugh (he didn't have any!). The other said, 'I had one in the back of my mind.' It made me realise the importance of leaders sitting and doing this exercise and then asking them, 'Do your staff know these outcomes?'"

Resource investigator

Because facilitators generally have a broad-sweep knowledge of education and educational issues, and because their work sees them range widely across the educational community, they have a good knowledge of the particular resources that leaders may find useful as they work towards achieving their goals. Resources can range from research articles and websites on a particular educational matter to advice and commentary from other leaders within a coaching community who have grappled with and found solutions to certain problems. Sometimes within the context of a coaching community of learning, a facilitator may suggest that a leader with knowledge or experience of an issue acts as a consultant to another leader or coaching partnership.

Providing knowledge from professional sources is a way of linking theory to practice and practice to theory. The role of resource investigator offers an effective way to affirm and/or challenge leaders' practices. During one research study, one leader with whom I was working as a facilitator said another leader had asked him to evaluate the culture of his (the other leader's) institution. While I was discussing with him a framework he could use for the evaluation, I was reminded of an article called "Good Seeds Grow in Strong Cultures" (Saphier & King, 1986), and I promised to send him a copy of some material in it. "It's got some really good norms for culture building in it," I told him. "I think it's relevant for you, because, if you look at the seeds here, you can see that your colleague asked you to do the evaluation because of your strength in this area."

"Your main role: putting new ideas to people and other people in front of us, to make us think through what we are doing and why we're doing it. Coaching has heightened my professional reading. All the snippets that you send out, I certainly look at."

Co-ordinator/convenor

Leaders don't have sufficient time to establish and organise professional development sessions for themselves. The work of setting dates for future meetings, circulating meeting agendas to leaders to add to and reflect upon, and organising speakers and consultants in relation to specific professional development matters is essential in establishing and maintaining coaching partnerships and fits readily within the facilitator's scope. Facilitators' knowledge of appropriate resources and appreciation of the limited time that leaders have available for professional development means they are well suited to setting up sessions that will bring maximum benefit to the participants. However, facilitators should not be complacent about what they provide. At the end of each session they convene, they should ask participants to comment on what they found valuable/not valuable so that they can continually improve their own practice as facilitators.

Catalyst/assumption challenger

In creating the conditions that are conducive to change, facilitators assume the role of catalyst. The observations and the reflective interviews of coaching are the most obvious opportunities to instigate change in leaders' practices. Facilitators can also use group sessions to create the necessary conditions for transformative change. The actual agenda of a group session can be organised around whatever the facilitator thinks is necessary to advance the coaching process and/or the leadership of the group.

Facilitators may take on the role of consultant during these sessions or bring in someone else in this role. Sessions will not work unless the activities used within them (e.g., role plays) are appropriate to the needs of the participants and the identified focus for the session (e.g., practising skills, developing community, setting professional goals, developing action plans). Nor will they work if the participants fail to work together as a "team" to identify and articulate their values and to utilise the strength of these values in pursuing their professional goals and bringing about changes in themselves and thus their leadership practice.

"I think there is somebody that has to have an overview, coming in with other ideas, because you see many more leaders than the partners do; because they only see one, but you see the lot."

The most successful sessions are those that challenge leaders to confront their leadership practice and the beliefs, assumptions and values underpinning it (their educational platform). Facilitators can act as challengers because they bring in the perspective of an outsider. The leader-as-colleague/coach is often too close to a particular situation or issue to provide the objectivity required to challenge certain "ways of knowing". One activity that brings in challenge is that of role-playing a contentious issue and then critiquing what went on and what was said during the role play. Another is conducting a session relating to various aspects of the political, cultural and social contexts of education and then having leaders critically evaluate the impact of these aspects on their leadership. Getting leaders to observe coaching leadership practice and then identify what they noted and its relation to their own practice can bring greater self-understanding.

Group dynamics advisor

During group sessions, the dynamics of the group need to be conducive to the developing coaching relationships. Leaders are most likely to work well together when the session takes place in a venue that is warm, quiet and comfortable and away from the distractions of their daily practice. There should be no phone calls or other interruptions. Music can be a part of these sessions, and food should always be provided. The one thing that the leaders who participated in my earlier research studies mentioned more than any other was enjoying the opportunity at tea breaks and lunch at conferences and workshops to talk to their colleagues. Leadership coaching is about capturing that energy and dialogue, and building on it.

Another aspect of developing group dynamics is affirmation that educational leaders are important people and that their commitment to the coaching model is valued. These points need to be made explicitly, but never patronisingly, to the group. Group dynamics are further enhanced when facilitators remind participants of how group dynamics operate. As such, the first in a series of sessions or the early part of a one-off session should contain activities that will help participants understand how they can use the dynamics of the group to collectively advance their aims. If time is limited, facilitators can simply emphasise the importance of everyone having an opportunity and the responsibility to participate. They can also highlight that groups are less effective when they try to achieve consensus about rather than a true understanding of an issue.

Norms establisher

The way the group operates, the success of a coaching partnership, and the relationship between facilitators and leaders will all be more effective when norms or expectations for behaviour and conduct are established early on. The most important ones are trust and confidentiality. For example, leaders will share much more of a personal nature with their facilitator on an individual basis if they know that the facilitator will never

"I enjoyed or benefited from [consultant's] session because he gave us a strategy that we are reluctant to use in a 'conflict' situation. Perhaps we need to be told that some strategies are OK."

> *"You never reveal anything about us back to the group. You don't just assume that would be OK."*

reveal what is said to the full group or to others with whom they work. Norms of openness, honesty and support should also be established.

These norms are basically those that come under the heading of "Professional ethics", and the group should discuss and commit to them before getting underway with the work at hand. The group may also choose to draw up principles that will expedite their work as a group, such as being open to ideas and building on them, and being willing to learn. Another important norm is that of the purpose of coaching—professional leadership development. All sessions should focus on this norm, and the facilitator may at first need to keep explicitly reminding leaders of it because it is one that is rarely evident in the other groups leaders meet in.

Observer/note-taker/scribe

Observing and note-taking are primary tasks for the facilitator. This work may involve noting down things that the leaders have decided to do or perhaps observing how the leaders are working in their coaching relationships. Importantly, it may also involve writing down, in the form of short case studies or case records of goals and/or issues, how leaders develop the theory of their own leadership within their work.

> *"I'm most impressed with all this. You write it down, and I read it back, and it sounds different, but that is exactly what happened. The key word is 'emancipated'. 'Counter-hegemonic'—I like that! I am never sure how to say that word, but that is exactly what it was!"*

Another consideration here is that leaders are often reticent about or too busy moving on to their next action to write anything down. The notes that a facilitator makes are only useful if they're given or sent as soon as possible after the observation to the leaders for their feedback and comment. Leaders find this outside perspective particularly useful in helping them reflect more critically about the processes in which they're involved. It lets them see their actions from another angle, and it gives them an opportunity to think about what they do in relation to theory and then to see how their practice influences and becomes theory.

Discussion leader/task facilitator

During group sessions in particular, facilitators often take the role of discussion leader and task facilitator by setting topics for discussion and then "chairing" that discussion. Facilitators generally choose topics by listening to leaders talking about what is important to them. Performance contracts and related objectives (or personnel, in general) are always a timely topic. Another is the dilemmas leaders face over review and monitoring of quality teaching and learning in their institutions. In regard to the second topic, leaders could work through the task of analysing the issues related to reviews, all the while looking for leadership actions and strategies that would best suit their individual circumstances. But whatever the topic is, it's important to ensure the discussion has a critical perspective and takes account of the current educational context. Good facilitators will chair the discussion in a way that allows everyone present to bring their knowledge to the situation and to hear the different views within the group.

Confidant

It's interesting that Everard and Morris (1985) did not identify the role of confidant, given that it can be one of the most important facilitation roles. This role is integral to facilitating the change process. Change begins at the personal level, and unless the facilitator comes to know the coaching partners as individual people, then it's unlikely that the intimacy and reciprocity required for openness, development and a more in-depth account of what is actually happening in the coaching partnership will occur. Leaders generally also require the active listening of a confidant to move into dialogue and problem posing. Facilitators who, during the first 10 minutes or so of the coaching session, actively listen as the leaders talk about the issues and dilemmas they're currently facing are likely to establish a very useful rapport very quickly.

"Coaching also engendered some self-doubt for me, and the facilitator's role as a confidant and conduit in providing relevant readings helped allay some of those doubts."

Advocate

A graduate student recently pointed out to me another important role for the facilitator (and the coach too for that matter)—that of advocate. The inside knowledge facilitators and coaches have of individual leaders' practice places them in a prime position to speak up for these leaders at interviews and performance appraisals and during conflict situations. Coaches in particular can also act as mentor and sponsor in highlighting career opportunities for their partner and assisting them to meet career goals. Good coaches advocate for their partners where possible, perhaps by bringing a job advertisement ("This is written for you!"), or speaking out in support of them in a professional situation.

Summary of main points
- The facilitation of coaching involves many important roles.
- The coach can also play each of these facilitation roles for the educational leader.
- Outside facilitation is often necessary to initiate the process of coaching between two leaders or groups of leaders.
- Outside facilitation can also enhance the professional coaching relationship.
- Groups of coaching partnerships in learning communities can be developed together with the aid of a good facilitator.
- Effective facilitation requires critical reflection on the continuing process of facilitation and coaching.

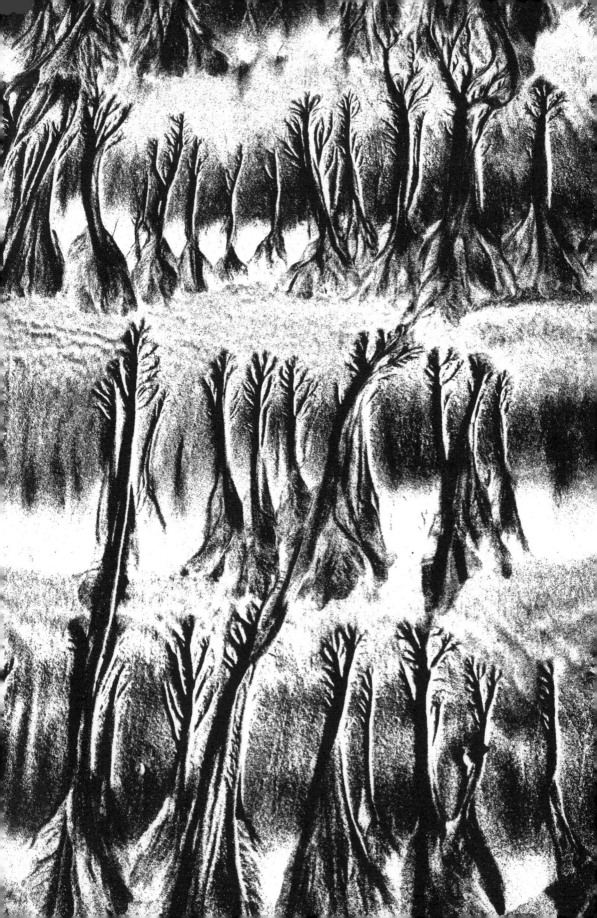

Sand *li* exist in infinite variety, and perfectly demonstrate the principle that simple causes can produce irreducibly complex effects.

Chapter 11

Leaders coaching leaders

Chapter overview

Once leaders have experienced coaching themselves, they move easily into developing coaching practices with their colleagues. For these leaders, coaching has moved to a new level, that of facilitator—of coaching others to use coaching skills. (For a full account of facilitating coaching, see the previous chapter.) This development promotes the building of effective leadership capacity throughout institutions or systems of education.

The case studies presented in this chapter tell the stories of using coaching leadership principles and practices to effect transformative change. The first case study (Case Study 1) presents the story of a foundation principal of a new school group engaged in coaching for transformative change in teachers' practice, especially practice aligned with team-teaching in 21st-century contexts. Case Study 2 shows how the paradigm of coaching leadership can underpin a system-wide development for aspiring principals. Here, the leadership coaching was directed towards ascertaining and then enacting leaders' moral purpose with respect to addressing educational injustice.

Case Study 3, from Australia, provides an example of how another system of education is moving schools towards performance-based, growth-learning cultures by building leadership for learning through coaching leadership. Case Study 4 presents a study of a principal who has been using and developing the practices and principles of coaching leadership for over a decade in his leadership. He has been intent, within the context of the learning culture of his current school (a recently established school), on intertwining inquiry-based professional learning with coaching skills in order to improve students' numeracy and literacy outcomes.

Taken together, the studies highlight that experience of coaching gives leaders confidence not only in their own practice but also in working with others to help them develop their skills of coaching and their own skills of facilitation and facilitative leadership practice. More importantly, facilitating coaching allows leaders to reflect on the change process and enhances their ability to use an action research process to guide their coaching intervention. The leaders tell their own stories here, and I follow each narration with a brief commentary.

Case Study 1: Coaching for transformation— the context and the challenge

Lesley Murrihy, foundation principal of a new school, reflects on the value of coaching and mentoring as tools for transformative pedagogy within 21st-century contexts.

Ten years ago when the first edition of *Coaching Leadership* was published, I was beginning my doctoral research (Murrihy, 2009), which explored whether the paradigm of coaching that Jan Robertson had developed assists the growth and development of educators in the multiple dimensions of spiritual, emotional, social and conceptual/intellectual. This project followed three participants through a nine-month Master's-level coaching and mentoring paper, with Jan and I revisiting them a year later in their schools. In brief, I concluded that coaching did lead to growth and development in the multiple dimensions. The findings also showed that, as a result of the integrated growth and development (across the dimensions), participants felt more empowered and agentic (more like leaders), enabled to make increasingly wise decisions. At the same time I was, as a first-time principal, using coaching leadership principles and practices in my rural school to support change in teachers' practice. Coaching was at the core of our professional development, not only in our school but also in our cluster of schools, and we were employing it in regard to a number of imperatives, including exploration of what it means to be culturally responsive in our practice.

Nine years later, I found myself considering anew these findings and the value of coaching and mentoring when I became foundation principal of Amesbury School. I was well aware that the expectation on the schools of today is for every child to be fully engaged in personalised learning programmes that take account of their needs, interests and desires, and that all students leave school with the skills and capacities to thrive in the increasingly complex and uncertain world they face. According to Wylie (2012, p. 3), "What we need from our public education system now, and for the even more challenging times ahead, is therefore even more demanding than it [ever] was."

The challenges we face are considerable. We work in an (apparently) confusing and conflicted policy environment—on the one hand government is pushing the 21st-century agenda of empowering student voice, choice and self-direction through the development of key competencies and future-focused learning; on the other it wants education—to use Biesta's (2014) words—that is "strong, secure, and predictable, and want[s] it risk free at all levels" (p. 1). As Biesta argues, education is not education if there is no risk. We accordingly need both approaches, that is, "strong" and "weak" education. Biesta proposes a theory of education in which education has three functions: qualification, which is the domain of knowledge, skills and dispositions; socialisation, which includes learning to become part of the existing social orders; and subjectification, which identifies the individual person as the subject, not the object, of education. I believe the overall challenge we face today is not that of swapping one educational paradigm for another but of bringing together what is relevant and good from all possible approaches into a complex whole system—a system which benefits *every* child.

Being clear about the purpose of education then looms large as we engage with determining what is "relevant and good". And if *every* child *is* entitled to an education characterised by high equity and high quality as Timperley, Kaser, and Halbert (2014) argue, then we must become urgent in our pursuit of it. While we take our time, some students languish. However, the pathway that leads us to realisation of this goal is not an easy one, as we have discovered. *"Every* child" requires *"every* teacher" to be highly effective and deeply reflective. Those attributes require increased intellectual capacity because the cognitive load of personalisation of learning is much greater. Collaborative practice and increased student agency require teachers to relinquish control and to find their joy in teaching in new ways. In short, our experience suggests that this transformation can strike at the very core of many teachers' understandings of what it means to be a teacher.

It was into this challenging educational landscape that Amesbury opened as a new school in 2012, with a great deal of expectation on us that we would be pioneers in this work. We were driven by a desire not to be side-tracked by the "bells and whistles" of a new school or technology or modern learning environment, but to steadfastly remain focused on high-equity, high-quality teaching for every one of our students. Our vision and educational purpose *is* for every child to experience what it means to be fully human and continually fulfil his or her potential. This is a noble endeavour and necessary, but we quickly realised that it was easy to say and that actually doing it was very, very difficult.

This was the point at which I questioned whether coaching and mentoring stacked up as transformative tools for the 21st-century challenge of assisting the shifts in teachers' conceptual thinking and instructional practices necessary for deep personalisation of learning and deep humanisation of education. I wondered how coaching and mentoring practices needed to evolve to "have more teeth" in a context where change is a moral imperative and therefore urgent. To dilly-dally would be to let some students down. However, Biesta's (2014) point kept ringing in my ears: it is not education if there is no risk. That is, change cannot be mandated; individuals have to choose it ... or not (hence the risk).

This conundrum is an interesting one for any school leader, including myself, who is strongly driven by a vision of every child continually fulfilling his or her potential and who knows that there are beliefs, practices and teacher capacities and capabilities that are essential to calling this vision into being but that are not yet fully part of the current teacher toolkit and identity. If change is an imperative and people have the right to choose to change or not, then what "teeth" does a leader have to enact the vision for learning that is meant to guide the development of a school?

Jan will tell you that questions like this have always consumed me, so as the school leader I couldn't wait until I'd resolved this moral dilemma and could take action. My colleagues and I wondered whether what we required was an intensive programme of professional development in which highly effective teachers would take the role of expert teachers. Their practices would exemplify the multifaceted roles of the coach: modelling, observing, reflecting, planning, monitoring, teaching, advising, questioning, appraising, assisting and exploring the practices that lead to deep personalisation of learning for every student. These expert teacher coaches would "walk" closely alongside small teams of teachers as they carried out their work from planning through to teaching and on to assessing and reporting; exploring with them and modelling for them the practices of highly effective teachers in the 21st-century future-focused context.

These coaches would help teachers to identify and challenge the thinking underpinning their practice within the context of these supportive coaching relationships. Coaches would then work with the teachers to make any identified and agreed-upon changes. We decided that this could be a useful way forward. So we identified the expert teachers in our school—those with a proven ability to shift achievement significantly and consistently, who were using practices that align with current best knowledge of future-focused learning and whose own practice was continually evolving to meet the needs of 21st-century learners.

> *"If change is an imperative and people have the right to choose to change or not, then what 'teeth' does a leader have to enact the vision for learning that is meant to guide the development of a school?"*

Each coach began working with a small group of team-teaching teachers as they together began implementing teaching and learning practices in an integrated literacy and inquiry programme designed to meet the needs of their 21st-century learners. All teachers were released for the same whole day each week, and each team met with their coach to explore effective practice while planning the learning programmes for their respective team of students. This approach was accompanied by one-on-one coaching sessions with teachers, followed by discussions after the observations as well as personalised professional development (aspects of pedagogical and curriculum content knowledge, for example). Also factored in were time—and space—for teachers to carry out the preparation and practices so necessary for deep personalisation of learning. The group of coaches, in turn, began meeting together regularly to share what they'd been doing with their teams, to share their notable experiences, to distil learnings and thereby develop their collective understanding of effective 21st-century practices, to plan the way forward and to identify what was assisting the growth and development of the teachers in their teams.

This "Highly Effective Teacher Programme" has been underway for one year now. Although it's early days, indications are that the programme is making a difference. Student achievement data show several significant changes, particularly for some previously "hard-to-shift" students. Teachers definitely feel that their practice is more evidence-based. They tell me they know more about their students and are making better decisions about learning programmes as a result.

The need for teachers to have time and space for new learning is as much an issue today as it has ever been. The propensity for the "urgent to drive out the important" is still a force we have to resist. In the demandingness of the school context, it is coaching that often becomes the victim of busyness: we do the "doing" but often don't get to the focus on "being". A strong need for coaching the coaches (supervision) has thus arisen not only to ensure that coaching conversations don't get lost in the busyness but also to help the expert teacher-coaches navigate ethically and wisely the different roles they carry out. However, the biggest realisation creating the greatest current challenge for us is discovering, all over again, what a risky business education is. Biesta (2014, p. 140) said:

> … without the risk, education itself disappears and social reproduction, insertion into existing orders of being, doing and thinking, takes over. While this may be desirable if our orientation is toward the reproduction of what already exists, it is not desirable if we are genuinely interested in education as a process that has an interest in the coming into the world of free subjects, not in the production of docile objects.

To conclude this brief snapshot, it seems that my initial question was unnecessary and came from my own feelings of impotence in the growing disconnect between what I want to see for children and the education we are providing. But then I came to realise that I could unpack, reflect on and become agentic through coaching. I also came to understand that coaching has always had teeth: its bite, paradoxically, is in its seeming weakness, its riskiness. But transformation cannot be mandated or forced; it must be taken up. In fact, it is not transformation or education if it's not chosen freely by the person, if it doesn't emancipate them. Paradoxically, it seems the more urgent the change, the more we need to remove the barriers to transformation, and the biggest barrier is often our own desire as leaders to control the situation and determine the outcomes. We can—and we must—assist teachers to know what is already known about effective teaching and learning through such strategies as the expert teacher coaching role. We need to help teachers gain knowledge of the inquiry process so that they have at their fingertips the skills to keep inquiring into their own practice and to keep developing future practices.

However, it's unlikely all this will be transformative without coaching. We, as leaders, therefore need to step back and, from a place of curiosity and a lack of self-interest, ask the deep, enduring and potentially transformative coaching questions of teachers so that they, from a place of self-awareness, can knowingly determine their destination. And maybe … just maybe … their destination will be better and more fruitful than any destination we would have hoped for. The power of coaching is in leaving transformation in the hands of the other. That is, to again use Biesta's words, the "beautiful risk of education" and the paradox of transformation. That is education.

"Student achievement data show several significant changes, particularly for some previously 'hard-to-shift' students. Teachers definitely feel that their practice is more evidence-based."

Commentary

I remember hearing Lesley speak at a conference recently about the "high-stakes leadership" she was experiencing. She promised parents that "all students will leave school with the skills and capacities to thrive". Importantly, she is working to give effect to the promise because of her accompanying moral purpose to step up into that leadership space with efficacy and agency. Many schools have such mission statements, but not always the capacity or commitment of leadership to fulfil the promise. Similarly, many countries have invested in forward-thinking policy documents that call for equity and quality of education, but few have put the same investment into developing the leadership capacity to ensure these policies are implemented successfully (Pont, 2015). Lesley states her commitment to that quest overtly.

However, leading transformative change in teachers' (and other leaders') practice is challenging because it asks educators to examine the very core of what it means to be a teacher, that is, their identity *as teacher*. Teachers often have no experience of the innovations in their teaching repertoire. For this reason, modelling of practice and observing others through the shadowing process (Chapter 8) is vital in terms of presenting opportunities for vicarious reflection on one's own practice. These processes also give teachers the strategies and skills—assuming they have the necessary support and challenge—to try out the new practices in their own teaching.

Lesley worries about how she can ensure that the coaching is "coaching with teeth". Her concern in this regard has implicit within it an important question—one that always needs to be asked. I frame it as "Coaching for what?" or "How intentional can we be, *should* we be, in terms of achieving those 'ends'"? Coaching always has teeth. Those of us involved in coaching relationships realise that the self-examination and self-work coaching entails is hugely challenging, and not just because it means opening up our practice to colleagues' critique. The challenge, of course, helps explain why some people are reluctant to be involved in leadership coaching. It also explains their lack of understanding of how powerful a tool coaching can be. Recently, I worked in a coaching capacity with a leader who had retired from his role as principal and was now coaching other leaders. He said to me: "I retired from principalship, and I got myself a coach for bridge and a coach for golf, but I never had a coach for the most important work I did in my career—the role of principal." There is no doubt that he'd come to see how powerful coaching leadership could be in changing his own practice and the practice of others he worked with.

Coaches themselves also need ongoing support. Supervisory-based support enables coaches to work through the difficulties and challenges they face in their coaching work. It helps coaches (in the same way their coaching work helps educators) to be deeply reflective about their coaching practice. Lesley highlights just how important this ongoing supervision is for renewal and maintenance of self-efficacy. I believe an ongoing peer coaching relationship would really support Lesley in her endeavour. She may argue that it will be difficult within the current competitive education environment to find another school principal who is not only committed to leading the open-plan collaborative learning environments that work to change teachers' paradigms of learning but also open to the partnered relationship that is coaching. I trust that difficulty will not be the outcome for her.

Case Study 2: Coaching moral purpose for equity and quality in New Zealand's National Aspiring Principals' Programme[1]

This case study focuses on a system-wide endeavour, of which I (Jan) was the academic director. The aim of this initiative was to develop new leaders with a strong sense of moral purpose for equity and educational justice and willing to act collaboratively and culturally responsively with their neighbouring schools to address issues of justice in their communities.

Deepening understandings of moral purpose

Most people who enter the teaching profession do so with the moral purpose of making a positive difference to people's lives through education. New Zealand's National Aspiring Principals' Programme (NAPP) takes the precept of moral purpose to a deeper level. It does this by engendering the shared values of equity and social justice through the values of culturally responsive leadership and pedagogy. The process is one that honours Te Tiriti o Waitangi (the Treaty of Waitangi) and thus New Zealand's dual cultural heritage.

Those of us involved with the year-long programme challenge these future principals to step up and, in accordance with their moral purpose,

---

1   This case study is adapted from an article published in the *Journal of Educational Leadership, Policy and Practice* and presented here with the journal's permission. The full citation is: Jan Robertson and Lorna Earl, (2014), Leadership learning: Aspiring principals developing the dispositions that count, *Journal of Educational Leadership, Policy and Practice, 29(2)*, 3–17.

actively address the under-achievement of particular groups of students (among them Māori) who are often poorly served by the current education system. In taking this step, leaders gain new understandings of just what moral purpose for equity means. With respect to Māori, leaders find that leading with moral purpose goes beyond just *doing for or on behalf of* Māori. Rather, it requires working *with* Maori and ensuring that the school is a positive place for success *for* Māori, *as Māori*, by inculcating and engaging in culturally responsive practices and pedagogies and having in place curriculum that honours New Zealand's dual cultural heritage.

> *"Leading with moral purpose ... requires working with Maori and ensuring that the school is a positive place for success for Māori, as Māori, by inculcating and engaging in culturally responsive practices and pedagogies and having in place curriculum that honours New Zealand's dual cultural heritage."*

For us (the programme team) the NAPP learning journey has been about evolving and transforming ourselves, particularly in terms of how we support leaders as they endeavour to learn leadership. When Te Toi Tupu (the Leading Learning Network) won the contract to deliver NAPP, I presented the team of kaiārahi (coaches) who would be facilitating the programme with a challenge to work in ways that would prepare the next generation of school principals (and the generations after them) to be "more than we had ever been able to be ourselves".

Being underpinned by a coaching paradigm

This aim has required us to exercise a more generative way of working so that the leadership capabilities of ākonga (the leaders who participate in our programme) can grow and extend. By generative, I mean two things. The first references the inquiry learning contexts that are the basis of the model we set for leading change and leading people. With their coaches, leaders generate inquiries into an aspect of their leadership of transformative change to address under-achievement in their schools. The second aspect of working generatively is that of coaching, conducted face to face, online and by Skype. Our kaiārahi use coaching as a conduit through which, right from the start of the coaching partnership, to powerfully question and challenge each ākonga to engage in deep learning conversations about the inquiry and what the findings from that inquiry mean for educational leadership and its impact on student learning. The important approach throughout for kaiārahi is that of the reciprocal learning within true dialogue. A "teach them all I know" stance has no place in this process, as it is the aspiring leaders' new learning about leadership that will influence *our* work, and the quality and equity within the New Zealand education system.

We tell new ākonga that NAPP is not about "doing a programme". It's about taking responsibility and developing the capabilities and mindset for self-directed learning *about* leadership and learning *in* leadership that they can take on into and right through their leadership career. In addition to having an experienced kaiārahi coach, every ākonga has a peer coach. All ākonga also participate in a regional learning community where group coaching takes place, as well as an online professional learning group where they are in constant reflective dialogue with their colleagues on the challenges of principalship. They are furthermore connected (via online learning groups) with their whole peer generation of aspiring leaders throughout New Zealand so that they can dialogue with one another and together develop deeper system-wide leadership. We want to develop *system* leaders who will work together to address the challenges of equity in New Zealand education—not just focus on their own schools as *school* leaders.

Our formative assessment within the programme tells us that these generative, personalised approaches to learning are successful. Every year, more than 90 percent of ākonga agree that working with a coach has developed their sense of self-efficacy (see Chapter 12), that they now know more about culturally responsive leadership, that they have a stronger understanding of their moral purpose, and that they are more focused on improving learning outcomes for Māori students.

Participating in reciprocal learning through coaching partnerships

Those of us in the project team approached the NAPP leadership learning journey as a means of evolving and transforming *ourselves* to new ways of thinking, doing and being. As a result, we found ourselves wanting to know how leaders *learn* some of the more complex concepts that we talk about in leadership—terms such as moral purpose, culturally responsive practice, efficacy and agency, and building capacity. We therefore decided to conduct an inquiry, a research study (Earl & Robertson, 2013), of our own.

We began by identifying the particular concepts we wanted to explore and used these to code and analyse the data collected from our ākonga at three different times in the year. Our aim here was to understand how these school leaders understood and enacted the various concepts under scrutiny. With respect to the concept of moral purpose, our analysis of the data showed that the leaders deepened their understanding of moral purpose and how to employ it in their practice across a four-phased continuum:

- focused awareness of the equity issues that define New Zealand education;
- self-awareness and examination of personal moral purpose;
- challenging, reinforcing or strengthening of beliefs and/or convictions; and
- acting with moral purpose.

Gaining awareness of the equity issues that define New Zealand education

The aspiring principals' reflections indicated that awareness of the pervasive inequity in New Zealand education is the starting point for developing moral purpose to address inequities. Within the New Zealand context of inequity, there has been specific government determination to develop schools that enable success for all students, especially those who are currently underserved. We found that as ākonga reflected on the complexity and importance of moral purpose, they emphasised the importance of *sharing* these reflections through discussion with colleagues. They agreed that this shared understanding is vital for moving the equity agenda forward in their schools and nationally. As one aspiring principal stated: "It's been critical to retain the moral commitment to students achieving academic success and to keep them to the fore. You cannot move the waka on your own but need everyone on board paddling in unison to get up speed and win the race."

Acquiring self-awareness and examining personal moral purpose

Knowledge of what inequity is and what inequity means for leaders typically prompts ākonga to examine their self-awareness of this issue and to critically examine their personal moral purpose with regard to it. For some ākonga, the idea of moral purpose as the driver of practice is a new and revolutionary one. It "made me stop in my tracks and think," said one. It "opened my eyes to becoming far more moral in my dealings with students and colleagues," said another. Some of the aspiring principals were relatively quickly able to connect their re-visioning of moral purpose to their self-identity as leaders:

- "This process and my entire inquiry have not really been about my [inquiry] project at all. It's been about my understanding of myself, my leadership and leading with moral purpose."
- "I've been able to reframe my leadership approach towards addressing under-achievement of these learners and to develop a stronger moral purpose in my leadership for change."

Challenging, reinforcing or strengthening beliefs and/or convictions

For most of the principals, though, getting to grips with their personal sense of moral purpose was neither straightforward nor easy. The process was one that troubled and challenged them, a situation that is, of course, integral to achieving the desired outcomes of inquiry-based coaching. These comments from participants were typical in this regard:

- "It has been quite a challenge to refocus my moral purpose in education."
- "I am still wrestling with moral purpose."
- "The process is 'helping' me develop and communicate a stronger moral purpose, but I personally have not yet fully developed that."

While challenging and reflecting on beliefs or convictions is an important part of the process of developing a moral purpose for equity, leaders who already have a strong sense of moral purpose can use the coaching facilitators of challenge and reflection to better appreciate and strengthen their existing beliefs and the manifestation of these in their practice. Our data showed that leaders who already had or who in time gained strong convictions about the importance and "rightness" of moral purpose were more willing and able to share their leadership thinking and skills with other leaders so that all of them could move forward. Phrases and comments such as "moral imperative", "holding moral purpose a little closer" and "reinforcing the importance of leading and communicating with strong moral purpose" show the intensity of such leaders' convictions.

Acting with moral purpose

For the leaders participating in our programme, moral purpose thus becomes not just a way of thinking but a way of acting, at times requiring courage and determination. It provides a foundation for educational leadership for equity and social justice. It is enacted every day, and that enactment is deeply connected to student needs and is modelled for everyone with whom the leader works and for whom he or she is responsible. In this way, moral purpose becomes a lived experience of leadership. A sense of urgency about what needs to be done and being intentional in doing it emerges: "I am more urgent in developing shared pedagogies within our school and ensuring we are all on the same page and that the children get the best deal possible. I am not prepared to compromise on high-quality teaching and learning."

Coaching more intentionally

Having completed our data analysis and reflections on it, we were in a position to ask ourselves this question: "Knowing what we know now about how ākonga learn about moral purpose, can we work more *intentionally* as coaches?" We took each of the four aspects of the moral-purpose learning continuum and developed coaching questions from our kaiārahi repertoire that would support ongoing exploration of these aspects. This work led to a question-based tool, depicted in Figure 11.1, that we use when working in coaching partnerships with leaders, to explore and strengthen moral purpose in educational leadership in general and moral purpose with respect to Māori students in particular.

"Knowing what we know now about how ākonga learn about moral purpose, can we work more intentionally as coaches?"

For us, as kaiārahi, the biggest challenge now

Figure 11.1: Questions to elicit reflective thinking about moral purpose

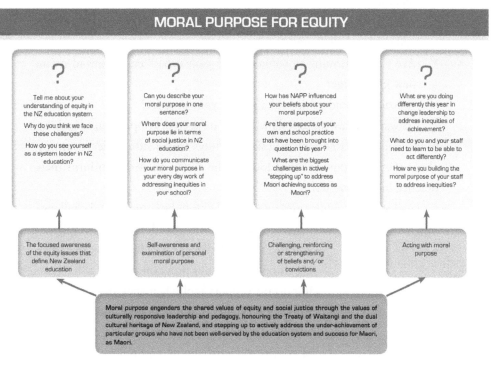

©Jan Robertson (2014)

is to ensure ākonga continue to carry their deeper sense of moral purpose into their leadership positions and practice long term. Our next piece of research will be to interview the leaders who have since become principals in their schools. Our aim in this regard is to assure ourselves that they are taking or have been able to take back to these settings what they've learned with us and that they've not been socialised into traditional ways of working. We want to know if they *are* acting as system leaders. Among the questions we'll be asking them are these ones:

- Do you talk about *your* moral purpose for equity and quality in your school?
- Do you talk with teachers and community about moral purpose for equity and quality when you are building a vision for your school?
- What have been the most important priorities in these early years?

- Do you feel confident and brave about leading change and addressing inequity?
- Are you working with other schools and centres in the region to help address local challenges?
- Are you continuing to connect with your NAPP colleagues to create new knowledge?
- Is coaching leadership still a part of your practice?

Answers to these questions will help us keep developing our coaching model and associated tools and skills in ways that ensure leaders' learning about moral purpose is embedded to the extent needed to inform their practice in the long term.

Leadership for equity and quality will always be complex and challenging, which is why leaders need support in order to address this complexity and rise to the challenges. Leaders who experience coaching through our programme have at hand an important support tool when they move on from working with us. That tool is peer coaching. Peer coaching provides leaders with an ongoing means of continually challenging and reflecting on their own practice and that of their colleagues, including teachers. But will the leaders who experience our programme coaching *continue* to support and challenge practice, whether their own or their colleagues, through peer coaching? We believe so.

> "Leadership for equity and quality will always be complex and challenging, which is why leaders need support in order to address this complexity and rise to the challenges."

Commentary

This case study recounts an effort to develop the type of leaders that Lesley (in the first case study) portrayed—leaders with high efficacy and agency who are able to rise to the "high-stakes" leadership required to address inequity and thereby improve the quality of education in New Zealand's education system. The NAPP case study differs from Lesley's, however, in terms of its intention to bring that leadership efficacy to "collective efficacy", wherein leaders connect and work with other leaders from other schools and centres, co-creating the knowledge they need to meet their moral purpose for equity. The NAPP leaders are also supported in this process by a peer coach as well as their experienced leader coach. However, the question remains of whether these leaders' experience of peer coaching will see them maintaining such a relationship on into their respective principalships?

The NAPP case study also makes clear the precept that moral purpose for equity is a lived experience. It's about self-examining values, beliefs, assumptions and decisions made on a daily basis, and it is this scrutiny that will lead to the strengthening or challenging of moral purpose. Questioning how far our moral purpose for equity extends and who it includes—My class? My school? The school down the road? New Zealand education?—is an important challenge within the process of asking whether we, as leaders, should more fully recognise our place in the education system and take our moral purpose to the system level.

Can moral purpose for equity be learned? The NAPP research indicates that it can, through intentional, structured, deep-learning conversations and accompanying reflection on practice, with this process occurring throughout the time leaders are working towards addressing the inequities evident in their schools. I firmly believe that school leaders are unlikely to gain awareness of the inequities they face on a daily basis until they are able to gain and increase their self-awareness of these issues. Leaders need to *be* asked and *to* ask the right questions of one another because deeper meaning is only likely to eventuate if our values, beliefs and assumptions are challenged. In short, the need for understanding of self is vital, and that understanding can begin with such questions as Who am I? Who do I take into my leadership every day? What am I not willing to compromise on? What does my moral purpose of education include?

The challenges and dilemmas of educational leadership often concern natural justice and fairness. As Meira Levinson of Harvard University stated recently, "A lot of everyday quandaries educators and policymakers face are dilemmas of educational justice, but we don't support or even acknowledge their struggle to address these challenges and make ethical decisions" (quoted in Anderson, 2014, para. 3). But are most of us even aware of the inequities and injustices in our communities today? And if we are, how readily can we identify the sources and nature of them? Are they, for example, related to

- school zoning,
- school scholarships,

- cost of housing,
- unemployment,
- competition between schools,
- insufficient resources,
- bullying,
- racism,
- poverty,
- lack of student and parental voice,
- differences in teaching quality,
- who gets the best teachers in the school,
- which subjects get the most emphasis,
- the quality of leadership within and across schools?

Because schools are a microcosm of society, educational leadership is about more than consulting or serving the community. It is also about enabling leadership that creates the community *with* the community. Leaders, moreover, need to support one another by working together, within their wider communities, in this endeavour. Most importantly, educational leadership needs leaders with a vision of "what might be". As Degenhardt and Duignan (2010, p. 17) state, "If you don't know where you're heading, how will you work out where to start, which direction to travel, what paths to take? ... [T]he answer is ultimately a matter of values, and what is understood to be the moral purpose of education."

Case Study 3: Coaching leadership to develop learning cultures

The emergence in Australia over recent years of a suite of nationally agreed teaching and school leadership "frameworks" has focused attention on the continual development of self-motivated and self-directed teachers, especially in terms of their professional practice and the capacity building of leadership for exemplary teaching and learning within and across schools. Sydney Catholic Education Office People and Culture Unit, led by Andrew Fraser, responded to the framework requirements by establishing policy direction for developing and sustaining a performance growth culture through a coaching programme conducted in collaboration with Jan Robertson. In this case study, Caroline Benedet, one of the "People and Culture" professional officers, endeavours to capture the learning arising out of the programme's inaugural years (2013–2015).

The Catholic Education Office Sydney (CEO Sydney) administers an education system of 150 primary and secondary schools and employs approximately 9,500 teachers and staff serving 70,000 students. The office continually seeks ways to engage its workforce in processes directed towards creating strong professional learning communities. In previous years, a number of coaching and mentoring initiatives designed mainly for individual principals, advisors and consultants were offered. Feedback from these participants indicated that while the initiatives were beneficial, they were not sufficiently goal specific and did not offer feedback robust enough to encourage learning of the kind the initiatives anticipated. Comments made clear that the type of feedback sought was that leading to the double- and triple-loop learning propounded by Argyris (2008).

In 2011, the CEO Sydney Senior Leadership Team endorsed the idea of utilising a coaching methodology with school senior-leadership teams in order to develop performance learning cultures. The People and Culture Unit of Sydney Catholic Schools then undertook research, scrutinised coaching models and sought an "expert in residence" to partner with the unit. That expert was Jan Robertson.

The developmental work in 2013 led to a revised leadership learning programme offering *Coaching Leadership: Developing Learning Cultures with Jan Robertson*. The programme, designed to encompass two years for each intake of participants, offers learning opportunities designed to provide school leadership teams with the principles, skills and support they need to develop and establish a learning culture directed towards grounding and strengthening school-based leadership and assisting the monitoring and improvement of teacher performance and development.

In line with the coaching model into which it fits, Coaching Leadership: Developing Learning Cultures focuses explicitly on developing reciprocal and collaborative learning partnerships through goal-oriented inquiry, practice and feedback. The programme requires leaders to participate in coaching partnerships with their peers, thus encouraging them to be learners in the process of continual transformation of self and, ultimately, of their leadership practice and team. The programme encompasses a suite of adult-learning strategies and resources that include:

- regular educational leadership research and input provided by the People and Culture Unit;

- regular face-to-face coaching leadership facilitated by Jan Robertson;
- provision and management of a web immersion for online collaboration and coaching; and
- annual presentation and celebration of each team's leadership learning.

The school leadership teams that opt into the programme must be prepared to commit to it for the full two years. A maximum of 10 teams can join the programme each year. Each team begins the programme by conducting an audit of their school's professional learning culture. From there, they identify an area of research inquiry they want to pursue via the coaching paradigm in order to bring about a change (the goal of the research) within that culture. The teams record their respective goals and the actions taken, and identify and evaluate the outcomes of their inquiries via a leadership case study.

By the end of the first year of our coaching-informed programme, our evaluation data revealed a positive impact on the leadership teams' practices and concepts of leadership. We also observed apparent positive influences on the development of the learning culture and the appraisal and accountability systems in the teams' schools. Data collected at the end of 2014 and 2015 confirmed these patterns. In the following sections of this case study, I look at the specific coaching-based skills and circumstances we and the leaders saw as facilitative of these changes. Each section is accompanied by a brief example from a different team as to the programme-based learning its members found most useful during their participation in the programme. The accounts also bring to the fore what these leadership teams specifically did to facilitate and develop a coaching-directed learning culture in their schools.

"Our evaluation data revealed a positive impact on the leadership teams' practices and concepts of leadership."

1. Changes in leaders' practice and leadership concepts

- *Ability to examine concepts of leadership and understand how to build leadership capacity for change:* Development of this ability was helping leaders look through a different lens at their capacity to lead and to build leadership in the teachers and other staff in their schools and particularly in the members of their senior leadership teams. Leaders were recognising the value of "developing an eye" for needed changes in teachers' practice in particular, and for detecting teachers' disposition to work towards such changes.

- *Opportunity to regularly practise coaching in peer-based partnerships:* Leaders said they now felt confident to ask colleagues questions that encouraged these peers to think about issues and how to solve them. Leaders also said they now knew how to actively listen to their colleagues' answers to their questions.
- *Time to think about thinking (metacognition):* As busy people, leaders were valuing the time to think about what was happening for them and others in and beyond the school and to reflect on the thinking that coaching in peer partnerships generates.
- *Lessening of collegial dependency:* Leaders said they were now noticing and embracing opportunities to build the leadership capacity (through coaching-based practice and skills) of their teachers. This approach was enabling teachers to take responsibility for solving issues and for developing and implementing changes in practice focused on improving teaching and learning.

> "Leaders said they were now noticing and embracing opportunities to build the leadership capacity (through coaching-based practice and skills) of their teachers."

Example 1: Appreciation and application of learning

When asked to reflect on their learning at the end of 2013, the leadership team of English as an Additional Language or Dialect (EALD) advisors (previously ESL advisors) had this to say: "As a group we grew in our understanding that coaching partnerships enhance our ability to be self-reflective." They saw their *key learning* over the year as extending the vision and use of coaching principles to a larger selection of EALD teachers from across the Archdiocese, a process that had allowed formation of a new professional learning community (PLC). They also noted as key learning activities:

- developing a framework of leading questions in order to open up dialogue in challenging conversations;
- scheduling time for reciprocal listening within a PLC structure in

order to connect teachers to a shared vision and to make them want to learn with and from one another and to move the PLC to a widely owned platform able to exert maximum influence within the education system.

At the end of 2014, the team provided this report:

> In 2014, a theme to explore how to expand our PLC members' understanding of leadership and their perceptions of themselves as leaders was central to our adviser group work. We maintained the rigour of moral purpose pivotal in driving change for our EALD students but included the notion of leaders as ones who empower others, build shared knowledge and lead change through action ... all qualities which our PLC members hold and employ.

2. Development of learning cultures

- *Recognising and appreciating their increased sphere of influence as system leaders:* Participants were eager to share their experience of developing a learning culture. They were now seeing themselves as people able to take risks in the interests of innovation and new learning. There was palpable energy among the teams with respect to purposeful learning conversations offering shared evidence of the impact that building leadership capacity has in terms of improving student outcomes.

- *Developing a shared language and understandings:* According to the leaders, these elements, gained through reflective dialogue with their coaching partners, was helping them gain greater awareness of self and others (roles and responsibilities), especially within the context of leadership for improved teaching and learning.

- *Detecting opportunities to promote a coaching learning culture:* Leaders said they were using staff meeting and senior leadership team meeting times to promote a coaching culture. They themselves were explicitly modelling the skills of coaching and inviting and encouraging learning conversations among all staff members, especially those not regularly working together. These developments, they said, were promoting "collective responsibility" for teaching and learning across the school.

- *Drawing on teachers' strengths:* Leaders said they were now better at identifying and drawing on teachers' individual strengths. They were helping teachers self-identify and maximise those strengths by encouraging them to observe one another's practice and model the skills of coaching. As a result, networks of expertise previously not recognised had become visible, thereby surfacing possibilities for development and change.

Example 2: Appreciation and application of learning

In 2014, the St Charles Primary School leadership team took as its goal "Creating a sustainable coaching process and culture at St Charles". For them, the challenge resided in this two-part question: How do we develop a sustainable system to ensure reflective practice continues and how do we model this to our teachers? When asked, at the end of 2014, to reflect on their learning, the St Charles team answered by stating what they hoped to accomplish in 2015.

> In 2015 and beyond, "Charlie's Changers'" are definitely looking forward to maintaining and developing the coaching culture throughout our school. We have the "stake" firmly driven in the ground and know where we want to be in the years ahead, especially after developing a [draft] Coaching Principles of Operation. We have made coaching a "high-energy" initiative for us in the next three years, as stated in our strategic Annual School Plan. We need to promote the importance and benefits of deep reflection and coaching to ensure coaching doesn't diminish to a compulsory one-off session that teachers feel obliged to take part in. We want to see coaching everywhere: in our staff meetings, PLC meetings, curriculum meetings, business meetings, staff development days and, more importantly, our executive meetings. We want to *be* the change and to *model* it. We want teachers to understand it, take part in it and reflect on it. The only way that this coaching process will unfold further in our school meetings is if we make a change to our executive meeting and foster other capable leaders to do so.

At the end of 2015, St Charles Primary School provided this reflection:

> Initially, a lot of the development was on the senior executive in order to impact on the staff so that we are all on the same path together, and a coaching culture was the way for that to happen. We linked it to our cyclical review, which validated many things but also challenged us as to what the next step forward should be. We have used many research texts this

year as an executive: for example, Robertson; Sharratt; Hattie. We have extensively explored data and want to link our goals to the professional teaching standards and the school's annual plan. Our conversations are much more professional, and the children are starting to set their own SMART goals. There is more student voice and more student feedback to one another. We are all learners together. We gave staff an opportunity to lead, related to their goals. In the PLCs, the coaching conversations have really been around the students' needs and achievement. We model the coaching practice in our executive meetings and in our staff meetings and when we are buddy to somebody else. We believe we have some great practices. In 2016, we will strengthen links and understanding of the professional standards. We will put more focus on teacher feedback. We will continue to model coaching practice. We will continue to get evidence that what we are doing is actually making a difference. In the end, it has got to make a difference to students' learning.

3. Appraisal and accountability systems

- *Examining the school's Personal Planning and Professional Review (PPPR) for effectiveness in terms of changing teachers' practice and building quality teaching:* Those leadership teams that had incorporated coaching partnerships into their PPPR approach reported that their teachers were now more able and willing to ask questions and to be asked questions in relation to their performance and so had become more reflective.
- *Developing shared understanding of what quality teaching and learning looks like:* Leadership teams had striven to develop this understanding across all leaders and teachers in their schools. They had been careful to include in this process middle leaders who often do not see their role and responsibility as relating to the quality of teaching in classrooms. Such leaders were being skilled and challenged to take responsibility for their own coaching-based conversations, with these informed by reference to and scrutiny of professional teaching standards

Example 3: Appreciation and application of learning

During 2103, the Patrician Brothers College (Fairfield) leadership team focused their leadership work on using coaching partnerships as a springboard to make changes to the PPPR processes at the college. They considered the PPPR "a non-productive framework for teachers to reflect on practice. We wanted teachers to engage in a process that supported their development as reflective, collaborative practitioners." The team therefore developed a personal reflective tool for teachers that referenced the Australian Professional Standards for Teachers. Teachers reflected on the current state of their professional practice and identified two areas that they would like to spend the year improving. The leadership team next provided opportunities for all teachers in the school to develop a "coaching relationship" with a chosen colleague that emphasised active listening. Each pair then set SMART goals for improving their professional practice. According to the college leadership team, this approach "was very successful".

During 2014, the team focused its leadership work on:

- continuing the practice of reflective partnerships, with the partners focused on 2013 SMART goal achievement and supported by Google's IT platform;
- consolidating application of the reflective tool so as to establish areas of professional focus throughout the year;
- implementing, as part of new staff induction, information on coaching expectations and tools;
- bringing in additional staff support to allow time for coaching;
- developing a programme for middle managers directed towards facilitating "highly accomplished" practice and complementing the school's "reflective partnerships" coaching culture;
- identifying, developing and implementing group professional learning activities that focused explicitly on the Australian Professional Standards for Teachers and thereby assist the thinking needed to transition all staff to seeing themselves as "leaders of student learning".

By the end of 2014, the team had achieved the following:

- launched a "professional learning groups" model in the school that led to the establishment of seven such coaching groups working together during a non-teaching period of two weeks and supported by a facilitator from the Authentic Learning Committee (an existing College committee);
- ensured that the principles and practice of coaching/mentoring/collaborative practice/deprivatising teacher practice underpinned the professional learning groups model;

- helped each staff member identify and work towards two professional learning goals;
- aligned teaching practice to the Australian Professional Standards for Teachers; and
- deployed a Google site where staff could share goals and strategies, collect evidence in support of inquiry initiatives and record reflections/notes.

By the end of 2015, 28 of Sydney Catholic Schools' senior leadership teams (from both primary and secondary schools) and its professional learning teams had been part of coaching leadership. All of these leaders noted their greater focus on educational leadership in terms of the quality of teaching and learning and on their ability to build the capacity for such leadership. The use of student achievement data was a major component of change. These leaders also recognised the change in mindset in regard to professional learning that had taken place. They had come to appreciate that *they* had had to change their leadership practice so as to enable the leadership that led to self-directed professional learning from their teachers and a much higher level of trust in relationships. Classroom practice had become much more open to observation and sharing of practice, with considerably more reflective dialogue. Schools more fully understood the practices that a professional learning community could share as an outcome of developing coaching leadership skills and principles to address student learning outcomes.

"All of these leaders noted their greater focus on educational leadership in terms of the quality of teaching and learning and on their ability to build the capacity for such leadership."

Commentary

Of interest in this case study was how the leaders themselves realised they'd been creating climates of dependency in terms of teachers waiting for them to tell them what to do, how to do it and then how well they had done it! This paradigm is such a strong one in education contexts. Once the leaders had developed their own coaching partnerships and experienced the power of facilitating and enabling their colleagues' learning, they began to change their practice with regard to the teachers in their schools.

For the participating teams, a strong desire to regularly connect with another leadership team surfaced and eventually became an integral component of the professional connections and opportunities for growth. Another major aspect was that many of the schools had established Personal Planning and Professional Review systems (their PPPRs) that were unlikely to lead to changes in teachers' practice but nevertheless met the guidelines for system compliance.. As the members of the teams developed their coaching expertise, they came to realise that formative, reflective, inquiry-focused learning relationships would develop a more effective professional growth culture in their schools.

At the beginning of the intervention, many of the schools were strongly immersed in a "project culture", such that when school leaders were asked, "Why are you doing that?" they answered, "Because we're doing RAMP or Early Years or IDEAS." What was very noticeable by the end of the second year was that these educational leaders now had a vision of leadership for learning and the type of adult learning culture that they aspired to achieve. They had developed school-wide pedagogies and begun to see the "projects" as resources that helped them to achieve the goals that they, as the educational leaders of their respective schools, were working towards. Their educational leadership capacity as senior teams had developed a shared language of learning, shared accountability and shared principles of practice directed towards enabling a sustainable, enduring leadership platform from which to improve teaching and learning. Classrooms were less 'closed' and teachers were sharing and observing practices that make a diffferent to student learning outcomes, much more readily.

At the close of 2015, the participating school leadership teams articulated their recognition of a distinctive and visible awareness of "professionalism" and leadership that they considered had been enriched through the research-based school inquiry and reflective dialogue modelled and practised among teachers and mirrored in their leadership relationships with parents and students.

Case Study 4: Taking an already successful school to the next level: The part played by coaching

In this case study, Mike Sutton, principal of Rototuna Primary School in Hamilton, gives an account of how he and other members of the school's leadership team used coaching to develop a strong inquiry-based learning culture in the school.

In 2010, our school, Rototuna Primary, reached the end of an era. The school opened in 2003 with 102 students; by 2010, the roll had passed 700. The leadership team that set up the school had moved on but had left the legacy of a school that the Education Review Office identified as a successful one. For us, the new leadership team, made up of the principal (myself), two deputy principals and an assistant principal, it was time to reflect on present gains and plan a way forward that would build on them. We wanted our school to be even more successful—to ensure that our students were meeting, if not exceeding, their learning achievement targets. But in order to realise this aim, we knew that we had to help our teachers grow in ways that would ensure continuous improvement in student achievement. In the words of Stoll and Fink (1996), we wanted Rototuna to be "a moving school". The support we offer teachers in this regard involves an inquiry-based model of teacher professional development. Coaching is an integral part of that model.

> *"We knew that we had to help our teachers grow in ways that would ensure continuous improvement in student achievement."*

Our approach to professional development

Whole-school professional learning and development (Timperley, Wilson, Barrar, & Fung 2007) has been common practice for many years at Rototuna School. To set the context for how this development is now exercised at the school, I need to explain that the school is organised into seven teaching teams. Each team is made up of all students of a specific class level (e.g., all Year 1 students) and is taught by four or five teachers, with one of those teachers fulfilling the role of team leader.

When I and my colleagues took over the leadership of Rototuna School, we identified *leading learning* as our most crucial role. We knew that in order to fulfil this role we needed to draw on and use literature to ground our decisions in best practice as we planned for the future. More specifically, in line with this research, we knew we needed to encourage development of a school culture committed to ongoing learning of everyone in it, because this culture would provide the solid base from which teachers could "grow" their work as highly skilled classroom practitioners. While securing student achievement remained Rototuna's primary purpose, we (the leadership team) needed to develop systems and processes that would enable all members of our school and everybody associated with it to "know our impact".

We decided early on to use coaching as one of the main means to our end. We wanted coaching to underpin all that we did, and we wanted to confirm our belief that all teachers are capable of coaching one another. Over two decades ago, Jan Robertson (1995) demonstrated that coaching leads to leaders growing and enhancing their practice. Ten or so years later, supervised by Jan, I showed through my research (Sutton, 2005) conducted at my previous school that coaching leadership enhances the effectiveness of school leaders' and teachers' professional learning and development. Of particular importance in terms of the obvious ultimate purpose of engaging in school-based coaching is Bryk and Schneider's (2004) finding that coaching and a coaching-based culture in schools contribute to raising student achievement within and across schools. Those of us in the leadership team at Rototuna drew on all these findings when determining how to transform our already successful school into an even better school.

We also realised that we ourselves needed to work collaboratively if we were to enhance our own professional learning and development and, from there, help teachers build their pedagogical knowledge and identify the impact of that knowledge on their students. For us, coaching was the key not only to achieving these interrelated aims but also to creating and sustaining a culture of schoolwide continual learning. The essential coaching skills that we identified, used amongst ourselves and then modelled for our teaching staff were based on Robertson's (2005) three levels of questions used during the reflective interviewing process of her coaching leadership paradigm. Over time, we positioned these elements within the inquiry-based model of teacher development that we now employ in our school. A description of this model and of how these coaching elements fit within it follows.

Teaching as inquiry

Our initial school-wide system of appraising the efficacy of our teaching (as reflected in student achievement) went through various iterations but was influenced throughout by action research (Cardno, 2003; Robertson, 2005). In time, it evolved into "teaching as inquiry", as advanced by Timperley et al. (2007). The influence of these researchers has been and remains crucial to our inquiry model.

Teaching as inquiry requires teachers to formulate a question or "wondering" focused on a group of students and then to endeavour to answer that question through research. Part of the research methodology employed in this regard at Rototuna consists of teaching colleagues coaching, the features of which are observing and providing feedback on one another's classroom practice and then discussing and reflecting on what that feedback means with respect to the student focus group.

Consistent across all of the iterations on our way to developing our model was our focus on needs-based student groups, heeding of student voice and adherence to the fundamental principles of coaching (Robertson, 1995). Work by Barbara Gottesman (2000) also influenced the development of our inquiry model in terms of teachers being the ones to identify the overall focus of the inquiry, which students the inquiry would focus on, what would be specifically observed and the context for both the observation and students' learning.

As we continued to develop our model, we noticed that the focus on, or the inquiry relating to, the observed group changed with each observation. When we discussed this matter with teachers, they said that the imperative to respond to the particular needs of their students during each observation session differed within sessions and from session to session. As a consequence, our model became spiral in form rather than cyclical in order to reflect the ever changing learning needs of the students and the consequent shaping and reshaping of the inquiry questions. Each inquiry is also a crucial part of whole-school professional learning and development because we try to be as evidence-based as possible in our work.

The iterative process of questioning and reflecting on observation findings helps determine and progress the direction of our overall school development programme. Over time, our school leadership team has been able to build the coaching-based skills level of our teaching staff's team leaders to the extent that they undertake the teaching-as-inquiry process with their team members. We coached these leaders during their initial observations of colleagues' practice and ensuing discussions, but once we and they deemed themselves sufficiently confident, they were able to fly solo.

The place of coaching

During the inquiry-based observations of colleagues' work practice, teachers use Robertson's levels of questioning to expedite the process. We encourage development of these question-related skills via the coaching process because we think these skills are the ones that enhance all learning discussions, whether conducted peer to peer, in team meetings, discussion groups and professional learning groups, or among all stakeholders in the school learning partnership. We believe that the more leaders and teachers develop and hone these skills, the greater and more useful is the knowledge they gain of the many facets of and influences on their own roles, praxis and student learning. Today, we see these coaching leadership skills being modelled and used in every aspect of life at Rototuna School.

In general, our inquiry model of professional development uses Robertson's Level-1 questions more in the pre-observation phase and the Levels 2 and 3 questions in the post-observation discussions. We also include on our observation recording sheets various starter questions to help observers get underway during the observation sessions. For example, our teaching-as-inquiry pre-observation sheet currently follows the ideas of Gottesman (2000) and Sutton (2005). Headings include:

• My inquiry
• Inquiry process model (after Timperly et al., 2007)
• Focus learners
• How am I going with my inquiry? How do I know?
• What do I want my observer to notice today?

These questions ensure that both parties are well prepared for the observation and the post-observation discussions. The learning is reciprocal. The coaches learn to critique their coaching practice, while the teachers are supported to co-construct their new learning with respect to meeting the needs of the student focus group.

As I had found (Sutton, 2005), coaching supports teachers as they implement the changes in their pedagogy that are needed to ensure alignment with the knowledge they gain from their professional learning and development. At Rototuna School, professional learning and development for teachers encompasses five call-back days over the year as well as in-class work with teachers and a number of staff meetings devoted to enhancing pedagogical knowledge and praxis.

In 2012, we began a three-year professional learning and development contract with mathematics consultant Bruce Moody. His role included facilitating the teaching-as-inquiry process and our once-per-term week-long intensive observation programme as well as being an integral support and resource during teacher call-back professional-development and learning days. During each week-long visit, Bruce observed the school's seven team leaders teaching mathematics in their classrooms and provided them with feedback on and opportunity to discuss their practice. He and (later) one of the mathematics team leaders then taught the group of leaders to model effective pedagogy. Each of these teachers then carried out this modelling in their classroom while being observed by the other teachers in their team. This aspect of the teaching-as-inquiry process required all teachers in a team to observe, twice a year, their team-leader colleague teaching mathematics. All teachers in the school thus received the same "message" about effective teaching at the same time. This encompassing approach accorded with our belief of the importance of whole-school or, in this case, whole-team learning.

After completion of the observations, Bruce and each team met to discuss what they had learned throughout the observation and post-observation processes and how they had implemented or could implement those understandings in their classroom practice. Each discussion session was driven by teacher questions and comments. During these sessions, Bruce used coaching to help each teacher explain their learning and any resultant changes to their pedagogical practices and to help the other teachers scrutinise and reflect on their colleague's commentary and descriptions.

Bruce also facilitated four after-school workshops during each of the weeks he was at Rototuna and helped the teachers identify and relate inquiry topics to the teacher and student learning needs they had identified since his previous visit. Teachers were expected to attend at least one of these workshops, but most of them usually attended more.

The impact of this initiative was huge. The weakest cohort of mathematics students in our school (based on national standards data) improved from 64 percent of students meeting the standard to a

90-percent achievement rate over two years. Overall, school performance in mathematics lifted by 10 percent to meet the school expectation of 90-percent-plus achievement.

At the start of 2015, we began an intensive writing programme that involved an in-school leader and team. Call-back days and teaching as inquiry continued to be part of the process. This programme was more intensive than the one we'd employed with the mathematics initiative in that the team worked with just one teacher over four days. On the first day of the writing initiative, the writing team observed the teacher. Over the next three days, they observed the teacher co-teaching with a member of the team, who modelled the techniques/pedagogy so as to take the teacher to the next step. Each classroom observation session was 45 minutes in duration, and it was immediately followed by a 45-minute coaching and discussion session that required use of all the skills identified by Robertson (2005) and mentioned earlier in this case study.

Once again, the in-class support focused on the two student cohorts with the lowest achievement rate. Data collected after two terms of the initiative showed an average 14 to 16 percent increase in achievement for these two cohorts and an average 12 percent lift in school-wide achievement. Data collected from at-risk students (student voice) showed all of them stating that they knew their teacher believed them to be good writers. The in-class support data also confirmed anecdotal evidence that all students could achieve as writers if they knew their teachers firmly believed they could.

The success associated with the writing initiative quickly piqued the interest of the teachers in the school who had not experienced the intensive in-class support. They arranged to observe colleagues and to discuss the teaching and learning of writing with colleagues from across the school. We also noticed teachers discussing writing pedagogy with colleagues in the staffroom, exploring this area of teaching on social media and accessing the writing Google docs set up in the school's intranet. The process of collaboration and coaching was indeed having a schoolwide impact.

In conclusion

Over the past five years, we've sought to make our school an even more successful one by exercising our belief that inquiry-based professional learning intertwined with coaching skills can permeate the learning culture of a school, resulting in teachers who are more confident of and effective in their practice and so better able to support all students reach or even exceed required achievement standards. All aspects of this learning culture are visible on a daily basis in our school, such that the Education Review Office recently commented on the strong, committed and collaborative ethos among Rototuna staff. As we have found, being part of a process where colleagues grow their knowledge and enhance their pedagogy so that students can and do learn is hugely motivating in terms of our work as leaders.

Commentary

This case study shows how Mike, a principal who started this journey by way of his own coaching relationship with another principal over a five-year period, brought the coaching paradigm to his school's professional learning culture. In his previous school, Mike started out by coaching four of his own expert teachers and developing their efficacy and skills to a point at which they became the coaches in ensuing years. Mike then became the *facilitator* of the coaches' ongoing development of their coaching practice, all the time drawing on current educational research, to inform, enhance and direct the process and practice. So here again was an example of the action-learning process of coaching complementing the inquiry process of professional learning, and confirming coaching as a discipline of research and practice. Mike's own earlier research into the process of coaching, moreover, cemented the importance of ongoing coaching skills development for teachers as a necessary investment in this process.

In his narration, Mike presents strong data in support of the power of coaching to change teachers' practice and impact positively on student learning outcomes. His coaching-related work at Rototuna School has enabled him and his colleagues to gather evidence confirming that coaching skills "enhance all learning discussions, whether conducted peer to peer, in team meetings, discussion groups and professional learning groups, or among all stakeholders in the school learning partnership." Drawing on understandings gained from this learning to further monitor and improve teaching practice and student learning has thus been key to

Rototuna's success in ameliorating student under-achievement.

Overall, Mike's case study illustrates how middle leaders can model effective pedagogy to their colleagues and how classrooms in a school can open up to the scrutiny of observation, with that opening initiated by the teachers themselves. The study also supports the claim that one of the most important parts of coaching is observation of practice—observation directed towards instigating reflection on one's own practice and thereby replacing judgemental assessment of teachers' practice with understanding of what new practices might and can look like in the classroom. Finally, Mike's study highlights one of the less-mentioned outcomes of a coaching culture: an energised staff, committed to high expectations for students' learning outcomes, and collaborative and collegial in their efforts to realise those expectations.

Summary of main points

- Observation of practice modelled by expert pedagogues is an important part of coaching practice.
- A coaching culture impacts positively on staff collaboration, expectations for student achievement and commitment to continual improvement and innovation.
- Leaders who have experienced coaching will more readily use this skill and knowledge to facilitate use of the process by others.
- Coaching other coaches builds leadership capacity within an institution as well as teachers' confidence and efficacy.
- Coaching creates structured opportunities for collegial dialogue and collaboration around shared issues.
- Student learning outcomes, such as engagement and academic achievement, are key outcomes of teachers' coaching pedagogical practice.
- Leaders who facilitate coaching relationships between and among colleagues take on the role of supervision and development of coaching practice.

That complexity can arise almost of itself and there is a connectedness
between every part of the self-created cosmos.

Chapter 12

Developing agency and efficacy

Chapter overview

Coaching relationships serve to strengthen the self-efficacy and agency of
educational leaders, an outcome that can then lead to the sustainability
of coaching cultures as leadership practice. This chapter highlights how
these qualities in educational leadership align to instil in leaders the belief
that they have the power to make a positive difference in their communities, particularly with collective efficacy through collaborating with other
leaders. This ability often entails working at the political level within an
institutional, regional or national context, and is illustrated in this chapter
through a case study of developing efficacy and agency through a system-wide coaching leadership model for aspiring principals. The chapter
is also concerned with the premise that leaders will not act with agency
on an ongoing basis unless they are equipped with the skills, support and
learning principles that allow them to constantly think about and re-
evaluate the values and beliefs underpinning their respective educational
platforms.

From apolitical to political

Critics of coaching argue that the process perpetuates a situation whereby ineffective and apolitical leaders simply choose to work together and consequently fail to challenge their current ways of working. However, my argument is that leaders who engage in coaching become politicised about the contexts within which they exercise the practice, to the point where they can act with agency and courage *if* the coaching model they are using disrupts their usual modes of thinking and operating. The disruption must be one that results in leaders questioning whatever "impressions" they've established of their leadership practice and the contexts within which it operates.

The coaching model in this book provides this disruption in two ways. First, it requires leaders to work in ways that differ from their usual interactions with their professional colleagues. Second, it brings into play the outside perspectives of the facilitator and/or the presence of the coach during reflective questioning and/or workplace shadowing. The challenges and disruptions that facilitators and coaches bring to leaders' practice requires leaders to question every aspect of what they think and do rather than leaving their thoughts and actions as everyday, taken-for-granted behaviour (Grundy, 1993).

The essential power (efficacy) of coaching lies in coaches' ability to stand outside the situation and outside of their own practice in order to ask their partners questions about their practice that will surface values and challenge assumptions. When assumptions are challenged, leaders are able to revisit (critically reflect on) their educational values and beliefs and deconstruct their multiple roles. In so doing, they come to see—and appreciate—that they're not alone, that other leaders face the same tensions and dilemmas.

These insights lead them to look beyond themselves to the bigger picture of their leadership and their educational context. They begin to view the social and political underpinnings of that context with a more critical eye, and come to understand how it shapes their leadership roles. Realising that they no longer have to hide behind a façade, they begin to speak out about the tensions and issues they face, particularly to the groups of people with whom they work. This "opening up" expedites shared ownership of the challenges and provides an ever stronger platform for group problem solving and posing, goal setting and action planning, all of which are the ingredients of agency and empowerment.

One of the most important aspects of leadership development, then, is raising the awareness of leaders about the social and political contexts within which they conduct their leadership practice. As I discussed earlier in this book, education is a political act, which means that educational leaders need to be aware of how public policy directions impact on decision making within their institutions so that they have the knowledge they need to act with agency. Neo-liberalism and its associated rhetoric of managerialism and choice have placed educational institutions in the invidious situation of having to compete against one another as private businesses in a public-service industry (Thrupp & Willmott, 2003; Wylie, 2012). To ask leaders to work collaboratively and develop collective efficacy across institutions can feel challenging at first in this low-trust environment.

My experiences with educational leaders during the time I was developing the coaching model made me realise that leaders tend to employ a bluff exterior and "impression management" (Goffman, 1959) when working with their colleagues in professional situations. Given that educational institutions stand or fall on numbers of enrolments, it's not surprising that many leaders strive to keep up an impression of "everything is going well around here". This demeanour not only hides issues such as bullying and underachievement but also isolates leaders within the cocoon of their own work, a circumstance that creates personal stress. Unable to share leadership issues and tensions with their colleagues, they believe that the problems are entirely theirs rather than ones that their counterparts also often experience.

My research also showed that educational leaders can feel very exposed and vulnerable under the ever watchful eye of colleagues and community—the "gaze", to use Foucault's (1977) expression. Leaders accordingly build up their boundaries with even more impression management and do

"My coach has been amazing. I wish he was 'on call' for the rest of my teaching career. He understands the pressures and is a skilled coach. He always knows when to ask the right questions in a non-threatening way."

not let anybody into the inner recesses of their institutions and practice. This façade, as I observed previously, is not conducive to systemic, institutional or professional growth because issues remain hidden rather than dealt with effectively. However, when educational leaders have the opportunity to debate not only the meaning of education but also the effects of managerialism and competition on education in general and educational institutions in particular, and what it means to be part of the power structures that maintain the status quo, they are supported and challenged to collaboratively lead transformative change in their communities.

Sometimes, leaders situated within the challenging environment that coaching creates initially experience loss of confidence in their existing practices, a situation that is also common in action research methodology. However, loss of confidence acts as a catalyst for change because it, too, creates a disruption by nudging leaders out of their comfort zones and challenging them to look at their beliefs and practices from a critical perspective. The coach as critical friend and trusted colleague provides support during this time, encouraging leaders to set their reflection and goal setting in positive directions and to recognise that the implementation dip is an inevitable part of the process of change.

Eventually, as goals are reached and new practices are tried, tested and found valuable, leaders regain their confidence. Their lived experience of coaching shows them that this process and its attendant skills equip them to work more comfortably within the constant state of flux that is education today. The process also helps to develop adaptive leaders who are comfortable with the not-knowing that such complex challenges bring. It furthermore shows them that they can act with agency—that they can bring about innovation in their own leadership practice and in the workings of their institution. Finally, it gives them the confidence to take risks and to step up into the challenges they see, with courage and bravery (McLaughlin & Cox, 2016), as they lead with moral purpose. Acting with agency inevitably involves trialling new ideas and practices, some of which will succeed and some of which will not. What is important here is that leaders see that both successes and failures are learning opportunities along the way to innovation and transformative practices.

The notion that coaching is an act of dissonance which leads to self-efficacy and agency is supported by the work of other researchers and commentators. Berger and Luckmann (1966) were among the first to propose that knowledge is socially constructed. They argued that change relies on creating dissonance within these constructions, and that dissonance is brought about by the picking apart (deconstructing) that critical reflection and analysis encourages. This picking apart creates new awareness or conscientisation (Freire, 1985) of issues and ineffective ways of operating as well as of how to

"Every interaction that I have had with my coach has challenged me to think more deeply and carefully and always in relation to my leadership and outcomes for children."

ameliorate them. That understanding, in turn, gives rise to feelings of empowerment (the "knowledge is power" adage). Giddens (1993) refers to these feelings as agency—the notion that it is possible to act differently to how one has acted before.

Bandura (2002) sees agency in terms of self-efficacy—the belief that one can make a difference. During his discussion of self-efficacy, Bandura highlights three types of efficacy—personal, proxy and collective. Personal efficacy is efficacy that is conducted by individuals, proxy is where an individual enlists someone else to take charge and to make changes on his or her behalf, and collective efficacy is where a group acts together as communities of learners to achieve what they may not be able to achieve individually. My coaching studies confirmed that the coaching leadership model enhances all three types of agency. The studies also showed that the more self-efficacious leaders become, the more likely they are to commit themselves to directing their leadership practice towards implementing innovations designed to enhance learning and teaching within their institutions and collaboratively across institutions.

Case study: Leaders learning agency and self-efficacy

The case study featured here is drawn from a broader programme of study that a colleague and I concluded relatively recently (Earl & Robertson, 2013; Robertson & Earl, 2014). The main aim of this research was to explore the effect of coaching on leadership learning among principals participating in New Zealand's National Aspiring Principals' Programme

(NAPP), an initiative introduced and described in the second case study in Chapter 11. The aspect of the study relevant to this current chapter relates to our interest during the research of adding to the knowledge base about how particular leadership dispositions are learned. We also wanted to provide examples and images of what these dispositions might look like when "translated" into practice.

We identified and focused on six key dispositions of educational leadership:

- moral purpose for addressing inequity in education (outlined in the previous chapter);
- efficacy and agency;
- receptiveness to learning;
- culturally responsive practice;
- building capacity of self and others; and
- principalship identity.

Analysis of our findings convinced us that these dispositions are inextricably interrelated. It is instructive, however, to consider them as separate entities before discussing the connectedness. For the purposes of providing a case study for this chapter, I focus on only one area, that of efficacy and agency. My account leads into a figurative depiction (Figure 12.1) of a tool that the NAPP coaching team developed to intentionally coach leaders towards agency and efficacy in the interests of providing them with the attributes they need to act as change agents, whether individually or as groups of learning leaders.

Building agency is an important part of the NAPP. We defined the process in terms of increasing participants' readiness and capacity to act, to lead and to respond to policy directions with moral purpose. Above all, the work was about developing leaders to feel efficacious and autonomous and equipped with the willingness to act as agents of change able to make a difference to the current situation of inequity in New Zealand education and to connect with others to do so. Such leaders are leaders who unrelentingly step up to the challenge of equity during their leadership. One item in a self-assessment survey that we asked the participating aspiring principals to complete two-thirds of the way through the programme showed that 96 percent of them agreed that they were developing a strong sense of efficacy.

A close examination of just what capabilities the leaders came to exhibit with respect to agency and efficacy led us to identify three such attributes (Earl & Robertson, 2013). They were:

- a belief in one's efficacy and authenticity as a change agent;
- a strong appreciation of the importance that social networks hold for providing support and a willingness to both access and provide that support; and
- a demonstrated willingness to take personal responsibility for the learning journey.

Essentially, the effective leaders in our study came to *know* they had the power or capacity to do what is required to effect change, and so were able to put that knowledge into practice. In short, they became agents of change.

For these leaders, the journey towards this knowledge was one of a growing belief in their personal worth and confidence. "The experience for me," said one leader, "has been life changing and affirming of my self-belief. I know why I have to lead change in education more now than I ever have." For some of the leaders, this growing self-belief involved affirmation of the knowledge and expertise they'd already gained during their careers but which they'd not previously recognised. We observed that efficacious leaders had a strong sense of their authenticity both as an individual and as a leader. One leader expressed this feeling as follows: "I've learned that I'm capable of leading people. I was starting to question where I was at and what was I doing because I had questioned my moral purpose. I've rediscovered [it] this year, and because of it I have a better understanding of self. I believe I am more authentic as a leader."

For the NAPP leaders, agency and efficacy was also underpinned by a growing recognition that leadership itself is about change and that agency is therefore about acting with confidence to bring about change—to take responsibility and have an ongoing positive influence within the many spheres of educational contexts and provision. One leader described his strengthening leadership identity as follows: "I've learned that I'm a significant agent for change within a school. I've also reflected on previous experiences of what I called leadership and [now know] that they were more likely to be called management, as they were certainly reactive."

The NAPP leaders also came to realise that a high level of agency entails confidence to challenge others by asking the questions that confront and problematise practice (Robertson, 2015) and by drawing colleagues into the conversations necessary to lead the change: "I've developed more confidence in my leadership,' one leader said. "I'm not afraid to have the hard conversations with staff now."

As the NAPP leaders discovered, needed support during their endeavour to act as agents of change through transformative practice came when they participated in social networks of other leaders experiencing the same or similar change-based challenges. There were comments about colleagues providing "a constant source of inspiration", and there were comments containing such phrases as "online learning communities" and a "national support network". According to the NAPP participants, when they had opportunity to share knowledge and create new knowledge with leaders from different schools, the process not only built collective efficacy but also inculcated a clear understanding of what was possible and could therefore be enacted, so strengthening agency at the individual leadership and school level.

Although feeling a sense of agency and efficacy is buttressed by shared learning, as is gained during engagement in professional networks and communities, it is also embedded in a sense of personal responsibility for one's individual learning. According to one NAPP leader, agency and efficacy came from stepping up and accepting responsibility for making a difference, even when it was tough: "I learned that I'd lost the moral purpose of education. The important thing I learned is that by being honest about myself and where I fit in New Zealand education, I can make a difference. I'm therefore more confident and able to challenge."

Leaders also indicated that this sense of personal efficacy was dynamic in nature, ever changing because of the ongoing process of risk-taking in transformative leadership practice, of reflecting on the insights gained and then integrating those insights into their knowledge and practice of leadership. Ultimately, agency and efficacy meant having the confidence to enact a greater sphere of influence, such as that encompassed by principalship. One aspiring principal who experienced this shift in confidence told us: "I have gone from thinking that principalship is something I may do in the future to actually wanting to get into it *now*!"

Our work with the NAPP leaders clarified for us that agency and efficacy are dynamic and evolving elements of leadership. As confidence and authenticity develop, leaders are able to take responsibility for their actions, more intentionally challenging the status quo and thus being ever more proactive in leading transformative change. So if we know these aspects of efficacy and agency and the impact of them on leadership practice, can we then coach leaders more intentionally towards increased efficacy and agency? We believe so.

Those of us involved in the coaching aspects of the NAPP came together as a team in order to identify and reflect on which of the questions we'd asked leaders had led to this type of learning. In other words, what were the questions most likely to facilitate deeper (deepest even) thinking about one's personal agency and efficacy? The questions that we identified allowed us to develop a tool, presented in Figure 12.1, to assist our coaching practice. The questions this tool contains serve as starter

Figure 12.1: Smart tool for coaching agency and efficacy

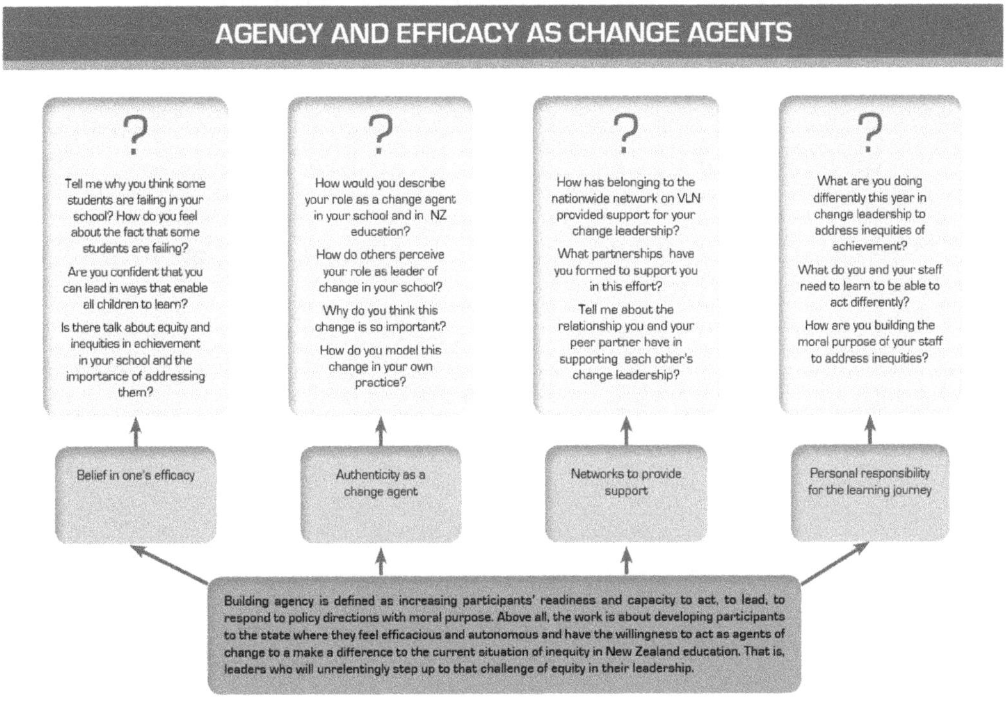

AGENCY AND EFFICACY AS CHANGE AGENTS

?

Tell me why you think some students are failing in your school? How do you feel about the fact that some students are failing?

Are you confident that you can lead in ways that enable all children to learn?

Is there talk about equity and inequities in achievement in your school and the importance of addressing them?

?

How would you describe your role as a change agent in your school and in NZ education?

How do others perceive your role as leader of change in your school?

Why do you think this change is so important?

How do you model this change in your own practice?

?

How has belonging to the nationwide network on VLN provided support for your change leadership?

What partnerships have you formed to support you in this effort?

Tell me about the relationship you and your peer partner have in supporting each other's change leadership?

?

What are you doing differently this year in change leadership to address inequities of achievement?

What do you and your staff need to learn to be able to act differently?

How are you building the moral purpose of your staff to address inequities?

Belief in one's efficacy

Authenticity as a change agent

Networks to provide support

Personal responsibility for the learning journey

Building agency is defined as increasing participants' readiness and capacity to act, to lead, to respond to policy directions with moral purpose. Above all, the work is about developing participants to the state where they feel efficacious and autonomous and have the willingness to act as agents of change to a make a difference to the current situation of inequity in New Zealand education. That is, leaders who will unrelentingly step up to that challenge of equity in their leadership.

©Ian Robertson (2014)

questions to move leaders into deeper thinking about each of the aspects of agency and efficacy for leading transformative change. Because these questions are starter questions, many other coaching questions will evolve out of the dialogue that ensues.

Summary of main points

- Because leadership is an isolated role, professional support and challenge through coaching can result in leaders gaining greater feelings of confidence, self-efficacy and agency.
- Educational leadership is influenced by social and political contexts. Leaders need opportunities to join in with other leaders to think about and gain awareness of their leadership roles within those contexts.
- Enhanced awareness promotes leadership as a political act. Leaders have a responsibility to take collaborative action on issues that are important in terms of educational justice.
- Coaching can lend the professional support and challenge necessary for critical reflection on leadership practice.

Clouds with their amorphous boundaries and turbulent structures are justifiably considered to be at the very edge of possessing a definable form ... Nebulous though they may be, clouds clearly show the imprint of the forces working on them; they express distinctive *li*.

Chapter 13

Beyond the boundaries

Deepening coaching: Breaking the boundaries

As has been demonstrated in this book, coaching challenges and supports educational leaders to develop their leadership practice in ways that advantage them, their institutions and education. If all educational leaders had ready access to "coaching organisations" with "learning facilitators", how might the work of education differ? But given that today's leaders will be developing tomorrow's leaders, we face the risk of getting more of the same in educational leadership and therefore educational institutions. What we will always need in order to ensure leaders are constantly challenged into new ways of thinking, being and acting are leadership initiatives that work alongside a coaching leadership paradigm. I was involved in one such research initiative over a decade (see Robertson & Webber, 2002, 2004; Webber & Robertson, 1998, 2004). Based on what I and my colleague term the "boundary-breaking model", this programme provided boundary-breaking leadership development experiences that provide the support and impetus called for in regard to developing and implementing practice which is not only new but also transformative. The boundary-breaking experiences can be between and across classrooms, schools, nations, cultures or roles.

Boundary-breaking principles

Incorporating boundary-breaking principles into the way coaches and leaders work together provides the challenge necessary to move leaders from inaction to action, from reactive to proactive and from perpetuating the status quo to challenging it and creating new knowledge. Coaching is thus a transformative process because it allows educational leaders to act with agency—to know they can contribute to and develop the system rather than be a cog within it. Surely this is the type of leadership that is required to meet the type of education demanded by the challenges of the 21st century?

The model is described fully elsewhere (Robertson & Webber, 2000), but what is relevant to note here is that it rests on eight principles deemed necessary to promote effective learning about leadership. These are:

1. *Developing a sense of community:* Here, the aim is to promote the personal wellbeing of leaders by ensuring they have access to pastoral care. Educational leaders, in turn, need to be generous with their leadership in the sense of moving their focus from individual gain to advancement of the group. In other words, they need to practise and model system leadership. Such leaders create space for other leaders to take up leadership, and they give of their own time to assist these others to realise this role.

2. *Including international perspectives:* This principle requires leaders to study other education systems, policies and practices on the premise that comparative studies aid critical reflection on issues (see Webber & Robertson, 2004).

3. *Using generative approaches:* Such approaches hold to the idea that rather than engaging with a prescribed curriculum, leaders experience guided professional study of the issues they encounter in theory and practice and then engage in dialogue and learning centred on these issues.

4. *Validating personal knowledge:* The notion at play here is that each leader brings valuable leadership theory and practice to the community, which all can learn from as they construct new knowledge and are challenged by these different perspectives.

5. *Encouraging formal and informal leadership:* This principle is under-pinned by two premises. The first is that every leader not only has the right but also has the responsibility to take leadership within the learning group or the leadership team. The second is that others in that team enable this right and responsibility to eventuate.

6. *Providing a forum for discussion:* The forum, within the context of the coaching model, offers opportunity for critique, debate and active participation, all of which serve as essential ingredients in the leadership learning process.

7. *Ensuring that construction of meaning is a shared process:* This principle maintains that developing understanding of concepts is a social and cultural process.

8. *Encouraging the growth of a counter-culture:* The process informed by this principle is that of putting forward possibilities and alternatives that are "deliberately at variance with the social norm" (*Collins Concise Dictionary*, 1999), thereby challenging leaders to consider, justify and articulate alternative ways of being and knowing as they create new knowledge together.

Relationships between principles and effective coaching practices

These principles should also form the basis of effective coaching practices. Together, coaches and leaders can explore additional opportunities that place leaders in situations where the principles underpin the pedagogy or design of professional learning. Professional communities of learning, international study tours, visits to other learning institutions, online discussion forums, conferences and formal study programmes are all examples of learning endeavours that support coaching practices and take leaders across the boundaries of individual learning contexts. Coaching provides leaders with the impetus, the conscience and guide to try out new ideas gained in these forums.

- When coaching partners employ the eight principles within their coaching process, they find the following learning practices are a natural consequence (Robertson & Webber, 2000):
- *Co-learning:* Leaders can learn more (and achieve more) *with* others than they can from learning alone.

- *Public learning and teaching:* Leadership as learning in the public arena provides powerful learning experiences.
- *Flexible timing:* Learning can take place at any time. Online coaching and reflection is equally effective.
- *Integration of technology:* Technology provides the space for and access to learning any time anywhere. The use of technology, so important to the boundary-breaking leadership model, can be harnessed for, as examples, email communication, online reflective journals, internet resources, and video-conferencing. Together, these assist the face-to-face coaching and learning community processes by providing an asynchronous and alternative mode of communication that offers leaders flexibility in their busy working lives.
- *Confluence of theory and practice:* Theory should inform practice as much as practice should inform theory.
- *Reduced control:* Leadership develops in contexts where it is encouraged to emerge and where leaders have reduced their control or "given away" some opportunities of exercising their leadership so that others can step into the space.
- *Shared/modelled leadership:* Validation of personal knowledge and generative learning approaches encourage the sharing of leadership, which should be modelled by those initiating learning opportunities.
- *Pastoral care:* The personal wellbeing of leaders is fostered by leaders engaging together on learning on a professional basis.
- *"Possibilising":* Possibilising is about creating "What if …? and "What might be …?" moments in order to explore alternatives and ideas. It is also a process where "ultimate hopes for the future are translated into action plans that seek to push out the boundaries of what is possible" (Halpin, 2003, p. 60).
- *"Big-picture" focus:* This focus becomes possible when leaders have opportunity to lift their heads up long enough "to climb the tallest tree to see what jungle they are in", to use an analogy from Covey (1989). It allows them to see the educational system as a whole and the part that they, as system leaders, do and can play in it. This type of opportunity also allows leaders to distinguish between the role and nature of leadership and the role and nature of management.

It is hopefully apparent from this book that the outcomes of the boundary-breaking model have direct relationships with the desired outcomes of leadership coaching. Table 13.1 provides a summary of these relationships.

Table 13.1: Relationships between the boundary-breaking model and coaching

Boundary-breaking model	Coaching
An emotional engagement with learning	Deep learning moves leaders out of comfort zones and established habits and ideas.
Movement beyond self	Vicarious learning and outside perspectives move leaders to a study of leadership practice and others rather than an examination of self.
Development of a critical perspective	Other ways of knowing assist analytical assessment of leadership practice.
Development of agency	Self-efficacy and confidence moves educational leaders towards other ways of being—to acknowledging they are agents of change who can make things happen.

A powerful learning methodology

Essentially, coaching is boundary breaking because it is a powerful learning methodology. It allows for the development of a particular kind of organisational culture in which authentic learning and leadership are the two key components for all participants. West-Burnham (2004) believes that "the most powerful means of developing leadership is to create an organisational culture which values the sorts of learning most likely to enhance the capacity of individuals to lead" (p. 5). He refers to the concepts of deep, profound learning. This type of learning is applied learning.

It is also learning "where knowledge is converted into wisdom and where understanding becomes intuition" (p. 5). West-Burnham considers that these two types of learning require use of two strategies in order for the outcomes of that learning to make a strong impact. The first is opportunity to reflect. The second is coaching, which he states is "the essential learning relationship" (p. 6). West-Burnham purports, as I have done throughout this book, that those who experience the coaching relationship with their colleagues bring these qualities and practices to their leadership and their everyday work because, for them, these aspects are a way of being.

Duignan (2007) similarly implores us to focus on leadership capabilities and heralds the advent of what he calls the "capable leader". In line with Duignan, I believe such leaders are leaders capable of

- constructing new leadership knowledge;
- creating boundary-breaking opportunities to gain critical perspectives and critical thinking; and
- crossing borders to new ways of being and knowing.

These leaders are also caring, committed, concerned, compassionate and culturally responsive. They are people who have the *courage* to create opportunities for critical conversations (Robertson & Allan, 1999) centred on continual learning and improvement. They are actively engaged in coaching relationships in order to build leadership capacity in themselves, their institutions and communities and with their colleagues. They have a strong moral purpose for addressing inequity.

Support in tandem with challenges to current practice is an important element with respect to releasing this potentiality of self and others. Professional colleagues are well placed to provide this element. The resultant communities of practice are built on notions of "colleagues as resource people" and "shared leadership and collective efficacy". More often than not, the answers the group is seeking will and should be found by the group. As Duignan (2004, p. 2) reminds us, effective leaders are people equipped and able to do the following: "Influence self, others and each other to: attain worthwhile and agreed goals; engage in meaningful relationship to generate and live a shared vision; use scarce resources responsibly; and elevate the human spirit through actions and interactions that are ethical, moral and compassionate."

Enhancing moral purpose for equity

Most educators will probably tell you they came into teaching to "make a difference", which is certainly an important part of the moral purpose of education, and thus teaching and leadership, but which is not a sufficient or sufficiently specific response to facilitate critical reflection and change processes. The big challenges for educators today—addressing inequity, developing modern learning pedagogies, being culturally responsive, teaching for diversity, teaching for sustainable futures—must be at the basis of any examination of strong moral purpose in education.

A commitment to equity begins with the children in teachers' and leaders' immediate care, most usually in the classroom. The pertinent question here is this one: "Are all of these children reaching their potential?" The question positions equity as a principle that is as much about the gifted student who doesn't get extended as it is about the student who is not reaching desired achievement standards.

As educators develop towards extended professionalism, they take responsibility for all students in their classroom and then in their school—and then all children in education in their community and all children in the system. When educators become system leaders, their level of accountability is rich and deep; or it should be. I consider that this level of accountability within the system as a whole has been chipped away by the external policy contexts of competition and choice. I often wonder if it's just too idealistic to think that teachers and leaders can actually be as concerned for the children in the classroom next door or the school down the road as they are for those in their own classes or schools.

But if they were, imagine what might change with respect to education approaches in our communities and our countries. What would we do in education if we could wave a magic wand, start with a blank slate, in order to offer the best education we could for all students? Every school a great school? (Hopkins, 2007). We know what we should do, but what would help us to do it? At the very least, educational leaders can and should be making a difference within their sphere of influence. Excellent examples can be found of school principals working together to address system challenges. But more needs to be done to develop leaders who can and will collaboratively step up to ensure that professional learning opportunities move teachers beyond practice isolated from that of their colleagues in other classrooms and schools and helps them bring a collective stance to the moral purpose of education. Coaching leadership supports leaders to be courageous and brave in this way.

Coaching questions that would help us to surface and examine our level of moral purpose might include:

- What do you know about inequity in student achievement in our education system?
- How do you feel about the inequity in the education system as a whole?
- Where do you feel we sit in addressing the under-achievement of students in this school?
- What do you believe will make the biggest impact on addressing student achievement?
- What are some of the most important things our students need to leave this school knowing or being able to do?
- What does equity mean for students in our school?
- Is it okay that some students leave our school without the necessary skills and capabilities for ongoing educational success? Why or why not?
- Are all students in our school community continually fulfilling their potential? Is it okay that some are not? Why or why not? And what is our responsibility as teachers in this regard?

The way we can support ourselves and our colleagues to be courageous and stand up for what we know is right in education and to act with agency and efficacy is through having the deep learning conversations that bring our moral purpose to account. We therefore need to ask one another the right questions, the hard questions, at the right time in order to keep our focus on the moral purpose of education and determine how we can shape our teaching and our leadership so it remains true to that purpose.

Many of the right questions can develop from research findings, policy and curriculum documents and education standards associated with quality teaching and leadership. As educators, we have to be a connoisseur of such knowledge because it helps us both lead and participate in the deep learning conversations with our colleagues that help increase our individual and collective feelings of efficacy and strengthen our ability to be agents of effective moral change.

Self-efficacy and agency for moral purpose

Some teachers in education not only feel their colleagues no longer care much about making a difference by improving the quality of their teaching as they should, but they themselves feel this way. Sometimes they have low self-esteem, low self-efficacy, do not see themselves as agents of change and do not fully see themselves as part of the *relationship* of change. Instead, their thinking is all about others needing to change if the situation is to be addressed, or it may reflect the attitude that "I've always done things in this way, and it works."

The intensification of our work and the expectations on us to process seemingly ever increasing and never-ending paperwork can make even the most energetic and enthusiastic of us feel jaded and tired about change. Addressing aspects of working conditions, resourcing time to allow participation in those aspects of professional learning that are important and monitoring and reviewing the implementation of initiatives can do much to help us and our colleagues feel more positive about the changes required of our practice.

An important part of the leadership work is to help teachers gain a coherent overview of policy and curriculum change and what it means for teaching and learning. If we can provide the structures, the room, the expectations, the energy, the time for change and therefore the opportunities that allow teachers to reflect on and develop their understandings of the broader educational context and of how that impacts on their work and their roles within it, then the changes in practice that we seek are far more likely to occur.

Deep learning conversations in these situations need to include questions that challenge assumptions and rebuild connection with moral purpose. These are the questions that help teachers increase awareness of how they see their identity in their role (see, too, the second case study and the coaching tool in Chapter 11). The coaching questions might be as direct as:

- What are you not willing to compromise on in trying to make a difference to these children's achievement levels?
- Who is responsible for the success of our school leavers?
- What would you stand up for when others might want you to sit down?

- What drives you in this work with students and gets you out of bed every day?
- Where, in this work, do you think you need more moral courage?
- How could you be supported further in exploring what new strategies will work most effectively?
- How would you define your moral purpose in one sentence?
- What are the barriers and how can we overcome them?

When we, as leaders and teachers, increase our awareness of our moral purpose in our work, when we surface and examine our values, beliefs and assumptions, we will often, *individually*, make the powerful decisions that favour needed changes in practice. Most importantly with regard to the value of deep learning conversations in this context is the support that comes from deep learning relationships: as teachers and leaders, we *do* need to feel supported, to feel we can be honest and go to our places of vulnerability; to feel that others are interested in our development and the fulfilment of our work.

Often, we need opportunities to see and learn what we don't know we don't know! Consequently, some of us may need to have practices modelled for us; to see what it all looks like. Others of us may need specific examples of strategies to try out and reflect upon in our next conversation. But once we do know what we need to know, we then have to meet the expectation that we will and can actively involve ourselves in our own professional learning, with that learning always directed towards transformative action with regard to our professional practice.

These processes are integral to deep learning relationships and to the deep learning conversations within them that can help us revitalise and strengthen our moral purpose as educators and remind ourselves of why we went into teaching. As with students, we teachers and school leaders need to see success, to experience the process of small successes leading to greater successes, of small achievements leading to even greater achievements as well as greater energy for change. However, the most important thing any of us needs is the courage to act: to try out new ideas, to take risks and to make the changes that we know in our hearts are essential and right in the world that is education today.

A further note

My research and development projects continue to confirm that coached leaders value the chance to learn from one another and the leadership relationships they have within and between their institutions as they create shared understanding and knowledge, and as they learn and model their leadership through their everyday actions. Educational leaders accordingly need to go on asking themselves:

- How effective are we?
- How do we know?
- Where do we want to be?
- What do we need to learn?

Too often, the word coaching is used ubiquitously and as a catch-cry, losing all relevance and meaning, because participants have no understanding of what it means to "coach". By using the skills described in this book, leaders can develop new ways of thinking and leading, and from there gain wisdom about appropriate leadership practice or what Duignan (2002, p. 17) calls "gravitas"—knowledge gained from deep reflection on practice. This deep reflection can lead to insights that change the way even experienced leaders work in their institutions, as the following comment from Nick Major, past principal and a coach with the National Aspiring Principals' Programme attests: "I have a lingering feeling of regret that I didn't have an understanding of the importance of coaching as a principal. Today I would be far truer to the model of being a leader who understands coaching conversations. I would go to work every day with the intention of having conversations with people about learning."

Going to work every day to have deep learning conversations is *exactly* what effective educational leadership is all about (Robertson, 2015). These conversations hold within them the transformative and innovative power for changing practice that is at the heart of the coaching model. For those of you who are leaders or about to become leaders or aspiring to leadership, development of self and operating according to your own full *potential* should always be your primary focus. Professional development is about *growth* of the individual and the institution. Growth requires change and transformation, support and challenge. *Influence* is what leadership is all about. It means using one's position and energy to harness the collective capacity that allows for a shared vision and shared accountability.

Everyone has the potential to contribute to that influence, and to influence that energy. As such, one of the most important roles a leader can take is to recognise and engage the potential that others have to contribute to the leadership energy in an institution and between institutions—to take that community on a journey from its current reality to a future that is desired and shared by everyone associated with it. Ultimately, coaching is the pathway to building leadership capacity of the kind that assists others to embark on that same pathway. I hope you enjoy and gain much professionally and personally from journeying along it.

References

Aas, M., & Vavik, M. (2015). Group coaching: A new way of constructing leadership identity? *School Leadership & Management* (formerly *School Organisation*), *35*(3), 251–265. doi:10.1080/13632434.2014.962497

Alcorn, N. (1986). Action research: A tool for school development. *Delta*, *37*, 33–44.

Anderson, J. (2014, July 17). *Getting to the root of educational injustice.* Cambridge, MA: Harvard Graduate School of Education. Retrieved from http://www.gse.harvard. edu/news/14/07/ getting-root-educational-injustice

Apple, M. (1986). *Teachers and texts: A political economy of class and gender relations in education.* New York: Routledge & Kegan Paul.

Apple, M. W., & Beane, J. A. (1995). *Democratic schools.* Alexandria, VA: Association for Supervision and Curriculum Development.

Argyris, C. (1999). *Knowledge for action.* San Francisco, CA: Jossey-Bass.

Argyris, C. (2008). *Teaching smart people how to learn.* Boston, MA: Harvard Business Press.

Bandura, A. (2002). Social cognitive theory in cultural context. *Applied Psychology: An International Review, 51*(2), 269–290.

Barber, M. (2002). *From good to great: Large-scale reform in England.* Paper presented at Futures of Education Conference, University of Zurich, Switzerland, 23 April 2002.

Barnett, B. G. (1990). Peer-assisted leadership: Expanding principals' knowledge through reflective practice. *Journal of Educational Administration, 28*(3), 67–76.

Barnett, B. G., O'Mahoney, G., & Matthews, R. J. (2004). *Reflective practice: The cornerstone for school improvement.* Moorabbin, VIC, Australia: Hawker Brownlow Education.

Barth, R. (1986). Principal centered professional development. *Theory into Practice, 25*(3), 156–160.

Bell, B., & Gilbert, J. (1996). *Teacher development: A model from science education.* London, UK: Falmer Press.

Berger, P. L., & Luckmann, T. (1966). *The social construction of reality.* London, UK: Penguin Press.

Berlak, A., & Berlak, H. (1987). Teachers working with teachers to transform schools. In J. Smyth (Ed.), *Educating teachers: Changing the nature of pedagogical knowledge* (pp. 169–178). Lewes, UK: Falmer Press.

Biesta, G. J. J. (2014). *The beautiful risk of education.* Boulder, CO: Paradigm Publishers.

Bishop, R., Berryman, M., Cavanagh, T,. & Teddy, L. (2009). Te Kotahitanga: Addressing educational disparities facing Māori students in New Zealand. *Teaching and Teacher Education, 25(5),* 734-742.

Bossert, S. T., Dwyer, D. C., Rowan, B., & Lee, G. V. (1982). The instructional management role of the principal. *Educational Administration Quarterly, 18*(3), 34–64.

Bryk, A., & Schneider, B. (2004). *Trust in schools: A core resource for improvement.* New York: Sage Publications.

Bull, A., & Gilbert, J. (2012). Swimming out of our depth? Leading learning in 21st century schools. Wellington, New Zealand: New Zealand Council for Educational Research. Retrieved from http://www.nzcer.org.nz/system/files/ Swimming%20out%20of%20our%20depth%20final.pdf

Caffarella, R. S. (1993). Facilitating self-directed learning as a staff development option. *Journal of Staff Development, 14*(2), 30–34.

Caldwell, B. (2002). Scenarios for leadership and the public good in education. In K. Leithwood & P. Hallinger (Eds.), *Second international handbook of educational leadership and administration* (pp. 821–848). Dordrecht, The Netherlands: Kluwer Academic Publishers.

Caldwell, B. (2003). Successful learning and the globalization of learning. In P. Hallinger (Ed.), *Reshaping the landscape of school leadership development: A global perspective* (pp. 23–40). Lisse, the Netherlands: Swets & Zeitlinger.

Caldwell, B. J. (2011). The great cultural divide in system leadership. *The Australian Educational Leader, 33*(3), 14–16.

Cardno, C. (2003). *Action research.* Wellington, New Zealand: New Zealand Council for Educational Research.

Carr, W., & Kemmis, S. (1986). *Becoming critical: Education, knowledge and action research.* Lewes, UK: Falmer Press.

Clandinin, D. J., & Connelly, F. M. (1995). *Teachers' professional knowledge landscapes.* New York: Teachers College Press.

Claxton, G., Chambers, M., Powell, G., & Lucas, B. (2011). *The learning powered school: Pioneering 21st century education.* Bristol, UK: TLO Limited.

Cochran-Smith, M., & Lytle, S. L. (1993). *Inside/outside: Teacher research and knowledge.* New York: Teachers College Press.

Cochran-Smith, M., & Lytle, S. L. (1999). Relationships of knowledge and practice: Teacher learning in communities. In A. Iran-Nejad & C. D. Pearson (Eds.), *Review of research in education* (Vol. 24, pp. 251–307), Washington, DC: American Educational Research Association.

Codd, J. (1990). Managerialism: The problem with today's schools. *Delta, 44,* 17–25.

Cohen, L., & Manion, L. (1980). *Research methods in education.* London, UK: Croom Helm.

Collins Concise Dictionary (1999). (4th ed.). Glasgow, Scotland: HarperCollins.

Covey, S. (1989). *Seven habits of highly effective people.* New York: Simon & Schuster.

Covey, S. R. (1990). *Principle centred leadership.* New York: Fireside.

Dawson, T. L. (2008). *Metacognition and learning in adulthood.* Paper prepared in response to tasking from ODNI/CHCO/IC Leadership Development Office. Retrieved from https://www.devtestservice.org/PDF/Metacognition.pdf

De Corte, E. (2010). Historical developments in the understanding of learning. In H. Dumont, D. Istance, & F. Benavides (Eds.), *The nature of learning using research to inspire practice* (pp. 35–67). Paris, France: OECD.

Degendhardt, L., & Duignan, P. (2010). *Dancing on a shifting carpet: Reinventing traditional schooling for the 21st century.* Camberwell, VIC, Australia: ACER Press.

Dempster, N. (2001). *The professional development of school principals: A fine balance.* Professorial lecture given at Griffith University, Nathan, Queensland, Australia, May 24, 2001.

Dempster, N. (2009). Leadership for learning: A framework synthesising recent research. *Edventures, 1*(13), 1–10.

Dempster, N., Lovett, S., & Flückiger, B. (2011). *Insights: Literature review strategies to develop school leadership.* Melbourne, VIC, Australia: Australian Institute for Teaching and School Leadership (AITSL).

Dick, B. (2009). Action research literature 2006–2008: Themes and trends. *Action Research, 4*(4), 439–458.

Duignan, P. (1988). Reflective management: The key to quality leadership. *International Journal of Educational Management, 2*(2), 3–12.

Duignan, P. (1989). Reflective management: The key to quality leadership. In C. Riches & C. Morgan (Eds.), *Human resource management in education* (pp. 74–90). Milton Keynes, UK: The Open University.

Duignan, P. (2002). *The Catholic educational leader: Defining authentic leadership. Veritas, caritas and gravitas.* Paper presented at the Catholic Educational Leadership Conference: The Vision and the Reality, Australian Catholic University, Sydney, Australia, August 4–7, 2002.

Duignan, P. (2004). Forming capable leaders: From competencies to capabilities. *New Zealand Journal of Educational Leadership, 19*(2), 5–13.

Duignan, P. (2007). *Educational leadership: Key challenges and ethical tensions.* Cambridge, UK: Cambridge University Press.

Dussault, M., & Barnett, B.G. (1996). Peer-assisted leadership: Reducing educational managers' professional isolation. *Journal of Educational Administration, 34*(3), 5–14.

Dweck, C. S. (2006). *Mindset: The new psychology of success.* New York: Random House.

Earl, L., & Katz, S. (2002). Leading schools in a data-rich world. In K. Leithwood & P. Hallinger (Eds.), *Second international handbook of educational leadership and administration* (pp. 1003–1024). Dordrecht, The Netherlands: Kluwer Academic Publishers.

Earl, L., & Robertson, J. (2013). *Leadership learning: Insights from the National Aspiring Principals' Programme.* Wellington, New Zealand: Ministry of Education.

Eaton, J., & Johnson, R. (2001). *Coaching successfully.* London, UK: Dorling Kindersley.

Ebbutt, D. (1985). Educational action research: Some general concerns and specific quibbles. In R. G. Burgess (Ed.), *Issues in educational research: Qualitative methods* (pp. 152–174). London, UK: Falmer Press.

Elbaz-Luwisch, E. (2001). Personal story as passport: Storytelling in border pedagogy. *Teaching Education, 12*(1), 81–101.

Elliott, J. (1991). Action research, practical competence and professional knowledge. In O. Zuber-Skerritt (Ed.), *Action learning for improved performance: Key contributions to the first world congress on action research and process management* (pp. 26–45). Brisbane, QLD, Australia: Aebis Publishing.

Everard, K. B., & Morris, G. (1985). *Effective school management*. London, UK: Paul Chapman.

Fadillah, M. I. (1997). *Professional partnership of teachers: An action research study for professional development*. Unpublished thesis, University of Waikato, Hamilton, New Zealand.

Foucault, M. (1977). *Discipline and punish: The birth of the prison* (A. Sheridan, trans.). New York: Pantheon Books.

Freire, P. (1985). *The politics of education: Culture, power, and liberation*. South Hadley, MA: Bergin & Garvey.

Fullan, M. (1993). *Change forces: Probing the depths of educational reform*. London, UK: Falmer Press.

Fullan, M. (2001). *Leading in a culture of change*. San Francisco, CA: Jossey-Bass.

Fullan, M. (2003a). *The moral imperative of school leadership*. Thousand Oaks, CA: Corwin.

Fullan, M. (2003b). *Change forces with a vengeance*. London, UK: RoutledgeFalmer.

Fullan, M. (2005). *Leadership and sustainability: System thinkers in action*. Thousand Oaks, CA: Corwin.

Fullan, M. (2007). *The new meaning of educational change* (4th ed.). New York: Teachers College Press.

Fullan, M., & Langworthy, M. (2014). *A rich seam: How new pedagogies find deep learning*. London, UK: Pearson.

Fullan, M. G., & Stiegelbauer, S. (1991). *The new meaning of educational change*. London, UK: Cassell.

Garvey Berger, J. (2012). *Changing on the job: Developing leaders for a complex world*. Stanford, CA: Stanford Business Books.

Giddens, A. (1993). *New rules of sociological method* (2nd ed.). Cambridge, UK: Polity Press.

Giroux, H. (1992). *Border crossings: Cultural workers and the politics of education*. New York: Routledge.

Glaser, B. G., & Strauss, A. L. (1967). *The discovery of grounded theory: Strategies for qualitative research.* Chicago, IL: Aldine.

Goffman, E. (1959). *The presentation of self in everyday life.* New York: Doubleday.

Goldhammer, R. (1969). *Clinical supervision.* New York: Holt, Rinehart and Winston.

Goleman, D. (2006). *Social intelligence: The new science of human relationships.* London, UK: Random House.

Goodlad, J. I. (1978). Educational leadership: Toward the third era. *Educational Leadership, 35*(4), 322–331.

Gottesman, B. (2000). *Peer coaching for educators.* Lanham, MD: Rowman and Littlefield Education.

Greene, M. (1985). The role of education in democracy. *Educational Horizons, 63*(special issue), 3–9.

Griffin, G. A. (1987). The school in society and the social organization of the school: Implications for staff development. In M. F. Wideen & I. Andrews (Eds.), *Staff development for school improvement: A focus on the teacher* (pp. 19–37). Lewes, UK: Falmer Press.

Gronn, P. (2002). Leader formation. In K. Leithwood & P. Hallinger (Eds.), *Second international handbook of educational leadership and administration* (pp. 1031–1070). Dordrecht, The Netherlands: Kluwer Academic Publishers.

Gronn, P. (2003). *The new work of educational leaders.* London, UK: Sage Publications.

Grossman, P., Wineburg, S., & Woolworth, S. (2000). *In pursuit of teacher community.* Paper presented at the annual meeting of the American Educational Research Association, New Orleans, April 2000.

Grundy, S. (1993). Educational leadership as emancipatory praxis. In J. Blackmore & J. Kenway (Eds.), *Gender matters in educational administration and policy* (pp. 165–177). London, UK: Falmer Press.

Gunter, H. (2001). *Leaders and leadership in education.* London, UK: Paul Chapman.

Hallinger, P. (Ed.). (2003). *Reshaping the landscape of school leadership development: A global perspective.* Lisse, The Netherlands: Swets & Zeitlinger.

Hallinger, P. (2011). Leadership for learning: Lessons from 40 years of empirical research. *Journal of Educational Administration, 49*(2), 125–142. doi:10.1108/ 09578231111116699

Hallinger, P., & Bridges, E. (1997). Problem-based leadership development: Preparing educational leaders for changing times. *Journal of School Leadership, 7,* 1–15.

Hallinger, P., & Murphy, J. (1985). Assessing the instructional management behavior of principals. *Elementary School Journal, 86*(2), 217–247.

Hallinger, P., & Murphy, J. (1991). Developing leaders for future schools. *Phi Delta Kappan, 72*(7), 514–520.

Halpin, D. (2003). *Hope and education: The role of the Utopian imagination.* London, UK: RoutledgeFalmer.

Hannon, V. (2011). *Designing innovative systems: Is "moving to scale" our challenge?* Keynote address to the OECD/CERI International Conference on Innovative Learning Environments, Banff, Alberta, Canada, October 2011.

Hargreaves, A. (2004). *The seven principles of sustainable leadership.* Paper presented at the Second International Summit for Leadership in Education, Boston, November 2–6, 2004.

Hargreaves, A., & Fink, D. (2004). The seven principles of sustainable leadership. *Educational Leadership, 61*(7), 8–14.

Hargreaves, A., & Fullan, M. (Eds.). (1992). *Teacher development and educational change.* New York: Falmer Press.

Hargreaves, A., & Fullan, M. (2012). *Professional capital: Transforming teaching in every school.* New York: Teachers College Press.

Harris, A., & Lambert, L. (2003). *Building leadership capacity for school improvement.* Maidenhead, UK: Open University Press.

Hattie, J. (2009). *Visible learning: A synthesis of over 800 meta-analyses relating to achievement.* New York: Routledge

Hay Group. (2001). *Identifying the skills, knowledge, attributes and competencies for first-time principals: Shaping the next generation of principals.* Melbourne, VIC, Australia: Hay Acquisitions Inc.

Hopkins, D. (2007). *Every school a great school: Realizing the potential of system leadership.* Maidenhead, UK: McGraw Hill Open University Press.

Houma, S. (1998). *A study of staff appraisal at the Solomon Islands College of Higher Education.* Unpublished M.Ed. (Leadership) thesis, University of Waikato, Hamilton, New Zealand.

Huber, S. (Ed.). (2003). *Preparing school leaders for the 21st century: An international comparison of development programmes in 15 countries.* London, UK: Taylor & Francis.

Isaacs, W. (1999). *Dialogue and the art of thinking together*. New York: Doubleday.

Jasman, A. M. (2002). *Crossing borders: Learning from, by working in, different professional knowledge contexts*. Paper presented at the Conference of the Australian Association for Research in Education, Freemantle, Western Australia.

Joyce, B., & Showers, B. (1982). The coaching of teaching. *Educational Leadership, 40*(1), 4–10.

Joyce, B., & Showers, B. (2002). Student achievement through professional development. In B. Joyce & B. Showers (Eds.), *Designing training and peer coaching: Our need for learning* (Chapter 5). Alexandria, VA: Association for Supervision and Curriculum Development.

Kaser, L., & Halbert, J. (2009). *Leadership mindsets: Innovation and learning in the transformation of schools*. London, UK: Routledge.

Kemmis, S. (1985). Action research and the politics of reflection. In D. Boud, R. Keogh, & D. Walker (Eds.), *Reflection: Turning experience into learning* (pp. 139–163). New York: Kogan Page.

Kemmis, S., & McTaggart, R. (1988). *The action research planner* (3rd ed.). Geelong, VIC, Australia: Deakin University.

Kolb, D. A. (1984). *Experiential learning: Experience as the source of learning and development*. Englewood Cliffs, NJ: Prentice Hall.

Kouzes, J. M., & Posner, B. Z. (2012). *The leadership challenge* (5th ed.). San Francisco, CA: Jossey Bass.

Lambert, L. (1998). How to build leadership capacity. *Educational Leadership, 55*(7), 17–19.

Landsberg, M. (2003). *The tao of coaching*. London, UK: Profile Books.

Lange, (the Hon.) D. (1988). *Tomorrow's Schools: The reform of educational administration in New Zealand*. Wellington, New Zealand: Government Printer.

Lee, G. V. (1991). Peer-assisted development of school leaders. *Journal of Staff Development, 12*(2), 14–18.

Lee, G. V. (1993). New images of school leadership: Implications for professional development. *Journal of Staff Development, 14*(1), 2–5.

Lee, G. V., & Barnett, B. G. (1994). Using reflective questioning to promote collaborative dialogue. *Journal of Staff Development, 15*(1), 16–21.

Lee, T. (2002). *Professional development for ICT using teachers in Hong Kong secondary schools: An action research*. Unpublished M.Ed. (Leadership) thesis, University of Waikato, Hamilton, New Zealand.

Lewin, K. (1948). *Resolving social conflicts: Selected papers on group dynamics.* New York: Harper & Row.

Leithwood, K., & Hallinger, P. (Eds.). (2002). *Second international handbook of educational leadership and administration.* Dordrecht, The Netherlands: Kluwer Academic Publishers.

Leithwood, K., Jantzi, D., & Steinback, R. (1999). *Changing leadership for changing times.* Buckingham, UK: Open University Press.

Louis, K., Leithwood, K, Wahlstrom, K. L., Anderson, S. E., Michlin, M., Mascall, B., ... Moore, S. (2010). *Learning from leadership: Investigating the links to improved student learning.* St. Paul, MN: Center for Applied Research and Educational Improvement, University of Minnesota and Ontario Institute for Studies in Education, University of Toronto. Lucas, B., & Claxton, G. (2010). *New kinds of smart: How the science of learnable intelligence is changing education.* London, UK: Open University Press.

Lupton, R. (2004). *Schools in disadvantaged areas: Recognising context and raising quality.* London, UK: Economic and Social Research Council.

Marshall, T. A., & Duignan, P. A. (1987). A two-stage approach to surveying opinions. In R. J. S. Macpherson (Ed.), *Ways and meanings of research in educational administration* (University of New England Teaching Monograph No. 5, pp. 171–188). Armidale, NSW, Australia: University of England.

McLaughlin, M., & Cox, E. (2016). *Leadership coaching: Developing braver leaders.* New York: Routledge.

Milstein, M. M., & Associates (1993). *Changing the way we prepare educational leaders: The Danforth experience.* Newbury Park, CA: Corwin Press.

Ministry of Education. (2015). *Interim professional standards.* Wellington, New Zealand: Author. Retrieved from www.education.govt.nz

Muijs, D., Kyriakides, L., van der Werf, G., Creemers, B., Timperley, T., & Earl,, L. (2014). State of the art: Teacher effectiveness and professional learning. *School Effectiveness and School Improvement: An International Journal of Research, Policy and Practice. Special Issue: A State-of-the-Art Review: Educational Effectiveness, Teacher Effectiveness and Professional learning, and School and System Improvement,* 25(2), 231–256.doi: 10.1080/092434553.2014,885451

Murrihy, L. (2009). *Coaching and the growth of three New Zealand educators: A multi-dimensional journey.* Unpublished doctoral thesis, University of Waikato, Hamilton, New Zealand.

Nofke, S., & Somekh, B. (Eds). (2009). *Handbook of educational action research.* London, UK: Sage Publications.

Oliver, B. (1980). Action research for inservice training. *Educational Leadership, 37*(5), 394–395.

Pont, B. (2015). *Perspectives of the OECD on educational (in)justice.* Plenary keynote address to the Education and School Leadership Symposium, Zug, Switzerland, September 2–4, 2015.

Popper, M., & Lipshitz, R. (1992). Coaching on leadership. *Leadership and Organization Development Journal, 13*(7), 15–18.

Resnick, L. B., Spillane, J. P., Goldman, P., & Rangel, E. S. (2010). Implementing innovation: From visionary models to everyday practice. In H. Dumont, D. Istance, & F. Benavides (Eds.), *The nature of learning using research to inspire practice* (pp. 285–315). Paris, France: OECD.

Robertson, J. M. (1991a). *Developing educational leadership.* Unpublished M.Ed. thesis, University of Waikato, Hamilton, New Zealand.

Robertson, J. M. (1991b). Dilemmas faced by school principals. *The New Zealand Principal, 6*(3), 17–18.

Robertson, J. M. (1992). Statespersons, connoisseurs and entrepreneurs: The educational leaders of our schools. *The New Zealand Principal, 7*(1), 14–18.

Robertson, J. M. (1995). *Principals' partnerships: An action research study on the professional development of New Zealand school leaders.* Unpublished doctoral thesis, University of Waikato, Hamilton, New Zealand.

Robertson, J. M. (1999). Principals working with principals: Keeping education at the centre of practice. *set: Research Information for Teachers, 1,* Item 9.

Robertson, J. M. (2000). The three R's of action research methodology: Reciprocity, reflexivity and reflection-on-reality. *Educational Action Research, 8*(2), 307–326.

Robertson, J. M. (2004a). Leadership learning through coaching. *set: Research Information for Teachers, 3,* 44–48.

Robertson, J. M. (2004b). *Leaders coaching leaders: A workshop kit.* Hamilton, New Zealand: Educational Leadership Centre.

Robertson, J. M. (2005). *Coaching leadership: Building educational leadership capacity through coaching partnerships.* Wellington, New Zealand: NZCER Press.

Robertson, J. M. (2009). Coaching leadership learning through partnership. *School Leadership & Management, 29*(1), 39–49.

Robertson, J. M. (2010). Learning through partnership: Challenging ways of seeing, being and knowing. *The International Journal of Interdisciplinary Social Sciences, 4*(12), 53–60.

Robertson, J. M. (2013). Learning leadership. *Leading & Managing, 19*(2), 54–69.

Robertson, J. M. (2015). Deep learning conversations and how coaching relationships can enable them. *Australian Educational Leader, 37*(3), 10–15.

Robertson, J. M., & Allan, R. (1999). Teachers working in isolation? Creating opportunities for professional conversations. *set: Research Information for Teachers, 2,* Item 3.

Robertson, J. M. & Earl, L. (2014). Leadership learning: Aspiring principals developing the dispositions that count. *Journal of Educational Leadership, Policy and Practice, 29*(2), 3–17.

Robertson, J. M., & Murrihy, L. (2005). *Developing the personal in the professional. Building the capacity of teachers for improved student learning: The missing basket—personal learning.* Nottingham, UK: National College for School Leadership.

Robertson, J. M., & Webber, C. F. (2000). Crosscultural leadership development. *International Journal of Leadership in Education: Theory and Practice, 3*(4), 315–330.

Robertson, J. M., & Webber, C. F. (2002). Boundary-breaking leadership: A must for tomorrow's learning communities. In K. Leithwood & P. Hallinger (Eds.), *Second international handbook of educational leadership and administration* (pp. 519–553). Dordrecht, the Netherlands: Kluwer Academic Publishers.

Robertson, J. M., & Webber, C. F. (2004). International leadership development through web-based learning. *International Electronic Journal for Leadership in Learning, 8*(12).

Robinson, V., Hohepa, M., & Lloyd, C. (2009). *School leadership and student outcomes: Identifying what works and why: Best evidence synthesis.* Wellington, New Zealand: Ministry of Education.

Rock, D. (2007). *Quiet leadership.* New York: Harper Business.

Saphier, J., & King, M. (1986). Good seeds grow in strong cultures. *Educational Leadership, 42*(6), 67–74.

Schön, D. A. (1983). *The reflective practitioner: How professionals think in action.* New York: Basic Books.

Schön, D. A. (1987). *Educating the reflective practitioner.* San Francisco: CA: Jossey Bass.

Senge, P. (1990). *The fifth discipline: The art and practice of the learning organization.* New York: Doubleday.

Sergiovanni, T. J. (1992). *Moral leadership: Getting to the heart of school improvement.* San Francisco, CA: Jossey-Bass.

Sergiovanni, T. J., & Starratt, R. J. (2002). *Supervision: Human perspectives* (2nd ed.). New York: McGraw-Hill.

Shields, C. (2002). Focusing a crowded leadership agenda: Social justice and academic excellence. *New Zealand Journal of Educational Leadership, 17,* 33–45.

Smyth, J. (1991). *Teachers as collaborative learners.* Buckingham, UK: Open University Press.

Smyth, J. (1993). Teachers' work and the politics of reflection. *American Educational Research Journal, 29*(2), 267–300.

Somekh, B. (1994). Inhabiting each other's castles: Towards knowledge and mutual growth through collaboration, *Educational Action Research, 2,* 357–382.

Southworth, G. (2002). What is important in educational administration? Learning-centred school leadership, *New Zealand Journal of Educational Leadership, 17,* 5–19.

Starratt, R. J. (2004). *Ethical leadership.* San Francisco, CA: Jossey-Bass.

Stenhouse, L. (1975). *An introduction to curriculum research and development.* London, UK: Heinemann Educational Books.

Stewart, D. (2000). *Tomorrow's principals today.* Palmerston North, New Zealand: Massey University and Kanuka Grove Press.

Stoll, L., & Bolam, R. (2005). Developing leadership for learning communities. In M. Coles & G. Southworth (Eds.), *Developing leadership: Creating the schools of tomorrow* (pp. 50–64). Maidenhead, UK: Open University Press.

Stoll, L., & Fink, D. (1996). *Changing our schools: Linking school effectiveness and school improvement.* Buckingham, UK: Open University Press.

Strachan, J. M. B. (1999). Feminist educational leadership: Locating the concepts in practice. *Gender and Education, 11*(3), 309–322.

Strachan, J. M. B., & Robertson, J. M. (1992). Principals' professional development. *New Zealand Journal of Educational Administration, 7,* 45–51.

Strauss, A., & Corbin, J. M. (Eds.). (1997). *Grounded theory in practice.* Thousand Oaks, CA: Sage Publications.

Sutton, M. (2005). Coaching for pedagogical change. *New Zealand Journal of Educational Leadership*, *20*(2), 31–46.

Thrupp, M. (2004). Conceptualising educational leadership for social justice. *New Zealand Journal of Educational Leadership*, *19*(1), 21–29.

Thrupp, M., & Willmott, R. (2003). *Educational management in managerialist times: Beyond the textual apologists.* Buckingham, UK: Open University Press.

Timperley, H., Kaser, L. & Halbert, J. (2014, April). *A framework for transforming learning in schools: Innovation and the cycle of inquiry* (seminar series, Paper No. 234). Melbourne, VIC, Australia: Centre for Strategic Education.

Timperley, H., Wilson, A., Barrar, H., & Fung, I. (2007). *Teacher professional learning and development: Best evidence synthesis iteration (BES).* Wellington, New Zealand: Ministry of Education.

Townsend, T., & MacBeath, J. (Eds.). (2011). *International handbook of leadership for learning.* London, UK: Springer.

Tschannen-Moran, B., & Tschannen-Moran, M. (2010). *Evocative coaching: Transforming schools one conversation at a time.* San Francisco, CA: Jossey-Bass.

Wadsworth, E. J. (1990). A vision of a pot of gold: School leadership and the emergence of practitioner consultants, *Delta, 44*, 49–57.

Walker, A., & Dimmock, C. (2002). Moving school leadership beyond its narrow boundaries: Developing a cross-cultural approach. In K. Leithwood & P. Hallinger (Eds.), *Second international handbook of educational leadership and administration* (pp. 167–204). Dordrecht, the Netherlands: Kluwer Academic Publishers.

Wallace Foundation. (2012). *The making of the principal: Five lessons in leadership training.* New York: Author.

Webber, C. F.., & Robertson, J. M. (1998). Boundary breaking: An emergent model for leadership development. *Educational Policy Analysis Archives, 6*(21). Retrieved from http://epaa.asu.edu/ojs/article/viewFile/588/711

Webber, C. F., & Robertson, J. M. (2004). Internationalization and educators' understanding of issues in educational leadership. *The Educational Forum, 68*(3), 264–275.

West-Burnham, J. (2004). *Building leadership capacity: Helping leaders learn. A thinkpiece for the National College for School Leaders.* Nottingham, UK: National College for School Leaders.

Whitmore, J. (2002). *Coaching for performance: GROWing people, performance and purpose* (3rd ed.). London, UK: Nicholas Brealey Publishing.

Whyte, W. F. (Ed.). (1991). *Participatory action research.* Thousand Oaks, CA: Sage Publications.

Wildy, H., Louden, W., & Robertson, J. M. (2000). Using cases for school principal performance standards: Australian and New Zealand experiences. *Waikato Journal of Education, 6,* 169–194.

Wiliam, D. (2011). Teacher expertise: Why it matters, and how to get more of it. In J. Hallgarten, L. Bamfield, & K. McCarthy (Eds.), *Licensed to create: Ten essays on improving teacher quality* (pp. 27–36). London, UK: Action and Research Centre.

Winter, R. (1989). *Learning from experience: Principles and practice in action-research.* Lewes, UK: Falmer Press.

Winters, S. (1996). *Developing classroom management styles in secondary schools.* Unpublished M.Ed. thesis, University of Waikato, Hamilton, New Zealand.

Wylie, C. (1997). *At the centre of the web: The role of the New Zealand primary school principal within a decentralized education system.* Wellington, New Zealand: New Zealand Council for Educational Research.

Wylie, C. (2012). *Vital connections: Why we need more than self-managing schools.* Wellington: NZCER Press.

Wylie, C., & Bonne, L. (2014). *Primary and intermediate schools in 2013: Main findings from the NZCER national survey.* Wellington, New Zealand: New Zealand Council for Educational Research.

Zeus, P., & Skiffington, A. (2002). *The coaching at work toolkit: A complete guide to techniques and practices.* Sydney, NSW, Australia: McGraw-Hill.

Zuber-Skerritt, O. (2011). *Action leadership: Towards a participatory paradigm.* London, UK: Springer.

Index